HELL IS ROUND THE CORNER

TRICKY

WITH ANDREW PERRY

BLINK
bringing you closer

Published by Blink Publishing
Wimpole Street,
London,
W1G 9RE

www.blinkpublishing.co.uk

facebook.com/blinkpublishing
twitter.com/blinkpublishing

Hardback – 978-1-788702-22-5
Trade Paperback – 978-1-788702-29-4
Paperback – 978-1-788702-30-0
Ebook – 978-1-788702-31-7

First published by Blink Publishing in 2019.
This edition first published by Blink Publishing in 2020.

Adrian Thaws has asserted his moral right to be identified as the author of this
Work in accordance with the Copyright, Designs and Patents Act 1988.

Every reasonable effort has been made to trace copyright holders of material
reproduced in this book, but if any have been inadvertently overlooked
the publishers would be glad to hear from them.

Blink Publishing is an imprint of Bonnier Books UK
www.bonnierbooks.co.uk

Born in 1968, Adrian Thaws had a tough and troubled early childhood. His mother, Maxine Quaye, committed suicide when he was four years old, making a deep, lifelong imprint on the boy who would grow up to become the artist known as Tricky. Admired internationally by some of the biggest names in music, including the late David Bowie, Tricky has released 13 studio albums, selling over 2 million copies worldwide.

CONTENTS

NOTE TO THE READER

We've got other people talking in this book apart from me, just because it's better! It's unconventional for an autobiography, I know, but that's alright. It's just how I wanted it.

Some of what follows in these pages, people might not believe if I say it. I'm sure when some people do autobiographies, they dramatise things. They exaggerate stuff, so some of the stories, if I told them, might sound like exaggeration. Like, 'He's not serious, that didn't happen!' Coming from someone else, maybe they'll believe them, because they *are* true.

There are family members talking about things that happened before I was born, or when I was too young to know what was really going on. And then there are friends who might remember things better than me – I had years of smoking weed, all kinds of drugs. Know what I mean? Sometimes it's more reliable someone else saying it.

LIST OF CONTRIBUTORS

MARTIN GODFREY – Great-Uncle
TONY GUEST – Uncle
MICHELLE PORTER – Cousin
ROY THAWS – Father
MARLOW PORTER – Aunt
WHITLEY ALLEN – Friend
RAY MIGHTY – Smith & Mighty
ROB SMITH – Smith & Mighty
MARC MAROT – Island Records MD
JULIAN PALMER – Island Records
TERRY HALL – The Specials
SHAUN RYDER – Happy Mondays, Black Grape
BEN WINCHESTER – Booking Agent, Primary Talent
PETE BRIQUETTE – Former Live Band Member
PERRY FARRELL – Jane's Addiction, Porno For Pyros
AMANI VANCE – Friend
LEE JAFFE – Photographer
CESAR ACEITUNO – Friend
MAI LUCAS – Photographer, Friend
CHARLES DE LINIERE – Friend
HORST WEIDENMÜLLER – !K7, Manager
MAYNARD JAMES KEENAN – Tool, A Perfect Circle
MARIE – Daughter

FAMILY TREE

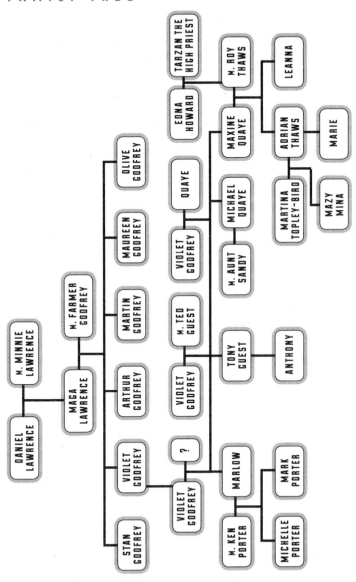

CHAPTER ONE
13 PADSTOW ROAD

My first memory is seeing my mum in a coffin, when I was four years old. In those days, when somebody died, you had the coffin at home for a week or two, so all the family could come and say their goodbyes before they buried the person. When you're that young, you don't really understand what's going on. Obviously I could see a lot of people were sad – family members coming into the house crying and stuff – so I knew it wasn't good. She'd committed suicide, and I didn't understand that, either.

They'd put the coffin in the room opposite mine, so I would go and stand on a chair and look inside when everyone was asleep. The coffin was kept open, and the body was right there. I didn't feel anything. I knew she was my mum, but I couldn't really get the concept. So that's my first memory: at four years old, going into that room.

I can't remember anything before that. I can't even remember my mum: that's my first memory of her, seeing her dead. I've never looked at it as bad or horrible. Most people's first memory is about school or home or whatever, but that's mine.

This was in my grandmother's house in Barnstaple Road, Knowle West – a white ghetto area of Bristol, which was built in the 1930s to help clear the slums out of the city centre. It was my great-grandparents who first moved there, when they were young, into a council housing development that had just been constructed.

People probably know I'm from a tough family, but no one knows the details. We were one of the first mixed-race families in England, going back three or four generations. My grandfather was an African serviceman briefly stationed in Knowle West. There's a tribe in Ghana called Quaye – but no one knows exactly where he came from. There's bound to be some slave history in his bloodline.

He met a white woman named Violet, and they had a kid together. He eventually left England, so their daughter – my mum, Maxine Quaye – grew up with the white side of her family in Knowle West. Even though she was mixed-race, culturally she was very 'white' and, given the area she grew up in, you would've thought she'd have gone on to marry a white guy.

Instead, she got together with a Jamaican man called Roy Thaws, and had me. I don't know for sure how they met. Roy was in London first, before he moved to Bristol, and his dad had a sound system, one of the best-known sound systems in England, called Tarzan the High Priest. My dad didn't come here and become Anglicised. He was still very Jamaican, and kept up the Jamaican traditions with the food he ate, and he even ran a dominoes team that played around England.

The first Jamaican my mum probably got to know well was my dad. They used to go to the same clubs, like the Bamboo Club in St Paul's, the black ghetto of Bristol, which was a very popular place for music with all locals, not just black people, so I like to think they met there.

They never got married, but when I was born, on 27 January 1968, my mum got him to give me his last name. If I'd taken my mum's name, I'd have been a Quaye, and if she had kept her mum's name, I would have been Godfrey, but back then, people wanted you to take your dad's name. It obviously wasn't something I chose: I was Adrian Nicholas Matthew Thaws, and that was that.

The rest of the family say I was very close to my mum, but I can't remember anything about being with her, apart from seeing her body in the coffin. One thing I found out later was that she wrote poetry. When

Channel 4 in the UK made a documentary about me in the mid-90s called *Tricky: Naked and Famous*, one of my family must've given them a poem she'd written, because my auntie Marlow read out the whole thing in the programme. I didn't even know about it until I watched the finished documentary: by that point, I'd made two or three albums, so it all began to make sense to me after that.

There was obviously no opportunity for her to go anywhere with her writing. She could've written until her hand fell off, but there was no way she was going to be able to publish a book. She wrote for her own pleasure, and apparently she used to do it a lot. That poem is about individuality, being an individual, which also kind of makes sense.

On the day of her suicide, in 1972, she got dressed in her best clothes and went visiting all the family. In those days, you'd really only get dressed up on a Sunday. So they were like, 'Where are you going? Why are you all dressed up?' And she was like, 'Oh, nowhere!' Then she went home, wrote a letter asking her auntie to look after me, and killed herself – with tablets, probably sleeping pills. I've always been told that none of the family saw it coming, because she didn't show any signs that she was about to do anything like that. There was no inkling. The only thing they thought was strange was, why was she all dressed up?

My dad found her, and he's never really got over that. He's still a bit fucked up by it, and he never talks about it. He rarely talks about my mum to me, come to think of it. He said to me once, 'Your mum would be proud of you,' but he has rarely mentioned her otherwise. He was a young guy when he found her. Imagine finding your girlfriend dead at that age.

Everyone in the family was cool with Roy up till that point, but afterwards things changed. My nan didn't like him very much. I think she blamed him for my mum's suicide, but it wasn't nothing to do with him. My mum had epilepsy, and what I think is, she had two kids, and you can have an epileptic fit any time, so it's hard for you to look after your kids. It's dangerous if you have an epileptic fit and you've got two kids in the house by yourself. I think she just didn't want to be here because of epilepsy. But obviously you're going to blame the boyfriend, ain't you, if you're her mother. It's easier if you have someone to blame.

Dad used to come and see me to begin with, but then my great-uncle Martin wrote a letter to my great-grandmother saying, 'Roy has a lot to answer for.' He was doing seven years in Dartmoor at the time. Basically, he was saying that when he got out, he was going to deal with my dad, and the news got back to him. Dad told me later, 'If I'd been around then, I wouldn't be around now.' He stayed away because my uncle Martin was threatening to kill him.

· ■ ■ ■ ■ ■ ·

You'd probably think I had a tough or unhappy upbringing, but it never felt like that to me. Knowle West was poor, but it didn't feel dangerous. You were just aware that people who weren't from Knowle West didn't want to go there. It had a rough reputation.

Because I'm black, people imagine it must've been a black neighbourhood, but it was actually almost completely white, including most of my own family. The funny thing is, even being one of a tiny minority I never experienced any racism whatsoever growing up. That only happened when I became famous and had money.

Our family is very ethnically mixed in itself. My great-great-grandfather, Daniel Lawrence, was a sailor, quarter Jamaican and quarter Spanish, who came over from Jamaica in 1915 to make his home in Cornwall, but my great-great-grandmother, Minnie, was from a totally white family, who I think were in the tin mines down there. They must have had a horrendous time with racism, because there were no black people in Cornwall back then.

Their daughter, my great-grandmother, Margaret ('Maga'), was mixed-race, and when she married my great-grandfather, his family disowned him. He was a Godfrey, which was the family name of a big landowner from Wales or Ireland. They might have even been a little bit royal or aristocratic – there's even a Godfrey crest. They weren't super-rich, but they owned farms and were wealthier than most.

When my great-grandfather was younger, he was a horse dealer, and everyone called him Farmer. He would import horses from Ireland to England – I don't know if it was legal or not. The Godfreys were dead against him getting involved with my great-grandmother, though, and when they married, that was it for his connection with them. It was them that moved to Bristol and ended up in Knowle West.

Going back a century or two before then, Bristol was a city built on slavery. It was where all the English slave ships got built. It's pretty dodgy, but the city's main seated concert venue, Colston Hall, is actually named after the guy who built them, Edward Colston, although I've heard there's plans to change the name. Bristol was also a big slave port, with hundreds of black people being trafficked in and out of the docks every year, which is probably why you've got street names like Black Boy Hill and Whiteladies Road.

A lot of the black in Bristol comes from the American soldiers stationed there in the Second World War – like my mum's father. But these black GIs weren't always welcomed with open arms: my great-uncle Martin saw a guy get kicked to death outside my great-grandmother's house.

When people see pictures of all my relatives over the years, they're like, 'Wow, there's so many different colours!' but for us it was normal. We never knew any different. It was totally normal to have my grandmother look white, and then my great-grandmother look American Indian, my dad black, my auntie Marlow a bit Spanish or Italian, and then for my cousin Michelle to look white as well. None of it mattered to us, and we are a very close family.

After my mum passed away, everyone rallied around to look after me and bring me up. I lived with my auntie Marlow until I was eight, then in Knowle West with my great-grandparents, Farmer and Maga, at 13

Padstow Road, and with my grandmother Violet in Barnstaple Road, and it was only a five-minute walk between the two houses. In those days you could leave your door open without any worries, so I could go back and forth from one to the other, and wander right in.

Although it was a rough area, it wasn't all tiny flats in council high-rises; more red-brick semi-detached houses on hill-top streets lined with occasional trees. I'm so happy I didn't grow up in a tower block. At my great-grandparents' place, it was just them two and me. I was really lucky, I think, because my great-grandmother was alive until I was thirteen or fourteen, and not many people get to see theirs. I've got pictures of three or four generations of my family – including me and my mum – all on the same doorstep outside that house at 13 Padstow Road. I've got that number tattooed on my neck – it's my lucky number, and my uncle Tony's, because it was obviously special to us.

Farmer used to play the thimbles, and Maga would whistle and play washboard and sing prison songs, because her son, Martin, was in prison so much. There was no carpet, just concrete floors, and a coal fire – my great-grandmother taught me how to make a fire. You didn't sit around watching TV there, because there was no TV, so we were out all the time.

Every June in Padstow Road, the whole street would come out for the Queen's birthday. It was like the Jubilee, every year. There would be stalls and tables laid out with food in the middle of the street, and everyone had cups with the Queen's face and the Union Jack on. It's weird: a lot of ghetto people are fanatical about that shit. Even though they're getting fucked over by the elite, they love them. You've got football thugs who love the Queen. It never made no sense to me.

I went to Connaught Road Junior School (now known as Oasis Academy Connaught), and me and my younger sister Leanna were the only black kids there. After Mum passed, Leanna lived at Nanny Maga's for a year or so, but after that we didn't grow up together and we've never had much to do with each other since then.

Connaught was right across the road from Padstow Road, and barely ten minutes from Barnstaple Road, so I could walk to school on my own – everything was right there, and I never had to leave the area. To a kid of five or six, that's a lot of fun, and it was safe back then because everybody knew each other. You didn't hear of dodgy stuff happening to kids, because there would be people on the gates. You'd come home from school, have your tea and then get straight outside. In those days, you were encouraged: 'Go on, get outside and play!' We'd be in parks, on bikes, hanging around outside chip shops, getting chased and stuff.

Me and my mates used to hang out on Filwood Green, right across from my nan's place and the local youth club. In the summer we all used to sit on the grass and play football. On the other side of the green, there was a chip shop, with pinball machines and arcade games. Sometimes the youth club would do bus trips to Weston-super-Mare, but mostly we would hang on the green, which I could see from my bedroom window – I've had some good times on that grass, I tell you, just sat in the sun, doing nothing.

One time, when I was about seven, my nan Violet was driving past and she saw me having a fight with a guy over a football. When I walked into the house later, she got me on her lap, and said to my step-grandad, 'Did you see him fighting, Winston? He done good!' She was proud of me. This was the guidance I was getting.

We weren't rich, but I always had good clothes. There's this great old picture of me from the '70s wearing a red tank-top jumper, a cream patterned shirt and beige broad-checked flares. I dressed dapper, mate! I wore a Marc Bolan T-shirt all the time, too – the first and only music T-shirt I ever had. I used to go into Weston-super-Mare wearing it, and Blackpool with my nan on holiday. I loved his lyrics. You know that song 'Cosmic Dancer'? It goes, 'I danced myself right into the tomb, is it strange to dance so soon?' Proper lyrics, and what's mad is, he died young. To me, that guy was just somewhere else – he was a psychic genius.

I was never a sad kid. I was a mischievous, naughty kid. The only time not having a mum used to frustrate me was when I used to go to school, maybe, or if I was going to pick up a friend from their house, and I'd hear them say, 'Alright – bye, Mum!' Hearing other people say 'mum' – that was the only time it really hurt. Otherwise I was mischievous, having loads of fun.

There was a picture of my mum at my nan's in Barnstaple Road, and I would see it every day when I got up. I'd go over to the window and say 'good morning' to her in the sky – because when you're a kid they tell you your mum is up there in heaven, don't they? I don't believe in that shit now, but when you're young everything's a cartoon. I suppose not having my mother around took me into an imaginative space. And later on, my music was these imaginary spaces – me imagining things.

My nan used to listen to Billie Holiday on an old cassette player. I would be sat in the middle of the room, aged about six or seven, playing on the carpet, and she would just watch me – not like 'don't put your fingers in the plug socket' kind of watching. She used to smoke a cigarette and just watch me. She'd put her ash into her palm, because she didn't have an ashtray, and rub her two palms together to get rid of it, then she would say, 'You look like your mum, you do!'

Billie Holiday is the first music I remember hearing; this haunting voice, and my nan telling me I reminded her of her dead daughter. She obviously missed her so much, because she was watching me like I was TV. My sister doesn't look like my mum – she looks more like my dad. I was too young to really know what was going on there. It was like I was my mum's replacement, almost. I was my mum's ghost.

· ■ ■ ■ ■ · ·

I can only have been five or six when I suffered my first asthma attack. My first memory of it is my great-grandad, Farmer, holding my hand at 13 Padstow Road because I couldn't breathe. That's what he always did whenever I had an attack, because he didn't know what else to do. He'd sit there holding my hand in the little room upstairs until it was okay and I could fall asleep. I didn't get a Ventolin inhaler till I was thirteen or fourteen, because living with my great-grandparents, their generation didn't really do the hospitals thing, or go to doctors. You know how everybody these days goes to the hospital for anything – they get toothache and they're straight down to the emergency room? In those days, you didn't do that, or at least they didn't. My great-grandmother never went to the dentist, and because sweets weren't in their culture, she never had a filling in her life. Any pain or illness, they'd just tough it out and let it pass.

I didn't have breathing problems until my mum died, apparently, and when I eventually saw a doctor, they said my asthma was probably brought on by the trauma of losing her. One time when I was about eight years of age, I was having an attack in the same house, sat on the concrete floor, while my great-uncle Martin was there.

'You know why he's having an asthma attack, don't you?' he goes to my great-grandmother, Maga.

'No, why?'

'Because he's a breed.'

'Shut up,' she spits back, 'don't say that in front of him.'

That one stayed with me. What's funny is, Martin isn't white neither: his mum is half-black, and his dad is white, so it was weird coming from him. I don't think he was being wicked, that's just how people thought in those days. He wasn't being nasty; he was my uncle – he loved me! It's just that our family say anything to each other; there are no boundaries.

At Padstow Road, we lived like gypsies. The only difference was we didn't travel around in a caravan, so, the way I see it, I had the best of both worlds.

I used to go rabbiting at night with Farmer and his son, my great-uncle Martin. To me, it was exciting creeping around the countryside at night, but of course it was illegal to trespass on farmers' land, so it was quite dangerous – you could get shot. We'd go out with netting and all this other equipment. You used little lamps or the lights from your car to get around, but often you would be going through hedges and ditches in pitch-black. Real fun, but scary too. As well as farmers with shotguns, there were bulls to contend with. There was one farmer who had a sign that said, 'You may be able to make it across the field in ten minutes, but my bull can do it in three!' It was risky, but that was part of the fun.

We had all the kit in my great-grandparents' house, with the long nets that Maga made hanging all over the walls, and ferrets in cages in the back garden, to send down the rabbit holes. Ferrets are one of my favourite animals: if one bites you, you have to burn its nose to get its jaws to unlock. After a good night's hunting, there would be rabbits hanging all over the kitchen walls, and we'd eat the rabbits. Rabbit is good! We had pigeon too, on occasion, but mostly rabbit. For us, steak was a rare treat. We lived off the land.

This wasn't something everyone my age in Knowle West did. It was because I was raised by older generations – old-school, eating rabbit stew, and bread and dripping and vegetables we grew in the back garden, like carrots, potatoes, runner beans and tomatoes. They didn't call him Farmer for nothing. We'd go scrumping for apples, too. It was just eating for survival, really.

At Farmer's funeral, they spread his rabbiting nets out all over the cars in the cortège. Martin was drunk and going on, so my nan Violet had a fight with him outside, and his sisters Olive and Maureen had a fight in the hearse, actually going at it right by the coffin.

Uncle Martin was well into rabbiting too, and he had the gypsy look – whippets, horses, big boots and a shotgun. After we'd been out at night he'd walk in the house, string around his trousers, rabbits hanging off his neck – we'd always come back with a couple, maybe four or five. I learnt how to kill a rabbit when I was still very young – you grab it by the neck and push up the chin to break its neck. It's the quickest death. Martin knew how to skin a rabbit and cook it. Hunting involves a lot of skill.

When I stayed in Totterdown for a while, there was a gypsy camp near where we lived, and my uncle Martin used to hang out there and go drinking with them. He was friends with them, as was my great-grandad, Farmer, and there was a kind of gypsy vibe about them both.

As well as rabbiting, my great-grandad and my great-uncles were bare-knuckle fighters. Farmer fought the king of the gypsies, and his son Arthur fought the gypsy king's son. I never went to any of the fights, but I saw enough in the way of street fights, bar fights and what have you, as I grew up. What I do know is, a lot of the guys doing the bare-knuckle fights ain't getting exploited, they love it. They grew up with it. They're doing it because they want to do it. Professional boxers get exploited by the big promoters, but not the bare-knuckle guys. You get bare-knuckle guys fighting for no money – gypsies fighting for the name of being the best.

My uncles were full-on gangsters. They did protection, so pubs had to pay them to keep trouble away. Also, they owned clubs themselves. Martin and Arthur, Farmer and Maga's sons, were known all over Bristol. Martin was feared by everybody – including my dad, after his threats from inside Dartmoor. When Martin was free to roam, he used to extort people. At one point he owned his own club in Manchester, and then burnt it down himself for the insurance. Ever since I can remember, his left eye was milky – I don't know what happened, but it was probably something to do with violence.

Arthur was just like his brother but less crazy. Where Martin was right in your face, people used to say Arthur was more sly – quiet but dangerous. He used to fight like fuck, but he was just more devious about it. Martin would slice up a fucking room of people – that vibe – whereas Arthur would get you on the quiet, smile at you, then do it. So they were different personalities, but they were together; they were known together and would do things together.

When he wasn't dressed in the gypsy style, Martin was a proper gangster, suited and booted. At seventeen, he'd been the youngest guy ever to be sent to Wormwood Scrubs, and he was often on the front page of newspapers for the crimes he committed. I wouldn't call them local celebrities exactly; people were just scared to death of them, especially Martin.

Their nephew, my uncle Tony, was a big guy up in Manchester, and known for violence. He'd moved up north from Knowle West when he was a kid, along with his mum Violet and his sister Maxine (aka my nan and my mum), but when the women returned to Bristol, Tony, who was fifteen at the time, stayed up there because he loved it so much. When I was little, we used to go up and stay with him for a couple of weeks for our summer holidays. Otherwise it was a week in Butlin's in Minehead, with six of us in a chalet – I never went abroad until I started in music.

In the mid-90s, I was out for dinner in the 'Curry Mile' in Manchester, with this guy who made a documentary about me. We'd been filming at my uncle Tony's house, and then we all went out to eat afterwards. Just as our food arrived at the table, the owner of the restaurant came in, saw uncle Tony and looked at our plates, and shouted something at the waiter in Indian, and the waiter came and chucked a napkin over the food and rushed off with the plates. The owner said to my uncle, 'That's for the punters, not for your family, Tony!' Obviously, he didn't want to offend my uncle, or piss him off.

Uncle Tony was a serious guy, but the women in my family also used to fight. My great-auntie, Maureen Godfrey, was a top female streetfighter in Manchester. If she got into it with a woman, she'd fuck her! My mum used to fight, too. The women in a gangster family are often tougher than the men. Most gangsters are mummy's boys – look at the Kray twins – and my uncles got into boxing through their mum. The person who first sent me to boxing training was my auntie Maureen.

One day, Maureen stabbed my uncle Martin, which I saw happen. I don't think Martin liked Maureen's husband very much, and he might have been trying to get money off him, so he used to go around and smash the house up sometimes. One day he went around there, and my auntie

Maureen opened the door, threw pepper in his eyes and stabbed him in the stomach.

Auntie Maureen was funny – a lovely, lovely lady. Once, I was walking home from school, and my mate goes, 'Look at that woman!' She was laid out on the floor drunk, with a bottle, outside a phone box. I pretended I didn't know her. She was a funny woman, but people thought she was nuts as well, so they left her alone. She had a scar because someone cut her with a knife, or so my uncle Martin told me, but I can't remember who.

This is the world I grew up in. I saw a lot of violence at a young age, and it was almost normal to me. I grew up around things like me saying, 'Where is Uncle Martin?' and Maga replying, 'Oh, he's in prison, but at least I know where he is.' Instead of Maga going, 'Aw, I wish he wasn't in prison,' she would look at it as, 'Well, at least I know where he is.' I grew up with that mindset.

I knew about my uncles, and what they got up to. Often when you walked into places with them, you could feel the respect in the room, but when someone's your relative, you don't see them as bad or good. If you're related to Al Capone, you ain't gonna see him as Al Capone like other people do. He's just family.

■ ■ ■ ■ ■ ■ ■

I feel like my dad had a really shit life. Growing up in Jamaica, his own father left him, and after that it was almost like Dad was basically chasing him around. I don't think his dad was very paternal: he was off doing his thing. Instead of you looking for your kid, it's your kid looking for you. My grandad moved to England, and if my dad hadn't followed him he might not have even had any further contact with him until Dad tracked him down. He wasn't the sort of guy to look back. Like, 'Oh, I left Roy there!'

My dad was a bit of a bad boy. He had a dominoes crew, and they ended up taking over my grandad's sound system, but then my great-uncle Martin threatened to kill him, and after that he had to stay away from me.

I'm going to hand over to him for a bit now, because he knows a lot of stuff about my background that I don't remember or wasn't around for.

ROY THAWS: I come from a place in Jamaica called Saint Catherine, down near Spanish Town, which was country then, not too ruffian. I was born in 1943, and when I was young there my mum and dad were working in Kingston, so I lived with my grandparents.

I was brought up Christian and went to a church school. As I got into my teens, school was very far away – too far! – and I never spent much time there, so when I was about fifteen, I came up to live with my parents in Kingston – in Greenwich Town, right by the sea, across the bay from the airport. I was in Kingston for four or five years. My mother did cleaning and odd jobs, and my dad worked at the sugar refinery at the wharf.

A lot of people in Jamaica lived very rough. I saw it, but, praise God, I never went through that. We always had our own light, electricity, water, everything. My memories of Jamaica are good, but it was hard for everyone living there. I used to work on the quarries for my money. From the day I was born, I lived independent.

My brother was the first one who came to England, then my father, then my niece, and eventually in 1962 I followed her. That quarry was very hard work, breaking the rock with machinery. My brother said, 'Oh, it's good over here,' so I'd dream of coming to join him.

I came over on the boat, and I paid a hundred pounds for the trip. My brother Rupert sent the fare home, because he was already in England for two or three years before me. The crossing took three weeks, and I didn't bring nothing from Jamaica, only my clothes. There were four of us in this little cabin in bunk beds. There was hundreds of people on there, and some were stowaways, hiding in the lifeboats, then at night time they'd come out.

At first I lived in Wolverhampton, because my brother and my dad were there, but I didn't like it. When I first came, I cried, wanting to go home. 'It too cold!' I got used to it soon enough, then after two or three months I came down to Bristol. Dad had been to Bristol before, so I followed him, and then my brother followed me. I just love Bristol, from when I first come here, and life was better, going to lots of nice parties and having fun. I never got myself into trouble.

I lived in Hartcliffe. It wasn't rough for black people and, telling the truth, I never had no problem with racism. I didn't have any time for that. My time was all spent going to work, to put food on the table. Before I met Maxine, I had two kids with another woman, Kevin and Julian, so I used to work very long hours, from six in the morning till six at night, in a bakery in Kingswood, north of Bristol. I would have to get up every morning at five o'clock, then I would also do nights, from 6pm until 6am. It was very hard, but I stuck it out.

I usually worked Sunday morning to Saturday morning, then I'd go back to work Sunday. I was getting good money. I used to send some back to my mother in Jamaica, but otherwise all my family was here. For a time, my father and my brother and I all lived together in St Paul's. So, we would be out at parties every Saturday night. Sometimes after leaving the party I would go straight to work – no clean clothes!

After my father got to England, he started up a sound system – he'd never done it before, in Jamaica. The music was all '60s reggae – ska and rocksteady and early Bob Marley. He would get imports straight from Kingston. He'd write to a friend back home, and the guy would send the records Dad wanted – the latest Jamaican records before anyone else had them. That's why he was so good, and we used to travel all over England – everybody want to hear 'Tarzan di High Priest'!

Dad never actually played the records himself, or got on the mic, he always got somebody to do it for him. My brother Rupert used to DJ a lot, and sometimes I would play on a Saturday night, but I couldn't do it the right way, and I had to go to work.

I still went around with him a lot. We would play in the Bamboo Club in St Paul's, against other sounds from London – that club was very good! A bloke in Bath used to have a sound, so we'd go down there and do a contest, to see who won. We'd go all over – Manchester, Liverpool, London, Cardiff – a network right around the UK. We used to do a lot of contests, sound against sound.

I met Maxine at a blues party in Albany Road in St Paul's. We just clicked straight away and started going out. The two of us were just good together. She was very lively, a very nice girl, and once we were together she kept herself to herself. Looking back, I never really had any time to do anything with her because I worked from six until six and I only had one day off on a Saturday.

Maxine's family were more established in Bristol, in Knowle West, which was a very white area. We were together there for quite a while, when she had Adrian, but she used to have fits, fits, fits, all the time. I couldn't do nothing about it. She said she wanted to keep the family together, the three of us, but all she would have was fits all the while, so she couldn't do it. After we had Leanna, she sent Adrian to live with his grandmother, Violet.

Sometimes I would be there when one of Maxine's fits started, and I had to hold her down and put my fingers in her mouth to stop her swallowing her tongue. She loved to go to a dance, but after a while she went off it because every time she came out and had a drink, she would have fits, so she didn't like to go any more.

Every day I still talk about her. She was a good mother. She had a good brain, and she used to tell good stories, but that's why she took her own life, because she wanted to look after her kids, and she thought she couldn't do it.

So I came home from work one evening and I saw that she had passed away. It was a terrible thing to live with, coming in and seeing her. I will never forget it. Adrian was at his grandmother's, but Leanna was there – she was only two, and hadn't had anything to eat all day. When I came in, I saw Leanna lying down on Maxine, and she was dead. Leanna ran up and grabbed me, and I saw the tablets beside her, and the letter she had written.

I fed Leanna, then ran over with her to tell Marlow, and everybody started crying. Maxine wrote the letter because she knew all her parents and family would carry on at me, thinking I had done something to her. The letter was saying, 'Roy doesn't have nothing to do with it.'

What I didn't know was that she'd tried to kill herself before. Her mother Violet knew, and if she had told me everything, and said, 'Watch her, otherwise she'll kill herself,' she would probably be alive now – I would've left two tablets out for her and hidden the rest – but her mother never told me nothing. Only once we'd notified the police and they started pushing me around did she say, 'No, he had nothing to do with it – she tried to do it before already.'

Maxine wrote this big letter to the family, to try and stop Martin from carrying on with me. They all knew that Martin was a very rough guy. Everybody in St Paul's used to be afraid of him, so that's why she wrote that letter, and said to tell him that Roy didn't have anything to do with it, and he should leave him alone. I gave Marlow the letter, and if Maxine hadn't written it, they would have blamed me and probably I wouldn't be alive today.

Still, Martin made it known he was looking for me, saying he was gonna hurt me. I heard that he was going to get me, so I had to keep away, from Martin and from my kids. Maybe he didn't see the letter Maxine wrote to them. I didn't want anything to happen to me or to anyone. I never moved far away, and I never left Bristol. I didn't know nowhere else except Bristol. I just moved from Hartcliffe and got a place down in St Paul's.

After that, I kept working to take care of my home. Sometimes I think I worked too many hours, and I should've given up the bakery job. All of my kids will tell you the truth: Adrian and Leanna were the only kids I didn't give nothing to. With the rest of my kids, I tried my best with what I had – I gave to them. In the end, Adrian phoned me and we would have a chat, and sometimes he came to see me, and I'm pleased about that. I always thought, 'When they come big, they'll know where to find me.' And it worked out that way. My life never separated from Adrian's. He's family. And I can never forget Maxine.

TRICKY: I didn't start seeing my dad until I was about twelve years old. For some reason around that time I'd taken to sitting on the stairs in my auntie Marlow's house, going through the phonebook. One time I found my last name, and I go, 'Who is this?' And she replies, 'That's your dad – give him a call!'

So I called, and his wife Christine answered.

'Hello, is Roy there?' I asked.

'No, he's not in at the moment,' said Christine. 'Who is this?'

'It's his son,' I simply replied.

'I'll tell him you called.'

After that, I started seeing him again. The first time, I went to his house without my uncle Martin knowing about it. I realise now, looking back, that my dad is quite a violent man, too. I must have been about twelve or thirteen when one day he took me to Eastville market. While he was parking the car there, he had an argument about a parking space. Voices were getting raised, and Dad pulled a flick knife out on the guy. He was going, 'You want me to cut you?' all in this Jamaican twang, and the other guy backed down. If he hadn't, the guy would have got cut, no doubt about it.

His manner seems gentle, but it's not when he loses his temper. He wasn't like my great-uncle Martin, but he would definitely cut you back then. Over the years, as he's got older, he has told me things every now and then, probably because Martin isn't around now – at least, he ain't like he used to be.

CHAPTER TWO
THE GODFREYS

Even though I lost my mum so young, I was brought up by women – Maga, Violet, my auntie Marlow and my cousin Michelle, all very strong women. There were men around – like Martin, when he wasn't in prison, and Tony, who would come down from Manchester to visit – but the main man who was around was Marlow's husband Ken. After Maga passed away, I lived mostly at Marlow and Ken's house in Hartcliffe. That was another busy house, with Marlow, Ken, me, their children Mark and Michelle, who were both a few years older than me, and another kid called Trevor Beckford, who wasn't related, but was like family – so that was six of us. It sounds like there was a lot of us, but when you're family, it doesn't feel crowded.

Ken worked as a hospital chef – he made the food in the Bristol Royal Infirmary – and he never got into trouble or any of that stuff. He used to spoil me, Ken, and he listened to music all the time. He was a white guy, but well into black music. He loved Sam Cooke, Marvin Gaye, and the first time I ever saw a music film was with him – *The Jazz Singer*, with Neil Diamond. In fairness, I was too young to think of it as anything more than just music.

Marlow worked too, in a restaurant, so we didn't feel poor. We always had food and clean clothes, and I would walk to and from school in Knowle West. When I was eight, my nana Violet moved from Knowle West to a top-floor flat in Totterdown, which was doing well, coming from Knowle West – it's a nicer neighbourhood, the next one up going north towards the city centre – and she demanded that I come to live with her.

With all these comings and goings, I didn't really go to school much. To begin with, I didn't even have to bunk off as such. Education wasn't important to my nan, so she didn't think it was important for me. She was just from a different generation. She was totally cool. If it was raining too much, she would come into my bedroom and say, 'Oh, do you really want to go to school? It's raining!' or 'It's really cold today, innit?' I think she was really just keeping me home for company, because she would otherwise be alone all day.

My senior school, Merrywood Boys School, wasn't great but it wasn't grim or rough-looking. All the rooms were nice, and warm. It was just a bad school because of area problems. I didn't mind going there from that perspective. I just didn't go because I had the choice not to go. Most kids go because they have to go, whereas if I didn't want to, I didn't. I had the worst attendance. One of my class teachers used to make fun of me. You know when they call your name out on the register, and you say 'Yes, sir'? He would pretend to faint, like, 'You're in – wow!'

The only things I was good at were English and sports. I could miss six weeks of school, then finally turn up and come top in an English exam, no problem! The one book I always remember reading was *Rikki-Tikki-Tavi* by Rudyard Kipling. I used to love that story, about the mongoose. Apart from that, I didn't know much about books. I like reading now in later life, but there weren't any books around when I was younger. I didn't know anybody who read.

Words, however, were a big thing for me, before music. I was all about words. From five years of age, I would apparently sit on my great-grandmother's concrete floor, writing poems – page after page, all afternoon – but unfortunately none of it has survived so we'll never know what was going through my head back then.

The only time I went to school was to see my mates, and it was a right laugh. My best friend, Danny Shepherd, was like Dennis the Menace. That kid, he used to do stuff. One time, he ripped some guy's box jacket from the back, almost tore it off him. Another time, he made like he was throwing a chisel at a teacher from behind, but threw it so it just hit the cupboards nearby. Danny must've been the worst, worst, worst kid in Merrywood Boys – if not the whole of Knowle West, which is saying something. I went all through school with him, and this other guy called Dean Reid – both white kids – right from the age of five at junior school. When you've got mischievous mates like that, and you bother to go in, school is funny.

Much later, in the 1990s, Merrywood got closed down and demolished, because it had such bad results. When I was there, I thought it had some really bloody good teachers, so I don't know if it got worse. One of them taught me really good handwriting – old-school, with fountain pens, in old English lettering.

The main problem was that everyone knew that you couldn't go anywhere from there. One really honest teacher told us once, 'If you fill out a job application, lie about coming from here – put a different postcode, because when people see you're from Knowle West, you won't get the job.' He was a cool teacher, telling us the truth, letting us know that coming from Knowle West, you've either got to work a bit harder, or lie. So that was good reality, more important than cramming something or being book smart – what education should be about. That served me well, all through my life.

As you got a bit older, you realised there were no prospects of getting out of Knowle West. There was just the Woodbine tobacco factory, where my grandmother worked, and Cadbury's, where a couple of my other family members worked. Those were the jobs that were available, but then the tobacco factory closed in the mid-80s, and all those jobs went – it's luxury apartments now. I think Cadbury's got shut down as well, so there wasn't a lot of work. If you wanted a legal job, it would have been construction or scaffolding.

There aren't many people who got well known out of Knowle West, apart from me and Julian Dicks. He was a footballer, who went on to play for West Ham United and Liverpool, known as The Terminator. I actually played with him at school – we were in the school team together. From the age of eight through to about fifteen, I was in the school team most of the time, but I didn't take it as serious as many kids do – like, it might be their route out of a hard situation. In my teens, it got to a place where I didn't want to use my Saturdays doing that. I just wanted to hang out.

I never went to football matches. I've only been to two in my whole life – one in Italy and one in Bristol. The only sport I watch is boxing, probably because I've done quite a bit of it myself, and I like to watch what they're doing technically. I grew up around it, and like football it's a very English working-class thing. As a kid, it might be your way out of a council flat. Most boxers come from very poor environments, and they get into it so they can change their lives. I can remember staying up really late to watch the Muhammad Ali fights on TV when I was just a little kid.

All the Knowle West white kids could fight, but I didn't feel it was particularly violent growing up, because I was just one of the kids. We used to run around, loads of us, all around the streets. I'm more aware of it now when I go back, because I'm not from there any more, so I can feel the atmosphere. If I go into a pub and it's all Knowle Westers, you can feel the vibe.

I never felt there was that much racial tension, although when I was a teenager I had police shouting 'black bastard' at me, or following me while I was driving along in a car, or someone shouting out 'nigger' from afar, which I can remember happening to me once in Hartcliffe. But I see all that more as a street thing. It's just how things were, and it never bothered me. You know: these policemen don't like me, and I don't like them – fuck 'em! But then I've seen white friends in Knowle West getting beaten up by police and locked up, so in my opinion it's more to do with the streets than the colour of your skin.

Back then, you were just aware that there were certain Knowle Westers who were dangerous people, like Wayne Lomas. He was a great guy, and a friend of my uncles. One time I was in the Robins pub, and Wayney had just shot some guy in the neck. I was sat at the bar, and my cousin was playing pool or something, and Wayne came in. I've known him all my life, and he goes, 'Do you want a drink?' So I goes, 'Yeah, alright, Wayne,' then he made the guy next to me buy me the drink. He goes, 'Aw, leave it out, Wayne!' and he put his fingers in the guy's neck like they were a pistol.

He was a bit crazy, Wayne. He went missing in 1988. Someone had killed him, and they eventually found his body five years later, chopped up into pieces and embedded in a concrete floor in a terraced house in Southville.

A handful of my uncles and cousins could have met a similar fate. In fact, one of them did, and when I really stop to think about it, so could I.

· ▪ ▪ ■ ▪ ▪ ·

You know how it's hard to understand what makes someone tick sometimes? My great-uncle Martin told me once that when he was in his late teens, he was in this home for naughty youth and he'd started boxing. He won some kind of Avon and Somerset competition, so he was through to the national finals in London. He'd qualified and everything, but the head of this place wouldn't let him go to fight in London. You can imagine, at that age it was such a big thing for him: he had already won at the regional level, and this was going national. After that, everyone in the family blamed the way he turned out on that guy who told him he couldn't go to London.

When he was telling me about it, I definitely got that vibe, too. I think that's what made him violent. He loved his boxing, and at that point it could've led anywhere for him, so this guy was killing his dream. Later on, when someone did something to him, and he was hurting them, it was almost like he was also hurting that guy. I don't know that for sure, but that's what I felt.

You can Google my uncle Martin, and you'll find stuff about him. He was on the front of the *Bristol Evening Post* when he was twenty-something

– this old article where they're looking for him because he's kidnapped someone or carved someone up. It says something like, 'THIS EVIL MAN' and there's a picture of him in a leather jacket, with the collar up.

If you want to understand me, and where I come from, you need to hear some of my uncles' stories.

MARTIN GODFREY: I was born in 1934, and grew up in Knowle West. It was such a poor neighbourhood, we had hardly any food – I remember my brother having to saw a loaf of bread in half because it was so stale.

Originally my father worked on a farm on the outskirts of town, and he used to come gathering pigswill from houses all around Knowle West and Bedminster – all the leftovers, for the pigs – until eventually he and Maga set up home there.

We lived at 13 Padstow Road, a normal, simply decorated council house with five rooms: downstairs had a kitchen and a living room, while upstairs there was one bedroom for Mum and Dad, one for my sisters – Olive, Violet and Maureen – and one for me and my brother, Arthur. It was a busy house, women cooking every night.

Knowle West was terrible during the war – I was five when it started. We got bombed a lot, because there were aerodromes, and lots of Americans stationed there. The house behind ours got bombed. Round the corner, there was blood splattered all over the gate where another house got bombed.

It was a violent place, anyway. It wasn't easy being a mixed-race family – my mother was half-black, and I'm quarter-black – and my dad had a lot of fights over it. My left eye is milky because, when I was about ten, some kid threw stones at me and hit me there; ever since, I've only been able to see out of the other one.

I saw a couple of Americans – two servicemen – getting beaten, and one of them died. I was playing down by the local pub, the Venture Inn, and I saw this Yank come out, and they all chased him, so I chased behind them, and he came to a little shelter on the corner, and they all piled on him – then they all went away, and an ambulance came, and I heard them say he was dead.

My mother, Margaret, used to take in these black squaddies and cook meals for them. She was very kind like that, but the neighbours didn't like it. They'd come and throw stones at the house. There was a big riot after that American got killed, and they came smashing our house up.

I was going to school one day, and the bombs fell and hit the school, so we had to run and get in shelters. Sometimes we'd be in there overnight, sometimes two nights, twenty of us or even fifty of us, women and children, all huddled in there like sardines. Loads got bombed, and because it was a poor part of town, it didn't get built up again for a long time after. People always looked down on Knowle West, but we were proud of it.

We had the rabbits, see, rabbits and hares, plenty of them, and that was how we beat the rations. We used to supply the whole neighbourhood with rabbits. Farmer used to take us rabbiting – long-netting at night, or ferreting with the dogs in the day. We used to sell the rabbits for five shillings each, and sometimes we'd catch twenty or thirty in a night. It put food on our table as well. I loved doing it, but it was dangerous – if you got caught, you went to court, and there'd be gamekeepers around with shotguns. We were at it almost every night, like the family business, and we'd go out miles on our pushbikes to do it.

They knew us well enough. One farmer called Hazel had a farm out Whitchurch way, and we used to go up there poaching. He caught me ferreting once and took the ferret off me, so Farmer went up to him and told him that he wanted my ferret back, but Hazel said he couldn't have it, so my dad punched him, knocked him down, took the ferret, and we came home. After that, there was always trouble with him. He'd put traps out, and had his sons out looking for us.

When I was about twenty, I followed my sister Maureen up to Manchester, and ended up living there for six or seven years. My niece Maxine came up there as well. She was a very nice young lady, very bright.

She used to write poems and was very good in school, read Shakespeare. She dressed well, and liked bright colours. Then she met this … she met Adrian's father, and then things went wrong. She moved back to Bristol, had the two kids, and then committed suicide. I don't know anything about him at all, but I don't think good things about him. She was epileptic, but I don't think that was anything to do with it – she'd had it since she was a kid. He was going with other women, and that played on her mind.

I was in prison, and I got a letter saying she'd taken her own life. I was shocked. I never thought she would do that. It was such a shame, terrible – all over her fella. So I wrote this letter back, making my feelings known. I just said I felt sorry for her, and how she was treated, that I wanted to run him out of town. I suppose I had a reputation at that time. A lot of people were scared of me.

The stuff I did, it was only little skirmishes around the pubs. Violence was what everyone was doing, and I was just the best at it. I got in a lot of trouble. For me, the violence was mostly for the excitement. It wasn't like I went around looking for it, but when you've got a reputation, they come looking for you, and you can't back down. It mattered to me at the time, but it was all stupid really, a load of rubbish. I regret it now.

We were a bit of a double act, me and my brother Arthur, and I got quite a reputation. To start with I'd just fight with my fists, but one time I was fighting a fella in a dancehall and he stabbed me on the head with a penknife, so that started it going where I carried a knife. I never saw that guy again.

These were just gang fights. It didn't feel like a gang as such, just a few of us used to get together, and we would go out and get in a lot of trouble together, just fighting. I went to prison a few times – always for stabbing with knives, once for two years, once for four years, another for seven years.

The first time, I got into a fight, and I cut a fellow with a knife in a pub. He survived alright. I went to court and I got two years at Horfield prison in Bristol, but after six months they transferred me to Wormwood Scrubs – supposedly I was their youngest ever inmate. I was alright in there; you just had to look after yourself. While I was in, I got beat up by the screws, and this MP, Peter Baker, who was doing a stretch for fraud at the time, saw it, and wrote about it in a book called *Time Out of Life*, saying it was the worst beating he'd ever seen.

It was a very good feeling coming out again, but not long after there was this bloke who kept telling stories about me and causing me a lot of problems, so I went for him this night and carved him up – got him on the floor and carved 'RAT' on his chest. I got four years for that.

Another time, I had a fight in a pub, and we both had broken glasses, and I cut him with the glass, and I got seven years. It was always different prisons. I was in Strangeways, Wandsworth, Gloucester. I can't say any of them stopped me reoffending – it didn't work like that for me.

I lost family along the way. Years ago, Arthur had a heart attack and died, and my nephew Michael was only in his late twenties when he got stabbed to death. This was in the early-80s: he was going into a blues called Ajax and they tried to charge him money to go in. He wouldn't pay, and the fella on the door stabbed him in the heart.

I got done over a couple of times, once on St Paul's Road, when a nurse found me bleeding to death. People come picking on you, and then they come down with more of them against one of you. I packed it all in eventually, and I do feel lucky to be alive. I kept on scrap dealing out in the country for a bit, around Wells and Glastonbury. Then a few years ago, I came back to Bristol, still doing scrap, then I retired.

When Adrian came to live with us at Padstow Road, he'd come rabbiting with us sometimes, but he didn't like the sitting around, the cold and the walking. He was just into music and dancing. He used to do that breakdancing on the street, then he would be out at night, every night, he wouldn't stay in. But he was a good little kid. He didn't get into much trouble.

TRICKY: While Martin was in Manchester, my mum's brother Tony was up there too, and he got quite a reputation as well, which all started from his bare-knuckle boxing. Martin used to fight him out like a dog. Martin had this club in Manchester, and all these gangsters used to go in boasting about their fighters, and he'd say to them, 'Listen, your boy won't beat my nephew!' Tony was only sixteen or so, and he would fight them and beat them. Sometimes he'd knock these hard guys out with one punch. That's how he became one of the top guys in Manchester.

TONY GUEST: I was a war baby, born in 1944. My dad was a black American soldier called Ted Guest, but he was never married to my mum, Violet Godfrey, Adrian's nan. I never had much to do with my dad because he went back to America, and I stayed here. Mum also had Michael and Maxine (Adrian's mum) by different men.

I grew up in 13 Padstow Road until I was eight, then I went to Manchester with a whole load of the family, so I was only in Knowle West when I went to Connaught Road school in the late '40s and early '50s. It was bad at school, because me and another lad were the only two black people there. My grandfather Farmer was white, and my grandmother Maga was a quarter black, and because he'd married a black girl people were always smashing our windows.

That was why you had to fight, if you were me, if you can understand that. You had to fight or run away, and I was a fighter. I wouldn't let no one take liberties. That was why I liked Manchester, because once I went there, you never got any of that – there were blacks, Indians, Asians, everything, whereas Bristol just seemed to be one thing: just Bristolians.

Maxine and Michael came with us to Manchester, and we lived in Chorlton-on-Medlock, near All Saints. I liked Manchester. I went to school and I had friends. I went to Webster Street School on Moss Side, then, at eleven, Cavendish in All Saints, and that's where I started boxing. I wasn't interested in any of the rest of the classes. The PT teacher worked it all out: he said, 'You know how you can do something good? You can do boxing,' so that's how I started. Before long I did bare-knuckle on the side. You got a few bruises but it was okay if you were good.

In our teens, Maxine always said I was too disciplined, being the elder brother. She went out with anyone, and I would say, 'Oh, he's no good.' I had to look after her. She was up in Manchester until she was about fifteen. She was a wild character, but the whole fucking family was wild characters, now I come to think of it! I think she met Roy when she was back visiting Bristol, so she moved down again, and it wasn't long before Adrian and Leanna were born.

We've been through a lot. I've lost my sister and my brother, and it wasn't in nice ways – Maxine committed suicide, and our Michael got stabbed to death – murdered. I got a phone call out of the blue about Maxine, just like I did about Michael. You never forget that stuff.

After us, my uncle Martin moved up as well – the mad one. I was close with him, and we went around a lot together. He was like a wildcat, man! He had a name and a reputation for fighting, and I got one too. How it happened: I was out in Manchester, right near Christmas, and I was going to the Wishing Well, which was a café that was open all the time, and then on to the club Martin was running. As I was going past the Wishing Well, they were all singing Christmas songs, so I go inside to join in and this Scottish guy came up and said, 'Hey, what are you fucking doing?' and he headbutted me, so I gave him a combination and punched him to the floor. His missus started at me with a high-heeled shoe to get me off him. I had no idea he was Danny Fieldings, one of the hardest men in town.

After that my name flew around town. That's how it happens. I was only sixteen, seventeen, and fit as a fiddle. I wasn't trying to be top man, it just happened after that. I kept up the boxing, but by the time I was twenty-five, I was on the door at clubs all around town. I was at the Bierkeller for eight years, Roosters, the Portland Lodge, and I worked at the pubs sometimes. There were a few places we were running.

The guy I did a lot of that with, Dave Ward, was close to the family of Shaun Ryder from the Happy Mondays, or so I later discovered. Dave was a moor man, like a gypsy. He ran Manchester for a long time, and I was his partner: I took care of the central clubs, and he looked after the south side.

Martin was dead smart back then. He had a club called the Edinburgh – not licensed, like a shebeen. I was security, always the one that made sure it was okay. It only started at night, and all the night birds would come out – black people and white people. There was good music and drinking all night and morning.

While he was up here, Martin stabbed a guy over on Moss Side. Me and Michael was in another shebeen, and at one point our Mike stood up and this waiter's tray went over. The waiter went mad: 'You've gotta pay for all this!' At that moment, Martin walked in, and because he was a handsome guy back then – they used to say he looked like a cross between Dean Martin and Tony Curtis – he had two birds with him, and they'd just been out on the town. We were close family, and they thought we were all brothers, so they went to our Martin, and said, 'Listen, you've gotta pay for all this!' Our Martin told them to eff off, so a fight started, and this waiter was a big guy.

Our Martin very slowly took his white mac off, put it over his arm, and then a fucking great big knife came out, and he stabbed the guy. God Almighty! It was chaos, they were jumping out of the windows to get out! It was a bad one – he got three years, Martin, and he said to the judge, 'Thank you very much, because in Bristol I would have got about ten for that!'

People said Martin should've been born in Apache days, because he had a right name. Bloody hell, in Bristol he got hold of this fellow at a party who was a grass. This guy was the king of the Teddy Boys, name of Webber. Webber's gang had got one of Martin's friends in a shopping centre and beat him up, and Martin went for revenge. He waited for him – he was like that, a dangerous man. He climbed up the drainpipe while they were having a party, broke in and cut 'RAT' on this bloke's chest with a knife. Branded him!

He was in prison a lot, Martin. I was with him the time he burnt down someone else's club. That night he came back from town to the Edinburgh, and he looked disappointed.

'Tone, where are all the people?'

'They're probably at the Birdland, at the bottom of the road,' I replied.

'Are they now,' he muttered. He called up two of the Scotch mob – Jimmy Boyle from Glasgow, he was on the wanted list, and they made a film about him later called *A Sense of Freedom* – and the four of us went down to the Birdland, via the petrol station, for two cans of petrol. The three of them went in, and it was packed in there, and they went sprinkling petrol from the cans all over the place, until they got to this open fire they had. Apparently the guy from the club started laughing – he thought they were helping with the cleaning up – and Martin goes, 'Yeah, I am!' and he throws the petrol can in the fire and the whole place goes up!

He had one of those long trench-coats on, and he was running off up the road with his coat on fire! You wouldn't believe it, man. They took me in, but I was only with him, I didn't do any of it, so I got off. He went to Strangeways for that.

As well as running security, I was also doing some minding, looking after a guy to make sure there was no messing about, no mithering. He was Dickie Ewing, from London, who used to do mock auctions. It was all legal, but if you ask me it was all a con. I got a shilling [5p] in the pound on what he sold, sometimes 10p in the pound. Those were good days. I did a lot of protection work for him, too. That was the dirtier side of it.

Dickie used to have a Rolls-Royce, and one time we went to Bristol in it. Adrian was only about twelve then and, as we pulled up, he was in the middle of the road shouting, '*Aaaaaww*, Uncle Tony!' Bloody hell, there wasn't much of that in Knowle West.

The Manchester clubs got rougher when the guns arrived in the '90s. They used to have little White Tony going into the Haçienda – he was only small, but he used a gun – and he got shot dead himself in the end. That was all about controlling the drugs that went in there, and all these different firms wanted to get in on it and run it. There was the Cheetham Hill Gang, the Salford Gang … That wasn't our scene but, Jesus Christ, you had to be able to look after yourself.

There was this guy with a big reputation – Paul Massey, his name was. I was in the Italian Stallion, and he comes down to the door, ten or eleven of them all wearing shell suits, and he goes, 'Alright?' I said, 'Yes, you're alright, Paul, but the rest have gotta pay!' And do you know what they did? They put their hands in their shell suit pockets, just like they've all got a gun. I said, 'Oh, do me a favour – for five quid you're gonna shoot someone? Go and do a bank!' It was okay then, you know? Unbelievable. But he was shot dead in 2015 outside his front door. They got the hitman that did it – he got life.

It wasn't long before I got involved with the music world myself, through Adrian.

TRICKY: Not all my family are gangsters. Uncle Tony's sister, Marlow, got married very young, almost because she wanted to change her name so she wouldn't be associated with the Godfreys anymore. Her daughter, my cousin Michelle, is like a sister and a mother to me. She has always looked after me, and her dad, Ken Porter – he's not actually my blood relation – always looked after me like a dad. I was like his favourite, and I think that, because he doted on me and she really loved her dad, she has always doted on me as well.

To look at her, people would think she's white, but she's actually a bit less than a quarter black. People didn't believe we were first cousins when they saw us hanging out together. They just couldn't get their heads around it.

There are a lot of dark secrets in her side of the family, too …

MARLOW PORTER: I grew up in Knowle West with the Godfrey family, with Martin and all of them, and I hated it. Oh my God, I just couldn't wait to get away from there. And then once I had, I thought, I'm never going back there – even if they offered me a house, two houses, five houses! It was horrific.

I grew up thinking that Margaret Godfrey, who everyone called 'Maga', was my mother. I was nine years older than Maxine, so I looked after her as an auntie would, but then one day, when I was fourteen, I was bickering with Maureen, who I'd always thought was my sister, and she suddenly looked up and said, 'Anyway, you are a bastard!' Maga, who I'd always called 'Mum', looked at me and said, 'Yes, you are, and Violet is your mother, but I fed you from my own breast!'

I went up into our bedroom to work it all out, and I thought, 'Well, my brothers Martin and Arthur are now my uncles, and my sister Violet is now my mother! How could they?' And they never ever spoke about it again. They didn't explain to me, nothing at all – not even in later life. When I went to see Violet on her death bed at eighty-eight years of age, I thought she would get it off her chest and say sorry, but she never said a word more about it after that day when I was fourteen.

The thing is, before that day, I sort of knew it, but I didn't understand. I used to go upstairs and look for things and read them, which a child shouldn't have done. One time when I was ten, I found this tin, and there was a baptism card inside that said 'Margaret Rose Godfrey' – my name – and then underneath, 'Mother: Violet'. There was nothing about a dad. I thought at that time, 'How can she be my mother?' That made me more withdrawn: I couldn't ask anybody, there was nobody I could go to and relay it to, so I kept it inside.

When Maureen finally told me in the most horrible way possible, I had one over on them all because I could say, 'I already know!' They didn't know how I knew, but I'd already known since I was ten. I ran upstairs and tried to rip up the card, and I stayed up there for two days. When I came back down, Maga said to me, 'Maureen has been really upset because of you staying upstairs.' She never asked me how I felt!

I couldn't wait to get out of that family, and out of Knowle West; a few years later, I married young to my husband Ken, but to start with, we couldn't find a proper place. Eventually we got a two-bedroom council flat in Hartcliffe, which was actually a house, one up one down, and we were overjoyed to have something of our own. We had this most amazing three-piece suite, and all this lovely furniture, and I loved cleaning! Give it a bit more polish! It was like my dolls' house, because I'd never had anything before. Ken had been in the merchant navy, so he taught me a lot of things about organising, because I had no knowledge of anything.

Of course, now Martin and Arthur were my uncles. Every girl worshipped Martin because he looked so handsome – he could have anyone. They would befriend me just so they could knock on the door and hope that he answered it. He was very smart, but it was fighting, fighting, fighting. I knew all about their violence.

By the time I'd had my two kids, Mark and Michelle, I went back to work and saved all this money to buy Ken a suit. In those days, there was no buying suits off a rack – everybody had their suits made, even though they lived in poverty. You went to Hepworth's or Burton's – they were the only two. You would go in, pick out what cloth you wanted, and they made the suit. I picked out a dog-tooth check for him, so he looked smart.

Not long after I'd had it made, Ken went out one night with my family and didn't come home all night. Imagine how worried I was. When he finally came home, the suit was thick with blood – I'm talking thick. Somebody broke a glass and slashed Arthur across the face, and the blood was from Ken trying to help. After that, Arthur had this massive scar right across his face: the scar burst because he was a haemophiliac, and it couldn't be neatly stitched back together, so it became more like an open scar. It made him look like what he was.

When Martin lived in Manchester, he used to do a lot of fighting with the Irish gypsies. He had something in him where he didn't feel pain. These guys broke both his arms, and he still went at them – he still acted tough, like nothing was wrong. He retaliated and he stabbed this fella several times, so then he went to prison, down on Dartmoor.

Maga made me and Ken go on a train to Tavistock to visit Martin. When we came out, it was misty, and we didn't know whether to go left or right, so we sat in the pub and they said, 'Oh, there won't be a bus for several hours.'

I said to Ken, 'Let's walk.' We kept walking until we came to a cross-roads, but we ended up having to walk back and sit in the pub. Maga was the Mafia mother, and that's what she made me do, every time they got put away. They all used to control me.

I never knew my dad, but Maxine's dad was a really nice person. We called him Quaye. I don't think we ever knew his Christian name, that's just what everybody used to call him. He was from Africa. He came over with the merchant navy and ended up staying here in England. He was very quiet, but there was something about him that made me think he was good. I can get feelings like that.

They used to call me 'the white witch'. I would say, 'Michelle, if you stay with that person, I bet you, blah blah blah.' And 'blah blah blah' would happen! You go by gut feelings, don't you?

Quaye was very tall, and he had a cataract on one eye, so it was milky. But he was very smart. He and Violet were together in Cardiff, that's where they met, probably because he was stationed there, and she had Maxine and Michael down there. Then she and Quaye decided to go to Manchester, so I didn't see so much of him after that, because they split up there and, like everything else in our family, he never got talked about again. Another skeleton in the cupboard.

Tony's father, Theodore Guest, was an American soldier, and he was also a decent person. In all fairness to him, he wanted Violet and Tony to start a new life over in America with him. She had tickets for the two of them to go there, but then all the family said, 'You won't have no family there, and what if it goes wrong; where are you going to run?' So she didn't go, and she never kept in touch with him after that, but I think Tony got some photos of his father. His father was very accepting of him, but he was in America, so that was the end of that.

I didn't go to Manchester with all the others. I did nothing with them. Maureen and Violet went up, and Olive was there for a little while. Maxine, who was really my half-sister, rather than my niece, as I'd thought, was only thirteen when they were going up there. She was at school and everything here, in Bristol, but she went up there eventually. When she came back, I took her in, and she lived with me. I was nine years older than her, so I was quite grown up, and I mothered her – and she treated me like a mother. At school, they said they'd never met anyone like her for writing, and that she should be a journalist.

By the time I'd had Michelle, and she'd had Adrian, we'd moved to another council house, and Maxine and Adrian would practically live with us. Sometimes the Godfreys would come and stay, and there was nothing I could do about it. They just dominated my life. And if I went against it, then they would get on the phone and say, 'You are obligated to my mother, she brought you up – you and your fancy effing carpets!'

I rowed with every one of them. I had worked all my life, where they didn't. I wasn't trying to prove anything. When I was young, I always thought, 'When I have children, they're never gonna get hurt like I've been.' I didn't have a clue about being a mother; all I knew was, if I do the opposite to what I had all my life, it'll be okay for them.

I brought up Michelle and Mark saying to them, 'Don't you ever tell people you know that there's a Godfrey in your family!' And they've grown up beautiful, haven't they?

Adrian was the sweetest little boy, too. When he came to live with me, I can't tell you anything wrong about him, except that when Maxine was alive and then just after she died, he used to have terrible screaming tantrums, and you never knew why. After Maxine died, because of his health, I had to give him medicine, and he *wasn't* going to have it. I thought, 'What am I gonna do?' I picked him up, took him upstairs, put him in the bedroom, and I said, 'Now you stay here until you say sorry!' I went in the other room, and I was trembling. 'Please God!' I didn't think I could cope, I didn't think I was going to do it right.

I wouldn't let him call me Mum. He'd had a mum, and he had to *know* that he'd had one – even if it was a vision that he didn't fully remember. So, no, he only ever called me Auntie Marlow. He was always writing on the floor. He never sat in a chair. That's how I know him – sat on the floor, leg out, scribbling away or watching telly, never in a chair.

Ken loved Adrian, but he used to say something naughty to him. He would say, 'Adrian Thaws, got no—', but he never completed the rhyme. One day the vicar came to the house for money, and Adrian came out and said, 'I'm Adrian Thaws, and I've got no balls!'

If he had stayed with me – who knows? But when he was nearly eight, Violet wanted him, so I went to Social Services or whatever it was at the time, and I was gonna adopt them both, Adrian and Leanna, and Roy came with me to say that's what he wanted, too. In those days it was so different.

They said, 'You've already got two children, we can't let your children be deprived.' We didn't earn great money then, so it didn't happen. But everything was okay, I fought them hard and I kept Adrian, and I thought that was always going to be the way.

Then Violet took him. It was like losing my own son, but they didn't see it like that. I said to them, 'You're too old, don't be cruel! He thinks of Michelle and Mark as a brother and sister – you can't do that!' Look how close he is still with Michelle now. I went to a barrister in Bristol, to see if there was any chance I could get him back, and he said, 'You would lose straight away because she is his full grandmother, and you are only a half-auntie.' I had no chance, so that was him back in Knowle West with Violet and her new husband, Winston Monteith, a *horrible* man.

TRICKY: I hated my step-grandad. I would've killed him if I could. I would've really liked to have poisoned him, if it wasn't for my nan, because he was the only company she had. Otherwise, I would have quite happily killed the bloke.

I was young when they got together, and what's really weird is, at that point, when I was four or five, he seemed alright. Then, when I was maybe fourteen, he started beating me up. He'd smack me around, so he was never grandad to me. He ain't my real grandad, know what I mean?

It was always Michelle who would drive down and pick me up. If she heard he'd been smacking me around, she would be down there within fifteen minutes in the car, and I'd go and stay with her and her family for a while.

No one liked Winston – my uncle Tony, no one. He would buy a bottle of lemonade, and he would mark it, so I couldn't drink it – he was one of them. Then, when I was sixteen, he started to pressure my nan to get me to move out. One day, I got up for breakfast and there was a paper on the table open at a page with adverts circled for bedsits. Like, 'Alright, it's time to go.' I knew that was him; my grandmother would never do that. It was him doing it, because he didn't like me, and I didn't like him.

I wasn't bothered and, by that age, you want to get out anyway. My auntie Marlow tried to intervene, and my nan broke her arm. They had a fight outside the house, and my nan grabbed her arm, and shut the door on her arm and broke it. They had fistfights.

If I'd have told my uncles, they'd have sorted him out, but I didn't think like that. If I had a problem with him I would just have a go back at him, but now I know I could've got one of my uncles to have a go back at him, and do something to him. He was an older guy as well, so maybe my uncles weren't gonna smash him up. Then it was for my nan's sake, too. I didn't want to cause too many problems for her, because then she would have to take his moaning. He was just a horrible cunt. He's dead now.

That physical abuse from him must have had an effect, because I didn't even remember that he used to beat me up until about five years ago, when Michelle told me about it, when I was talking to her on the phone. I genuinely couldn't remember it, so I must've shut it out, and it must've affected me.

I saw so much violence as a kid. My uncle Michael was generally a very quiet man. One day I was down at his house with his wife, my auntie Sandy. After, Michael was taking me back to my nan's house, so we got in a taxi. I was about ten years of age, and we were driving from Montpelier, where he lived, going to Totterdown. He was quiet anyway, but he was especially quiet all the way.

When we got to Oxford Street, where my nan lived, he said to the driver, 'Pull over here,' and I thought, 'My nan's house ain't here, it's about five or six doors up. He knows where my nan lives – it's his mum!' But I didn't say anything.

He got out of the car and I stayed in the back. He said to the driver of the taxi, 'You took me the long way round, do you think I'm stupid? You're taking the piss.' He dragged him out of the car and *battered* him. I was watching from the back as he beat him up – he'd got him on the bonnet, punching him in the head, smashing him up.

After he'd knocked the guy senseless, he opened the door, got me out, walked up the street, then turned to me and said, 'Don't tell your nan!' And that was it, we never spoke about it again.

I don't like violence to this day. Maybe that's just my reaction to my violent family. I'm uncomfortable around violence.

I've got friends from Knowle West who are not worried at all about it, so it must have affected me if I particularly shut it out. I was never a fighter. My uncles and their nephews and my grandad Farmer could all fight, and even my mum, my aunties and my nan could fight, so really, I should be a fighter, too. I should be a well-respected guy that people are scared of, but I never had that, which is unusual coming from a family like mine. It's kind of strange what happened to me.

I've done plenty of boxing training, but I never competed, whereas my uncle Tony is not a big guy, but there's no man on earth he wouldn't fight. In his day, there's no man on earth my Uncle Martin wouldn't fight. He looked at it as, alright, if I can't put you down, this knife will put you down. But I never had that mentality. It wasn't at all that I was scared. I would be around violent places, but I didn't have a dark mind like my uncles. If some doorman came and told me to get out of the club, I would get out of the club. But my uncle Martin and my uncle Tony? Nah, that ain't gonna happen.

CHAPTER THREE
FOUNDING FATHERS

In my teens, all the signs pointed towards me leading a life of crime. I was hardly ever in school. I would just be going out, smoking weed, getting into trouble, getting harassed by the police. Just kids' stuff, you know – thieving and hustling. Very occasionally we'd do a bit of shoplifting – put on a long leather coat and run out with stuff – but we weren't really into that so much as robbing houses, breaking into offices and selling weed.

If I'd stayed in Knowle West, all that kind of activity could have become a bigger part of my life. But it wasn't like I had some master plan to become an artist and get the fuck out of there, because that was something that just didn't happen to people like me.

Still, I knew I couldn't become a gangster, not the way my uncles were, because I was a lot softer than them. I knew it wasn't in me, just from knowing how they operated. They were tough, tough, tough men. So I did illegal stuff, but not the same kind of stuff as them.

I was always tiny as a kid, and you know how council flats have those really small bathroom windows? Well, one of my cousins used to put me through those so I could open the door and he could rob the flats. How it would happen was, I would go and visit this cousin at his house, just to hang out, then he would persuade me to come out with him, we'd stop outside a house or flat, and he'd end up putting me through the bathroom window. Just because I was small.

So, I'd already been breaking the law from a young age when I fell in with a guy called Nicky Tippett. He was different, Nicky. He was a total rebel, and a bit of a legend in my area. I was about sixteen, and he must have been about fourteen, but he was simultaneously younger and more street than any of the people around him. It was almost like Nicky was born street, and a proper Knowle Wester, though he was mixed-race.

I started doing naughty stuff because of him, so it was a younger guy getting an older guy into trouble. It's supposed to be the other way around. He was as naughty as fuck. It was just robbing everything that moved, stealing cars, breaking into places.

I had such good times with him. I was having a total laugh, but for Nicky it wasn't about thrill-seeking. He wasn't the sort of guy to just throw a stone through a window or knock on a door and run away. The most he might have done for fun was steal a car to joyride. When I knew him, from when he was about fourteen, it was all about money. Business, at fourteen years of age! I've never seen him act like a child, ever. I can't ever remember playing football with him or doing anything fun with him, unless it was to do with money.

One time, I'm walking past a house with him, completely oblivious, and he suddenly stops dead.

'Listen!' he says.

'What?'

'Can you hear that?'

'What?' I say. 'It's just a phone ringing.'

'Yes, but no one's answered it,' he replies, smiling, and he's straight over the garden fence.

We used to call him Nickodemus. He was the only person I knew who drove when we were young. He must've been driving a car when he was fifteen, all without a licence. Me and him went halves on a beautiful Ford Cortina – I think we paid £250 each for it – but Nicky knew how to steal a car, too.

It was me and Nicky mostly, and sometimes our mutual friend Whitley Allen would join us. Nicky's no longer with us, unfortunately – he died a couple of years ago – but Whitley remembers those times better than I do.

WHITLEY ALLEN: I first met Adrian because he was seeing this girl who was friends with my girlfriend. He was living at his nan's in Totterdown at the time, and I'd been hanging around there because of this girlfriend, so our paths finally crossed. We quickly found out we'd each grown up in a slightly different part of Knowle West, both black, but we'd been going around with the same people, all from the same group.

Once we finally met, we just sort of clicked. It was just one of those connections – weird. We found out we had the same sort of interests, and we started always being together. Even when we were in a group, it would always be me and him. We very rarely talked about doing things together, we just did them. We weren't followers, we led. He had my back, and I had his. I would walk through fire for him, and vice versa.

One time, we were walking in Easton, and his dad pulled up to the kerb. He goes, 'What are you doing here?' And *my* dad is in the passenger seat. We were both like, 'Are you for real?' Then they just drove off – they didn't even give us a lift! That was like, 'Oh my God,' – we obviously had so much in common without realising. I suppose that was why we were hanging out together. We were linked.

We've done a lot of things, but he used this term – we were curious. We were getting up to all sorts, including with women. We got into – no, I should really say, *he* got into a lot of situations, where I'd be like, 'Oh dear!'

For instance, my sister hated him with a passion. Every time he would come in the house and Grace was there, she would get up and walk out. I've got to give it him, mind, because one day, he said, 'I'm not having this, Grace, what have I done to you?' And she was like, 'You know what?' and they were cool after that. But that's him. Just like, wow, no messing.

We got up to a lot of naughty stuff with Nicky Tippett. Again, I knew Nicky's mum and family, and he knew Nicky separately, then we all met up altogether. Nicky was mixed-race, but he was a real Knowle Wester, and the original straight-out criminal – a cat burglar. He lived and breathed crime. One time, Adrian was supposed to be there with Nicky, and he didn't turn up, so I went instead – and it was a profitable job, as it turned out!

Nicky's older brothers were more into fighting, because if you were mixed-race up there in Knowle West, you had to make your mark, otherwise you got walked over. There was Lloyd, Michael, Stephen, Ivan, and then Nicky was the youngest, so he didn't really have to do anything physically, because he had all that family behind him. He was less violent, just more criminalised. He was shrewd and cunning, but a wicked, lovely guy, so we both spent a lot of time with him.

He thought about housebreaking every minute of the day. It was always, 'Let's do a job!' Once, we were doing a job, and we were in the house, and I was like, 'Right, we're good to go,' and he was like, 'Nah, there's more stuff in here!' I was getting jittery – come on, Nick! He would spend all day in there, till he'd gone through every drawer and cupboard. This dude is different. I'm not on that tip – I'm more, get in, get out. Whereas he didn't panic, just carried on …

We weren't earning *loads* from it. For us two, it was just to continue survival, because we were sixteen, seventeen, and we weren't working. It was, 'How are we going to go out on the weekend? Right – let's go hustle!'

We didn't rob houses in Knowle West. You didn't shit on your own doorstep, so we would branch out to the more middle-class and wealthier areas. To begin with we were on foot, though, so we couldn't go too far, and that's where Nicky's plan for a car came in.

Nicky had his eye on this car – a gorgeous red Cortina E with a wooden dash. He was like, 'I want that car!' because it was up for sale, but he didn't have the money then, so he set us up to do a burglary, and our payment was, we'll get the car and so much cash. We made some good money, but then we were mobile.

Nicky was too young to drive, but he drove anyway. I think I was the only one who didn't drive it, but it was like, 'Right, now we can go anywhere,' so we ended up moving out to Southmead and all over. For Nicky, it was all a means to that end. He was a fourteen-year-old kid on that level. Most fourteen-year-olds ain't thinking that way.

There were other people we had in common, like Dean Reid, who he went to school with. Dean's family were from Southmead originally, then they moved to Brislington. A funny fella, tiny like Adrian, all the family were, and there were loads of brothers, all fighters.

Adrian will probably say that Dean was the first black guy who used to wear eyeliner. He used to have the wet-look hair, with eyeliner, and they'd go to Reeves – this club in a white middle-class area, but they ran it, always fighting. The club was adjoined to a hotel, and one time we were in the hotel, and this taxi driver started looking for trouble – and the problem with that is, they always pick on the smallest one and it would either be Adrian or Dean's brother Junior – I was bigger so I always got a bye. Junior had a bag in his hand, and the dude was getting lairy, so he dropped the bag, swivelled round and just banged him. The bloke hit the floor, then Junior was just – normal, like nothing happened.

Then there was Gripper, which was this guy Chrissie Morgan's street name. Another wayward soul, also mixed-race. His grandad used to beat him hard – an old Jamaican-style grandad, mad as hell. There were three brothers, and he controlled them all. The two girls, I wouldn't mess with them either. The oldest one was Melita, I wouldn't touch her, and the other was Maria. I go over to their house one time, and Maria's beating up Gripper in the street. They'd had an argument in the house, both fighting, then he walked away, just like not having it, and she wouldn't stop hitting him. Rough!

Gripper was a lovable rogue – massive, but fast as hell. He should have done boxing. When Tyson was around, this trainer guy wanted to get him into boxing, but he didn't have that mindset. He was just a crook, into stealing bikes – motorbikes and pushbikes – that's all he used to do. Then he got into burglary and got hooked on crack, but that was after we left. When we were around, he was still clean – he didn't even smoke pot.

He was the same age as Nicky. They were about the same, but on different levels – Nicky was supreme compared to Chrissie. Nicky was in the elite class.

TRICKY: HMP Horfield, a Category B men's prison, sits in the north of Bristol. It's way up on the other side of the city centre from Knowle West, but most of the kids I knew in the neighbourhood were kind of resigned to the fact that they'd be locked up there at some point. My uncles had been there, my cousins had been there, my friends had been there, and even my friends' sons went there later on, so I almost knew that I was going there as well.

I'd been arrested a few times and taken into the cells at Knowle West police station. You start getting into trouble before prison, and you get locked up for the night. That would be for just fucking around, but you are too young, so they can't keep you there. So that's where you start, and deep down you know where you're going to end up. Going to prison is almost like the next step.

When I was finally sent to the young offenders' part of Horfield, aged seventeen, it was hardly a shock at all. How it happened was, a mate and I used to buy forged £50 notes – for a fiver each, I think it was. We'd buy loads of them, and then send people into shops, or go into shops ourselves, and buy stuff and get the change. It was like small-scale money laundering, but they called it Forgery of the Crown, which makes it sound really serious, and I eventually got nicked for it when the mate I did it with grassed me up – at least, that's what I think happened. There's no way they could've known about it unless he'd told them.

It wasn't like he gave evidence in court or anything. I was just a young guy from Knowle West who couldn't afford a decent lawyer. I was going to jail, it's as simple as that. Money makes a difference in these things. They don't have to have someone stand up in court to send you to prison. If I'd had enough cash to get a proper lawyer, there's a good chance I could've got off with it, because there was no proof of me having those notes, just hearsay.

I wasn't surprised when the judge sent me to prison, because before me was a woman who had two kids, and she couldn't pay a fine. The guy sent her to prison, so it's obvious where I was going. This judge was just a horrible rich dude. To be a magistrate, you've gotta come from a good family. You ain't getting judges or magistrates coming from Knowle West, so it was a rich guy who had no idea what real life is like. If you can send a woman with two children to prison for not paying a fine, what kind of person are you? My case was up next, so I knew I was going to jail. It was just fucking obvious.

My nan was there in court, and she spoke a little bit. She was a good actress, my nan. She was all tearful, like, 'Oh, he lost his mum when he was four.' She might have been able to get me off, because the judge was listening to her, he liked the fact that she was pleading. He liked the power, it puffed him up, he was getting off on it, but I wasn't gonna let her do that for him. He was nothing compared to my nan. My nan was like a soldier. There's no way I was letting this coward – that's what he was – reduce her to that, because she was a lot stronger than he would ever be in his life.

I said to her, 'Sit down, Nan!' and she sat down and changed from looking all sad, to looking more normal. I could see him looking at her, and then straight off he sent me down for two months. I thought, 'I'd rather go to prison than have my nan beg this fucker for anything.' I sent myself to prison, really. I'd rather go to jail. I didn't give a fuck.

Seriously, my nan could've got me off with her acting skills if I'd kept quiet. After I got sentenced, she came over and gave me a little slap and said, 'Look after yourself!' Then she walked straight out of the court –

from, 'Oh, he lost his mum' to that casual farewell! She didn't visit me in prison or anything. She knew, she had been through all that.

As they led me out from the courtroom and down into the little holding cell below, I honestly wasn't scared. It wasn't a shock. It was just part of the journey. When you're that age, it's almost like just another adventure. You ain't seeing it as prison, more like, this is where you knew you were going to end up, and here it is.

After waiting around for a bit in the holding cell, they put you in a van, which is divided up into tiny cubicles narrower than your own body, and you are chained through these armholes to the person in the next one along. If you're claustrophobic, or if they have an accident, you're fucked.

When you arrive at the prison, they take you in, and you're put in another holding cell, where all the other new prisoners are. One guy I felt really sad for. He was a lot older than me, probably in his late forties, and he was picking up dog-ends off the floor to make himself a roll-up. He was in there because he murdered a guy for cheating with his wife. He shouldn't have been there, really. He wasn't a hardened career criminal. Affairs of the heart make people do crazy things. I don't know how much he got, but it must have been fifteen years.

Then my natural instincts kicked in. Someone came and offered me, like, 'Hey, you want some cigarettes?' I said, 'Nah,' because if you take a cigarette, then you owe him two. Your natural instincts kick in. I also realised that it's important where you are in line. A guy two people before me said the wrong thing and got a smack from one of the screws, so I knew what not to say by the time he came to me. You learn from someone getting a smack in front of you.

While you're still in the holding cell, you get fed, and the food's disgusting. I've always been a really fussy eater. I grew up with good food. With my uncle Ken, we'd eat spaghetti Bolognese, roast dinners, and then even with my great-grandparents, it would be fresh fucking rabbit, with vegetables out of the garden.

In there it was worse than school dinners. I had this thing on my plate – this lump of fish, peas and mashed potato – and I was just looking at it.

'You gonna eat that?' asks this guy next to me.

'Nah!'

He takes my plate and starts scoffing it down.

'How long are you in for?' I goes.

'Two years.'

He said it like it was two minutes. There was another guy who was doing seven years for arson, and he was just the same. I immediately realised: I ain't like these people. Just that mentality … I mean, I didn't care, but they *really* didn't care – there is a difference. I was there because I had to be there. They seemed like they'd been there before, and they were gonna go there again, and they were totally comfortable with that. I wasn't. I knew I hadn't got nowhere better to go, but how was I gonna be a prison guy if I couldn't even eat the food?

I was just watching everything, and that's what hit me, how conditioned you could get, and how he ate the food like it was fresh rabbit or spaghetti Bolognese. That was like, wow.

· ■ ■ ▨ ■ ■ ·

After the holding cell, you see a doctor, and you get all your stuff – pillow, bed sheets, blankets and all of that, and carry it through to your cell. And that's it – from then on, you are locked in your cell for twenty-three hours a day until they let you out again. Every other day, you get what they call 'association', where you go into a room for an hour where there's a television, pool table, darts.

At eighteen, you go to the full adult prison, but I was only seventeen, so I was in the youth custody wing. My cell was at the front of the building, overlooking the main road. There were just two of us in there, me and this other guy. He had a picture of his girlfriend on the wall – a ballerina, not professional, but she did ballet – and he drove himself crazy about this girl, wondering if she was cheating on him. He was there for longer than me, and he'd been in before as well, because he knew how to make the beds and stuff – you have to make the beds a certain way, and if you do it wrong, you can be given punishments.

In that respect he knew the game more than me, but he was driving himself crazy about this girl, worrying about who she was cheating on him with. I think if you go to prison, you can't be worrying about your girlfriend. He was totally comfortable there, he had his roll-ups, he was totally cool – it was just his girlfriend.

In the first couple of days, I had an asthma attack, because they'd taken my inhaler off me. The other guy in my cell, who I didn't even know at that stage, he was scared to death, even more than I was. The screws outside could obviously hear me but they just didn't come to give me my inhaler, so I could have died in there, and they wouldn't've given a fuck. Only the next morning did they bring me my Ventolin – gave me two puffs and took it back off me.

As you can imagine, that made me a little bit angry. I could understand sending someone to prison, but letting someone nearly die of an asthma attack? That experience made me even more anti-authority than I was before I went in.

Otherwise, I never had any problems in there – no bullying, none of that. It wasn't that I saw terrible things in there. The only thing that really got to me was the boredom. Prison is just mind-numbing. Unbelievable. You're in a cell the size of a bathroom for twenty-three hours a day, with literally nothing to do. You just sit in the cell and talk with the other guy, smoke a roll-up, and talk some more. You aren't like, Oh, I wish I could listen to music now. You are just bored. Twenty-three hours a day, watching the walls. I never got one visit when I was there, so it wasn't nothing except boredom. Nothing else came into my head except wanting to get out.

That, in a way, was my journey. Shit food, bored out of my mind, and people saying, 'Yeah, I've got seven years, I've got two.' That really got into my head in all those empty hours and days. I was only in there for two months, but it was that mentality, just seeing how conditioned you can get.

When I got out, it felt like it had been a rite of passage. I felt good. I was seventeen, and I can remember going back to Knowle West, like, 'Yeah, I've been to prison!' Because when it finally happens, for some reason you almost feel a little bit good about it. I was at my auntie Marlow's house, and I remember my cousin Michelle said to me, 'How was it?' And I said, 'Easy!' And she said to me, 'No, it wasn't easy – you did it because you had to do it!'

Because of the boredom, and the conditioning, and the Ventolin episode, I really didn't like it, and it was like I made a life choice right there. I won't say I didn't get in trouble after that, but I knew that that life wasn't for me, so I didn't go into it full-on. So sometimes, when I didn't have money, I'd get an agency job and other work instead of robbing or doing something dodgy. But without seeing that little prison stint, who knows?

My uncles were hardcore, and it's only because I'm not tough that I didn't end up like them. I really admired them, how they had a name in Manchester and Bristol. If I was a tougher person, I would definitely have chosen that way, because if you admire somebody, you want to emulate them. It's only the fact that I'm not a tough guy, and luckily I realised I'm not, that set me on a different path.

There were definitely people around me at that time in my teens who weren't sure I'd be around for long. I met this guy who was writing a book about the streets of Bristol, and he said in the book, 'If this boy makes it to twenty, he could really be someone.'

Some of my relatives and old friends say they always knew I would do something with my life. Whitley always says he knew it as well. He says that I could go in a room and it would go quiet, or I could walk into a club and the vibe would completely change, or if I started telling a story, all of a sudden everybody would stop and listen. There were little signals telling me I was going to be who I am now, but I couldn't see them yet. It was almost like people were telling me a story I didn't know. Because sometimes I do wonder: how the fuck did I get where I am now?

CHAPTER FOUR
TARZAN THE HIGH PRIEST

The Specials changed everything. Their first album was like my life on a record. Just called *The Specials*, it came out in 1979, and I was only eleven then, so I can't quite remember how old I was when I first actually heard it, but I knew right away that they were the ones for me. Seeing them on TV was the first time kids like me had a band representing us – someone like myself on television!

Suddenly it was like, 'Ah, now everything makes a bit of sense ... I have a voice.' I used to think, 'Where do I belong? I'm in Knowle West, growing up with white people, then I go and visit my dad in St Paul's, where it's predominantly black.' It was like I had two different lives almost, and then I myself was mixed-race, surrounded by a family of varying colour.

When I saw The Specials – black and white people together in one band – it was the first time I could relate to anything. Like, 'Ah, there's people who feel like I do.' All the songs on that record were describing life as I lived it – getting chased on the street, hanging around council estates, and later on going to nightclubs – so they were the first artists I ever heard talking about stuff I had experienced.

When Terry Hall sang, he was a white guy in a band with black guys, so it was almost like the reverse of my upbringing in Knowle West, but still he spoke to that little black Knowle Wester. Then you had Neville Staple in there. The only time I'd ever heard Jamaican being spoken in music was on reggae tunes that were actually made in Jamaica, but here was a British bloke dropping proper Jamaican patois on an English record.

The Specials became a huge part of my life, and it was the same for thousands of kids growing up in our multi-racial generation across England. They arrived just at the perfect time for me, as music in general was quickly becoming more and more important to me. After hearing Billie Holiday with Nana Violet, Marvin Gaye at Ken Porter's, and reggae on the streets around my dad's, I'd got into Marc Bolan, and then I'd gone into a little electronic phase, listening to Gary Numan of all people.

When I was fifteen, I got into skinhead music, which is weird seeing as some of those Oi! bands, like the 4-Skins, were supposed to be racist. I was into it for the music, not the look so much, but you end up getting into the fashions – Dr Martens, Crombies, Fred Perry's, Sta-Prest trousers and all that. I wouldn't have called myself a skinhead, and I wasn't actually a skinhead with a shaved head, but I definitely dressed like a skinhead. Shiny boots, braces – it was all part of the culture. I used to polish my boots every night before going out. We'd go to skinhead clubs, where they played Prince Buster and stuff like that, and all your mates would be there with their Dr Martens on.

From there, I made the natural progression into rude boy, with the brogues and the slacks, and I was just ripe for discovering The Specials and Two-Tone. I could so relate to them, in a way that I couldn't with anything else. Like, when I was in my teens, I remember seeing Prince on TV with my cousin Michelle, and thinking, 'God, what the fuck is this? Who's this in high heels doing this strange music?' I realised that he was an incredible artist, but I couldn't identify with him at all.

Seeing Terry Hall, it was, 'Okay, I could do that one day.' With Prince, even if I wanted to be a musician, it was like, 'Well, I can't do that – I don't wear high heels, I can't play every instrument, and I can't dance like he does,' but when I'd seen The Specials, I was like, 'Fuck, I could be a musician, because they are all like me.'

Terry Hall made me want to be in a band, because he wasn't a natural singer. He was self-taught, and he had his own thing going on. I used to lie in bed listening to the album and pretend I was singing the songs onstage in The Specials. I'm sure some of the other big rock bands who were around at the time were from council estates, too, or at least from humble backgrounds, but with The Specials, it wasn't like they were from council flats and now they were swanning around behaving like rock stars. When they got famous, it seemed like they'd stayed exactly the same as they were before.

My excitement about music as a way of life was my own little discovery. Although there were certain sounds I'd been exposed to through various family members, music didn't have that kind of place in their lives. My great-uncle Martin wasn't into dancing – he stabbed and glassed people. If any of my uncles went to a club, it was to take it over, or to burn it down or to hurt someone who'd disrespected them. They weren't in the club for the music, that's for sure.

Although, actually, Martin once informed me that he was a creative type. When he'd carved 'RAT' on that guy's chest, he did it again on his forehead in smaller letters. I asked him, 'Why did you do the little one?' and he goes, 'Because I'm artistic,' so I guess he must've been. Someone told me Martin may be able to play piano a little, but he's never confirmed that.

In the houses I grew up in, nobody was painting or writing or playing music, and there were certainly never any concerts in Knowle West. Nothing ever happens up there. The only music event I've ever heard about took place after I'd moved away: Tim Westwood came and DJ'd, and apparently he got robbed – some people broke into his bus and turned it over. There was only ever the one boozer, the Venture Inn, a red-brick estate pub in Melvin Square: that place was famous for violence, which is probably why it eventually got closed down.

⬛ ⬛ ⬛ ⬛ ⬛ ⬛

When my nan moved to Totterdown and I went to live with her there, it was, as I've said, a step up for both of us. It was a better area, more expensive. It's closer to town, right near Temple Meads, with shops and pubs and decent schools nearby. It's more multicultural, too. Living there was literally the first time I met Indians and Pakistanis, so I guess you'd say my horizons were broadening. It was a nice community, very small, very family, but still a bit ghetto – it certainly wasn't a posh neighbourhood like Clifton.

Nana Violet always encouraged me to go out as late as I wanted. I never had anyone saying, 'No! You've got to be in bed!' Whitley was the same, so from the age of fifteen the two of us would go out all night. None of that, 'You've got to be back at eleven o'clock,' like some of our mates had. Maybe that's another reason why we gravitated to each other because, out of all the bunch of us, me and Whitley were the tightest.

It was the same when I stayed at auntie Marlow's. I don't think it's because they knew what we were up to, which was increasingly going out late to hear music after hours, but they always encouraged me to be independent. I can even remember one Christmas Day when I was living with my nan, when I went out on the street after we'd eaten the turkey or whatever. I used to hate Christmas Day, because once you've eaten your Christmas dinner it's so fucking boring. I went to hang out on the street corner and smoke a spliff, and I was the only person there, because all my mates had to stay in and do Christmas with their family. But my nan was like, 'Alright, go on!'

Whitley and I started smoking weed when we were fifteen, and my first musical experiences were with him. At the same time as we were out housebreaking with Nicky Tippett, we discovered the Saxon Studio International, a sound system from Lewisham in south London who came to Bristol regularly because of the Jamaican population there.

To start with, we didn't even know what they looked like. They would make a cassette in London, then that cassette would go all around England. You'd get a tape off someone, then you'd pass it on to someone else. It was literally word of mouth, and we felt like we'd found the coolest thing around. We'd constantly listen to those tapes, full of the latest early-80s dancehall rhythms from Jamaica, with them chatting over the top.

Me and Whitley were obsessed. We eventually saw Saxon when they came to Bristol, and then we'd check out all the other reggae sound systems, like Jah Shaka and Sir Coxsone Outernational to see if they were as good, but Saxon always had the edge on them. For us, they had the best MCs, and they were renowned for their 'fast chat' style.

I doubt that anyone involved made money out of what they were doing. Smiley Culture was the one who went on to be famous – he got in the charts in '84 with 'Police Officer'. A couple of years after that, Tippa Irie almost made it as well, and also Maxi Priest, who was more of a pop-reggae singer, made a load of albums after his association with them.

There was a lot of personal tragedy within Saxon: Tippa Irie's sister got murdered in some gangster thing, and then, in 2011, Smiley Culture died during a police raid on his house, although the inquest said he committed suicide – stabbed himself with a knife. I think he was quite a notorious guy.

For our part, we'd be smoking sensimilla and listening to those guys' latest cassette, and that really sent me another big step further along my musical path. We became obsessed with Saxon, and sound systems in general, and everything me and Whitley did – all the robbing and stuff we did to get money – was so that we could go out and hear music. We didn't do it to buy a flash car, or a TV, or trendy clothes, like other kids do. We basically hustled money just so we could go out and party, and it was virtually every night of the week. In a way, I think that's what kept us out of real trouble, because our goal was different from everyone else's. Listening to Saxon was where music really started to take over my life and send it in another direction.

One time in those mid-teen years, we were on our way to rob some-where – a warehouse, if memory serves – and I realised I'd forgotten my gloves, so I took my shoes off, and put my socks on my hands so I wouldn't leave fingerprints. I think back now, like, 'What kind of brain is that?' What is going on there? It certainly wasn't going anywhere up the ladder.

On nights out, we used to walk everywhere, from Totterdown or Whitley's place in Knowle West to a club in town, and then all the way back again afterwards. You're talking a walk of often an hour or more, but that was nothing to us, walking these distances. You would get into mischief while you were going there, it was just part of the fun, so I never really felt like I needed to learn to drive.

Our primary objective in life was to hustle for money for the essentials of our lifestyle: some weed, a couple of drinks, and then a bit of food when you leave the club, because then you will be starving. We used to go to this place, Slix – a dirty, greasy-chicken place: we'd come out of the club, go to Slix, then walk home, even if it took an hour and a half. That was a good end to the night.

We didn't go to the commercial clubs in the centre of Bristol that often, only on the rare occasion when there was nothing better to do. There were always fights in the centre of Bristol, between guys from different areas of the city, especially around the taxi rank after closing. With a lot of those more normal townie clubs, we couldn't actually get in anyway. You had to have a white shirt on, and proper shoes, so we used to go to the reggae clubs, or illegal blues or shebeens, or pubs, or this club near Temple Meads station called The Rockpile. That place was on three floors: bikers and Hell's Angels on one floor, Knowle Westers on the next, and Hartcliffe people on the other.

There was so much violence in there the doorman had a crossbow behind the counter. One of the doormen was an older guy from Knowle West, called David Kissack. I probably only met him four or five times, but he knew my cousin Mark well, so we'd have no problem getting in. Before it changed its name to The Rockpile, my uncles used to go there. I can't remember what the music was like, because it wasn't a place you went for the music. You'd go there to have a late drink and hang out – a horrible place, rough as guts, but I didn't see it as rough at the time. It was just where I'd see loads of people from my area.

Sometimes me and Whitley would just meet up, smoke a spliff, walk somewhere, and see what club we could get into. Sometimes you might get in, but sometimes you might stand outside for hours, not getting let in, then just walk home again. We were always very curious. 'Oh, there's a new club? Let's go and try and get in!' And if we didn't get in there, we would have a bottle of Cannai, smoke a spliff and stand around outside, and probably have a right laugh doing it.

The funny thing is, sometimes we'd be out and about, maybe coming out of somewhere at two in the morning, and we'd run into my grandad Thaws doing 'Tarzan the High Priest' out on the street. Grandad would be playing all the old reggae classics from the '60s – ska, rocksteady and early reggae – and while that was blasting out, he'd also be cooking Jamaican street food. He would bless a goat before he killed it, and all that old-school shit. When he was younger, he played in clubs obviously, but I know him from the times where I'd come out of a bar or a club, and he would be right there, set up on the street. You could buy some food off him, and you'd stand there eating and listening to reggae.

He didn't get on the mic, he'd just be selecting. The guy was a legend. I didn't really know that at the time, but these days you can actually Google him – Google my grandad! People would write articles about him. Until I saw him the first time, I hadn't even made the connection that sound systems were in my culture. It wasn't like me and Whitley had been led there by our Jamaican dads, though; it was just what we naturally gravitated to.

Obviously, as a kid you like girls. You're young, there's girls – that's normal. But we went to clubs because of the music, and before long we'd be following the music out of town, to London, Birmingham or Manchester. We were obsessed.

■ ■ ■ ■ ■ ■

The first time I wore a dress for a night out, I was only fifteen. It wasn't exactly that I wanted to look like a girl. I wanted to look like those girls in the video for Malcolm McLaren's 'Buffalo Gals'. Through Saxon and some of the other sound systems, we'd been exposed to early hip-hop, and 'Buffalo Gals' went a step further, into the charts, so everyone was talking about it.

Malcolm McLaren looked like an idiot to me, but the little kids body-popping and the little girls in the dresses with the black make-up across their eyes – to me, they were the coolest ever. So that was the kind of look I was going for – not so much a cross-dressing female thing, but as an early hip-hop thing, in my head at least.

When we'd got ready to go out, my nan was just, 'What is he like? Look at that silly bugger!' She hardly batted an eyelid. Then, me and Whitley went into town and had a great night. We got the bus into town – not in a car or anything – and just went to some bar in the city centre.

For a guy to wear a dress into the centre of Bristol – I wouldn't advise that. I definitely wouldn't advise a young *black* kid to do that, not in the 1980s. Looking back, I think, 'You were fucking mad,' because I certainly wouldn't do that now. And we didn't go to an exclusive club, like Soho House or somewhere, but some bar where street guys go to have a fight. Apparently, I once described my actions as 'a mixture of nosebleed attitude and not taking myself seriously'. It was just a stupid thing to do, really.

Over the years, I think I developed the outlook that feminine men are more interesting, or more intelligent, than masculine men. To be really tough, you've got to have a bit of ignorance or narrow-mindedness about you. For instance, someone who is a proper fighter doesn't think they can lose. They narrow things down to this tunnel vision. That's why I'm not a tough guy, and not a good fighter, because I don't have tunnel vision.

To me at the time, going out in a frock was just a recipe for a good night out. Everything was fun, everything was adventure.

Very early on, we cottoned on to Glastonbury festival. I went every year, I think, between the ages of fifteen and nineteen. It was very different then, back in the mid-80s. It wasn't all about the music being beamed out on live TV – it was a hippy and squat-punky kind of thing, all about the whole atmosphere of the place, the weekend away, and the vibe.

We'd either get a lift down there with friends, or bunk the fare on the train, or hitchhike. We always jumped the fence. We never paid to get in – ever. There was always a way in there! Then we'd walk around, drop a microdot, sit in a field tripping out and watching people, and then maybe walk around some more and accidentally see a band. Back then, you didn't know who was playing, but we'd try and search out bands we'd never heard of, and which weren't famous. It wasn't all about going to the main stage and seeing whoever the biggest artist of the time was.

You'd be stumbling around hearing interesting music coming from an outlying tent, so you'd go in and end up listening for two hours to someone you'd never heard of before. Then you'd sit by a fire outside and watch the fire-eaters, surrounded by all these weird sculptures. It was a real outdoorsy, alternative thing.

I can remember seeing big reggae bands like Black Uhuru, Burning Spear and Aswad, but even then the productions weren't as big. A band was just onstage playing music, end of story, without all the lights and the smoke and the dancers.

One time I went with my cousins Michelle and Anthony, who was my uncle Tony's son, and me and Michelle were watching Aswad, I think, when suddenly we notice Anthony with his face painted, dancing around smoking a spliff on the main stage. In them days, you could get to the side of the stage if you had a bit of hustle about you. I can remember getting backstage on the main stage a few times back then, but try doing that nowadays! It was a much simpler operation then, less corporate, more hippyish and disorganised.

The drugs were different, too. It was weed and microdots and maybe a few beers. Now it's cocaine and ecstasy, like a huge club. It doesn't feel like the Glastonbury I used to go to any more.

． ▪ ▪ ▪ ▪ ． ．

You could say me and Whitley were moving into a more alternative lifestyle, and back in Totterdown, not far from my nan's, there was a squat where we used to buy weed or hashish, and hang out, smoking, chatting and listening to music. From the people who lived there, we learnt all about squatting, and how they'd hear by word of mouth about a squat that had become available in another town up country, and literally just pack their stuff up, hitch over there, and move straight in. Coming from Knowle West, it was pretty mind-blowing.

One day, the guys in Totterdown said, 'Oh, there's this squat in Birmingham,' and me and Whitley hitched up there when I was about seventeen, and we ended up living in this place in Moseley for about nine months. A big part of it was, there was a huge reggae scene up there, so we'd be partying the whole time, checking out their bands and sound systems, and doing a bit of work every now and then to get by.

We'd hook up with Whitley's brother, Mervyn, who took us to an illegal blues in Handsworth, home of Steel Pulse. There was another blues up there, which was right by Burger Bar, where the infamous Burger Bar Boys gang were from. Obviously, coming from Bristol, we didn't know any of that was going on.

On the squat scene, you'd meet all these interesting characters. We met this guy who'd travelled all around the world, and I'd never met anyone like that before. It ain't that I didn't want to travel, I just didn't know what travel was. I didn't know you could go off to South America. This guy Gary was always barefoot and he would tell us all these places he'd been to, where he was sleeping on beaches and stuff. I didn't even know you could do that! I didn't know you could go to a different country and sleep on a beach, so me and Whitley used to sit there and listen to all his stories with our mouths open.

He would come back to England, live in a squat, work for three months or so, save his money, then fuck off to Africa or Israel. The only reason he worked was so he could get money to travel. That was his life: travelling.

Then he would come back to England for two months, do some scaffolding or whatever, save all his cash up and then be away again on his adventures.

We met a lot of travellers, like this bloke from Peru. I'd never met anyone from Peru before and, believe me, he looked very Peruvian – old-school! I didn't even know where Peru was, so the squats really broadened my outlook – not just music, but life. I've been all over South America now, but back then I didn't know that a place called Peru even existed. I was a council estate kid, so to be in a squat all of a sudden with a guy from Peru was totally mind-blowing.

When my grandmother died, she had never left England. She had never been on a plane in her life, and she died at eighty-eight, so I had no business on a plane. I never had a passport, and neither did Whitley. We weren't even signing on, I don't think. We always heard that, if the police are looking for you, they'll catch you when you're signing on – so we avoided it altogether. We had no passport or ID, because you didn't have to have it when we were growing up, and we didn't need it either. It was a totally different world.

We noticed that we didn't meet any other young black guys squatting, and living that lifestyle. We can't remember ever bumping into any other black guys, in all the squats we ended up living in. To us, the people there were very different. If you came from the reggae culture community, this was a different world. We used to see a couple of dread guys who went to squat parties in London, but they weren't actually squatters. I don't think black kids squatted. There is black culture and there is white culture, and squatting was white culture, but perhaps coming from Knowle West we hadn't seen it like that before.

Whitley was my main mucker. It was like, if you see Whitley, you see me. Whitley is black but, like me, he's very white as well. He is very Knowle West. We had the black culture, and we used to go to all the reggae, but we were very white as well. I've got black friends who say to me, you act just like a white boy. Whitley is like that, too – very white English.

We started chasing music all over the country. We'd rustle up some cash by selling a bit of weed, maybe, then get up to London or Manchester, to check out a sound system, like when King Tubby's came to the UK, or to see Saxon or Coxsone. A lot of what we got up to in these teenage years, I've forgotten. I guess I was too busy having a good time, but Whitley has a better memory than me: he knows where we went, and who was really around.

WHITLEY ALLEN: In my teens, I'd go to the football, Bristol City matches, with these white Knowle West guys I knew, and the reason I stopped was, they were making monkey chants. I was like, 'What?' That's when I realised, this ain't for me. Your eyes are opened, and you realise they have a real mob mentality. Me and Adrian, we'd categorise Knowle Westers as hyenas – they travelled in packs, whereas we both travelled singly, and that scares them because they're used to the crowd. I think that's how I met him, and he met me, because we were curious to go wherever they weren't going.

We didn't follow any code. Our fashion sense was just what was good to us. He did skinhead when he first got to Totterdown. He was hanging around with this other guy called Rob Claridge, who I ended up knocking about with, and Rob was a skinhead. Two-Tone was coming in, and rude boy, so we were all going through that phase, but we only realised after the fact that rude boy originated in Jamaica. We just liked that look, then it's like, 'Why am I drawn to that? Oh, that's why – it's my culture.'

We also didn't really connect why we then moved on to the sound systems: it was our childhood. My mum brought me up, because my dad wasn't around: she is full Jamaican, so it was a Jamaican household. Being in Knowle West, all my mates were white, but reggae music was always being played, and obviously Adrian's grandad did a sound system, so we naturally gravitated towards that scene, then you start branching out.

We'd see Saxon all the time: they'd play quite often at the Inkworks (now known as Kuumba), which was just off Stokes Croft, and Malcolm X, the deconsecrated church in City Road that got turned into a community centre. Then there was Sir Coxsone, and local sounds like Inkerman. We'd see Daddy Freddy, the ragamuffin toaster who moved over from Jamaica, and went into the record books as the world's fastest rapper – all those sorts of people.

Reggae was just going into dancehall, but we were wherever the music was at. This is 1984, '85, so hip-hop was just coming in fresh – if it was a reggae night, we would go to a reggae night, and if it was hip-hop, soul, funk, then we're going there.

I'm a year older than him, and a few inches taller, so when he rocked up with me, looking too young, that's probably why he got in – he's smart, know what I mean? So we'd go to the Moon Club in Stokes Croft, then as soon as we'd get inside the door, I would only see him briefly for the rest of the night, if at all. He is definitely good with his mouth. He'd go off chatting, like a social animal, whereas I'm more reserved, and if someone chats, fine. Then, at the end of the night, he'd suddenly appear and be like, 'We're going on here, let's go!' That was how we used to roll.

We got around a lot. We'd maybe go to a club like that first, where there was a bit of hip-hop, then to somewhere more mainstream in the centre of town, and end up in a blues – a shady unlicensed place where we could have a smoke and a drink, and relax in the early hours – and there it'd be reggae. For instance, we used to go to Reeves, then we'd walk all the way from there to St Paul's to go to a blues like Ajax, which went right through the night, and then come home Sunday morning – sleep all day, party all night. Mad!

There used to be a blues near a little roundabout by City Road, and we were over there all the time. Then there was Ajax, which was less relaxed, more serious. That was where his Uncle Michael died, and he was like, 'I wonder where it happened?' I remember the person who done it – I didn't like him, never did. It was uncomfortable for both of us, and I felt the vibe from the dude. He was horrible, and they were all horrible people – not the Ajax venue people, just these people who did the music that night. They'd play heavy lovers rock, and proper grind-up music, but the funny thing is, there were no girls in there.

Through all this period we were just hustling for money to finance our night-time habits. One time we went to Swansea and stayed with a wicked guy up there who used to grow his own weed. He lived right out in the sticks by Sandy Bay, up near the golf course, and we ended up coming back with a kilo of weed in bags on the back of motorbikes. 'Shall we do it?' 'Yeah, come on!'

The idea was, the proceeds would put money in our pockets for weeks, but that didn't happen because we flooded the market in Bristol. We had that much, that every time we went to somebody, they were like, 'Nah, mate, I've already got that one.' There was no one left we could sell it to.

One time, I was at home after work, and there's a knock at the door, and it's Adrian in a car, with two girls we'd met in a club in Swansea. They were going up Wells Road and they recognised him – 'Come to Glastonbury!' He was like, 'Yeah! I'll get my mate!' So he came and got me and off we went. He ended up getting on with one of them, and stayed down there for three days. I was smarter – I was going back and forth, commuting from Bristol with an Asian guy from Totterdown who had a burger van. So I would meet him, he would bring me home and then back down again in the morning.

Somehow I bumped into Adrian every day – a massive festival, before mobile phones, but I'd always find him. Random! Ruthless! Glastonbury was crazy, man, but by the '90s it started getting a bit cliquey. A lot of the black St Paul's guys started going down, dealing, so there would be altercations.

In Totterdown, there was an older black guy who kind of took us under his wing. His real name was Mike – he's passed away now – but everyone called him Balkie. He was very instrumental in our musical journey. He had a sound system himself, and he was a lot older than us, but when older people latch on to you, it's probably because they can see you're different from other kids. We were just on a different mission to everyone else.

We used to go to Balkie's family house and smoke, and then we'd go off and do stuff with him. He used to have a green BMW with a wicked system installed, so he'd pick us up and drop tracks, and we'd be like, mouths open. One time, he got us in this car, and he dropped Eric B & Rakim's 'Check Out My Melody'. That was like, wow! By the time we got out at the other end, I'd decided I wanted to be a DJ, and Adrian was going to be an MC. So Balkie was literally our instigation to go off and do music.

One time, he took us to Newport, and coming back he ran down the back roads, with the music on loud. We had been up all night, but he was driving, and he was falling asleep at the wheel. We just thought he was mucking about, and he would come awake with a start, almost like he was making a joke out of it, then he would go off again, and the next thing we were crashing along the central reservation – we nearly died, know what I mean? Then he just drove back, to standard, and we went home to bed, and he went straight to work.

He turned us on to a lot of music, but he also told us about ways we could make some money. He was like, 'Go join an agency, do some night work, fruit picking or whatever.' We were like, 'Okay,' and went down to the agency and we started making money, legit. He was sort of looking after us, and helped us to go legit, with regular money coming in.

TRICKY: The other people I went out with at night were my cousins Mark and Michelle. I was too young to get into clubs in Bristol on my own, so they'd take me to these places and, because I was with them, I could get in. We'd go to some of the townie clubs in the city centre, but more often than not it was the Dug Out on Park Row, near the university. The Dug Out has gone down in history as this legendary place where the so-called Bristol scene started, but I never saw that. For us, it was just a hangout place, and for me particularly it was exciting to be somewhere I could get in without too much hassle.

To be honest, I can't really remember the music specifically but it was probably early hip-hop, and soul-y, rare-groove kind of stuff. It was a really grimy place – not ghetto grimy, because it wasn't ghetto people in there. Just a grimy basement club.

When me and Michelle were out on the town, people just couldn't understand that we were family. Back then she had freckles and really blonde hair, so people couldn't get it. I don't know if it would be different nowadays, but people found it strange that our skin was different colours, and that we were related – and first cousins, too, not a distant thing. People thought we were taking the piss.

MICHELLE PORTER: We'd be in a club, and he'd obviously be trying to chat some girl up, and they'd be giving me dirty looks, and he'd say, 'Oh, this is my cousin,' and they'd say, 'Yeah, right!' He'd say, 'No, it is! This is my cousin Michelle.' And people would look at us, obviously thinking, 'They're together, because he's black and she's white – and then he's got the balls to chat me up while he's out with his girlfriend!' People thought we couldn't possibly be related.

My mum, Marlow, was his mum Maxine's half-sister. Mum's surname was Godfrey, but she didn't find out that her sister Violet was actually her mother until she was fourteen, and then it wasn't talked about. She just carried on as she was before, and to me, Violet was always auntie rather than great-auntie. It wasn't something that you confronted, and you're never sure how much is true and how much not. There are quite a few skeletons in the closet.

My mum isn't like the rest of the Godfreys. She didn't like the things they did as a family. She just wanted to get out of there, get married, have children and live happily ever after. As soon as she could, she moved away from Knowle West. She still went to visit Violet in Barnstaple Road, and if there was ever a crisis or anyone needed money, they would all come to Marlow's, but as a child, she'd hated being part of that family.

So she married my dad Ken and moved to Hartcliffe, which is your typical white working-class area. I think there may have been one black family, and one of their lads was in my class at school. Adrian came to live with us when his mother died, when he was four, and it was a happy house with Al Green and Ray Charles playing, and security. Growing up, I certainly didn't see Martin very often, and we had a much nicer life than that other side of the family, but then unfortunately Adrian's grandmother demanded that he come and live with her, and he wasn't treated as well there as he was when he was with us, with his step-grandad beating him.

Me and Adrian have always been close, since we were kids. We didn't go to the same school, because I'm that bit older than him, and seven years is quite a big difference when you're that age. When I had my daughter, Natasha, I was only twenty-one, and he was only fourteen then.

But when he moved out of his nan's place, pretty soon he came and lived right close to me. We always lived close by each other, so if there was ever a crisis, or if he had a bloody asthma attack or something, it would always be me who would come to the rescue.

My mum had always shielded us from the dark side of life, so I don't know if I ever saw Adrian going to Horfield [prison] as him descending into that. I always knew he was a good boy really, I just knew he was going to be alright – he was going to find his path, and whichever way he went, he was nice inside and that would always shine through. I never had any doubts about him and the way he would turn out.

Once he was in his teens, we'd be out clubbing all the time, with my brother Mark, who's three years older. It'd be places like the Dug Out, which was a grotty little downstairs dive where your feet stuck to the carpet. You know, one of those places you wouldn't want to go in with the lights on – but at the time, you couldn't care less. Otherwise, it was lots of parties, and nights at warehouses, where we knew someone who was playing. It was always grotty places, none of the glamorous places – backstreet clubs, which attracted the people who came to hear music, dance and have a good time.

TRICKY: By 1983/84, early rap was coming through, and I fell for it completely. It wasn't on the radio or on TV much, so I don't know how I heard it. I guess it was from people like Balkie and my mates, and then in clubs once I'd got into going out. It seemed like it snuck into England, dead underground. It was so different, no one really knew what hip-hop was, which is hard to imagine now, as it dominates the charts here and in America. Back then I didn't even know it was hip-hop. I just knew I'd never heard anything like it. Like, 'Whoa, what's this?!'

The first records I was buying were things like UTFO and Roxanne Shanté – really good stuff – then once New York hip-hop started getting established, it was EPMD, Eric B & Rakim, and Public Enemy, who everyone was listening to, and maybe a little bit of LL Cool J. I was into the clothes, but not so much total hip-hop fashion. It wasn't the full kit, except for the trainers, and maybe a baseball cap – it was mostly just the music and the dancing.

One of my half-brothers was a very good body-popper. There were five of us – my dad's sons – and one of my two older brothers, Junior, was one of the very best around. Junior was more in the black community, and his brother Kevin played for a black football team in Bristol, a ghetto football team. My two younger brothers, Aron and Marlon, even though they are mixed-race like me, grew up in black neighbourhoods. For kids like us, hip-hop was the future.

CHAPTER FIVE
TRICKY KID

The first time I started getting on the mic was round at a friend's house in Totterdown. It was with a guy called Neville Lewis, whose parents were Jamaican. He was doing some low-key sound-system stuff in Bristol, and he had a little turntable set-up at his place, so sometimes we'd have a spliff, and he'd hand me the mic – what, me?! – and I'd do some 'off the top of the head' stuff. They called it toasting back then, voicing in that Jamaican DJ style.

What's funny is, Neville was actually a very talented guy – one of the best toasters I ever heard. He could have been a star, but in those days there weren't any opportunities in that kind of genre in the British music industry. Who was going to find you and sign you? There was just no way, so it wasn't about that. It wasn't about hoping to get famous through it. It was just for the fun of it.

I was about sixteeen or seventeen then, and it gradually became something I'd do round at other people's houses and squats, while we were hanging out, smoking weed – not even a sideline to all the naughty stuff I was getting up to with Nicky Tippett and Whitley, just something I did for a laugh without really thinking about it. It was nothing I ever thought I could get a career out of, or would be doing later in life. It was like going to a club, or hanging out with my mates in a pub, or meeting a girl – just fun stuff I'd get up to.

I wasn't looking for it at all, on that level, when I got involved with the Wild Bunch. They were a hip-hop crew crossed with the kind of

Jamaican-style sound system that me and Whitley had been attracted to. My connection was Miles Johnson, aka DJ Milo, who I'd known since I was seven years of age.

Miles was one of the main members, and through him I got invited in, because I think he knew I was good before I did. I was never like, 'Oh, I'm going to be a rapper.' I was doing it more like a hobby at various squats, at night, and I suppose my name must've started to get around. He was the one who kept saying, 'Come down!'

It was Grant Marshall who actually started Wild Bunch. He was the first one to have the reggae/hip-hop idea. Grant was calling himself Daddy G, but I think he was working in a bank at the time. He was well educated, but he lived in St Paul's, on Campbell Street, right around the corner from the front line – a proper dodgy area. A lot of the early Wild Bunch parties were literally in the corner of a room in G's house in St Paul's, just a pair of decks on the floor, no lights, people dancing.

Even if it was in a club, maybe in a smaller side room, I can't ever remember being up on a stage. It was always down with the people. Wild Bunch came from sound systems, and that was how sound systems used to do it. The only difference between Wild Bunch and sound systems is that Wild Bunch wasn't Jamaican, and they played hip-hop and funk as well. Maybe G played a bit of reggae, but it was mostly hip-hop and funk. I loved that mix because hip-hop had become such a big part of the culture, it took over everything.

I'm pretty sure I was technically still at school when I first started doing stuff with them. I would get a call to go down to St Paul's at twelve o'clock at night, and my auntie Marlow would say, 'Just go – go down there!' and I'd be out till 4am.

St Paul's had a late-night thing going back there in the mid-80s. The clubs in town would close at one or two in the morning, but you could go to St Paul's at whatever time, get a beer and smoke some weed. It was the place to go, even if you just wanted food after hours. It was a hangout.

For me and Whitley it could be a bit dodgy, because we weren't from there. We knew certain people, but it wasn't our turf, and for stepping on someone's toe you could get stabbed. That very Jamaican attitude: something like that happens, and there could be a problem. You had to be careful how you moved around, because if you step on the wrong person's toe, or you bump into someone and don't apologise, it's gonna go off. It's going to turn from nothing into getting stabbed, and it can escalate very quickly.

So, we'd go there, be at G's house, then walk back to Knowle West, Hartcliffe, Totterdown, wherever. As I remember it, though, the crowd that came down wasn't that 'black'. Those guys were not in the black community. They crossed over. It wasn't a St Paul's crowd; more middle-class white Clifton people, coming down to St Paul's. It was black, because of some of the people in it, but it *wasn't* black, if you see what I mean.

Previously known as Robert del Naja, 3D, their main rapper, was a white student at the local art college. He'd met Grant, because G was working behind the counter at the local record store, Revolver, in the early days of the post-punk times. That's how Nellee Hooper came into the picture, too, and he became one of the DJs to begin with. Nellee was a ghetto boy – he grew up in a white ghetto, Barton Hill – and he was the go-getter. In the early '80s he'd been a percussionist with Pigbag, who had a Top 5 single with 'Papa's Got a Brand New Pigbag', and he seemed to have connections in the London music business from that.

As for Mushroom, aka Andrew Vowles, he grew up with his grand-mother in Fishponds, which is not an affluent area. Another of their MCs, Claude Williams, aka Willy Wee, was seeing my cousin Michelle, and he grew up in Redland, a decent area, and went to quite a good school in Cotham, same with Miles. Miles was a ghetto boy, as was I, so it was us two and Nellee who were more from that Knowle West, Redcliffe, Barton Hill, council estate background.

It was a right mix of people actually doing it, and in the crowd too. You might get the odd St Paul's guy wandering in, but mostly it was 3D's kind of people turning up – students from Clifton and Cotham, who were into 3D's whole graffiti thing.

There was definitely no money in doing the Wild Bunch. Most of them had day jobs – G worked in a bank, Claude was plastering. As for me, I was younger, and at that age you don't care about the money so much. It was just fun. Cool people, though I didn't know everybody – it was a very different crowd for me. Everybody seemed to get on, and there wasn't a lot of trouble. It was just a good night out – like going to a club without going to a club. You could smoke a spliff there, have a drink, and you ain't got a doorman watching over you. You could go on till whatever time you wanted. When the night ended was when the night ended, sort of thing.

Other times, we'd play out on the streets. In the summer, G would set up the turntables outside, on the street corner. It felt like freedom, you know? The police didn't bother anybody, didn't shut it down, because it was in St Paul's, so there was no stress. It didn't seem people were bothered with St Paul's. It was its own community, so the police didn't bother with it. You could go to an illegal blues all night, like Ajax, and the police just seemed to let it go on.

The Wild Bunch was great music. It's different now: DJs play what they think people want. Back then, DJs played what *they* wanted. It wasn't so regulated. The Wild Bunch was the first time I ever heard Public Enemy, from Miles. We were in St Paul's and he played 'Bring the Noise', and I thought, 'What – the – fuck – is – this?!' I couldn't really believe what I was hearing. Back then, DJ-ing was about playing music that people didn't know, rather than playing something that's popular. You were a good DJ if you got the music first. That comes from the dubplates thing in reggae. If you got a dubplate from someone, and you could play a tune that no one had ever heard before, you were the top guy. That was important back in the day, but now it's different. It's playing the biggest song from last year, kind of thing. And DJs weren't superstars back then. Now all these guys are as famous as fuck – more important than the music, which ain't right.

The Wild Bunch was very competitive, but we had a good feeling about what we were doing. You wanted to be the best DJ or the best rapper in England. But there was also a community, like, we used to play with people from London. Even though it was competitive, there weren't no bad vibes. It wasn't like, everyone's got to have a beef with each other. If there was a great rapper in London, I knew who he was, and he would know who I was, and we had no problem with each other. It was like, 'That's a really good rapper there,' and there was nothing negative between you.

Part of what hip-hop was about, was this: a rapper is someone who don't know how to sing, getting on the mic. I can't sing, but I can rap. Kind of like The Specials, hip-hop was a voice for people that didn't have a voice. Rap gave ghetto kids a voice, and it's easier to get over the first hurdle if you're in a group. It's not just me on the mic, it's D [3D] as well, and there's others coming in and out. I was a shy kid, and you can hide almost, because it ain't all about you.

I was writing, but I wasn't like, 'I'm going to be a big rapper, working it.' The writing started when, say, there was something big coming up, like the St Paul's festival. Because you wanted to be the best, it was, 'Ooh, I better start writing.' You always wanted to have new lyrics for the next show. You couldn't come with the same rhymes all the time. Being the best was all about having fresh rhymes. It was a continuation of what I'd always done, scribbling down words on my nan's concrete floor.

At that time, I was just writing about my everyday life, and observing people. Never any ghetto stuff, funnily enough. I'd write about Margaret Thatcher, no opportunities, that kind of thing, but never like, 'I'm a bad boy'. I never mentioned prison, selling weed or robbing. That stuff I didn't want to dwell on, more on not being able to get a job. After I came out of prison, I forgot about it straight away, and I certainly didn't write about it. Some of the words like the 'trendy Wendy' bit in 'Five Man Army', and most of 'Daydreaming', date back to Wild Bunch days.

One time, me and Milo were in Grant's house, and G was on the turntables and I was on the mic. At some point, it was just Milo cutting up and me voicing. There were only thirty or forty people there, and when I did the vocal, you could hear a pin drop. Afterwards, people were whistling and going mad. I've got no idea what the track was, but we were taping that night's session onto cassette, and the tape went all around Bristol and became a little classic thing. It was almost like my very first record, my first release or recording – like, 'I'm here.'

I didn't even know I was any good. I liked rap, and I liked writing words, so I used to rap them. I didn't consider myself good, however, or even really a proper part of Wild Bunch. It was a loose thing for me, something to do. I can remember being out walking with Whitley, and there was a poster up on the wall for the Wild Bunch and it had my name on it. That was the first time I realised, 'Oh, okay, I must be in the Wild Bunch then,' because I really wasn't looking for it.

· ■ ▦ ▮ ▦ ■ ·

Here's how committed to it I was. Whitley and I had been up in Wales for a long weekend. We'd come back and were just heading over to buy some weed at the squat in Totterdown, when we bumped into these people who lived there, Dick and Joanne, on the street. We went to the pub with them and they were like, 'We're moving to a squat in London – come up!'

At that point we didn't know anything about the culture, or how you got by in the squatting lifestyle, but a couple of days later, on the Friday, we each got all our stuff together in bin liners, jumped on a National Express bus, and made our way to an address in King's Cross – and we ended up living there for the best part of two years – all from a quick chat over a pint in Totterdown.

The squat was in a council block called York Way Court, five minutes' walk around the back of King's Cross station, where you'd see a lot of prostitutes. It was as dodgy as fuck, quite a notorious estate, and was a dangerous area in those days, with hard drugs everywhere, but me and Whitley were cool there. People had somehow squatted all these council flats, which you accessed through Copenhagen Street, and we were in one on the second floor. There were two rooms, and it was just sleeping bags, and you'd sleep wherever – no curtains, no furniture, no nothing … and there was only half a sink.

On arrival, we were totally broke. How were we going to survive? Luckily, the barefoot squatter-hippy guy, Gary, taught us how to live with nothing. He was from Bedminster in Bristol – a bit of a surfer, long hair, suntan, Hawaiian shirts, and really into his Northern Soul. He took us to the markets early in the morning to pick up vegetables that had fallen on the floor, before they'd been kicked around and turned to mush, then we'd go home, clean them up and make a soup with them, or a vegetable spaghetti Bolognese. We'd then go down with a big cardboard box, gather up unwanted veg, and even steaks and poultry, and go home and eat like a king for nothing.

That whole area behind King's Cross was a total wasteland, not like it is now, all gentrified for Eurostar. There was a pie and mash shop, selling jellied eels, a shady little gay club, and that was about it. There were a lot of drugs, though, especially heroin. York Way Court was fucked. I never did heroin or any of that. Coming from the reggae thing, it was always weed for me and Whitley, but we definitely saw it.

We used to hang out at this old woman's flat, and one time we went in there, there was this guy shooting up on the couch – really well dressed, like a bit of a cockney wide-boy. He was definitely local, but he had a nice shirt on, a smart pair of slacks, bit of a gangster, and there he was, nodding out.

We used to go to these amazing parties right across the road from the Copenhagen Street squat. They were in these old warehouses behind King's

Cross, which eventually went legit as a nightclub called Bagley's. The people who put them on were the beginnings of that mad collective Archaos, with the motorbikes and the mohicans – the whole Mad Max thing.

Going to London wasn't about furthering my music career – anything but! For better or worse, I didn't give a fuck. It was just to go to clubs and parties. I wasn't even thinking about making music, or that there would be more opportunities up there. I went there just for the adventure, and to go out and hear music. By now I was eighteen, nineteen, and me and Whitley were still obsessed with music. Yeah, I was chasing girls, but music more – always listening to it, always going to see it.

How we'd finance it was, we would work a couple of weeks, so we could then go out partying for a couple of weeks. We would do agency work, then sign on for a bit, then do scaffolding for a month, then sell a bit of weed. One agency job we got was polishing the brass outside this posh office building in the City. That was such an easy job because it was winter. We'd give the brass a quick scrub, then slope off down to the boiler room in the basement and sleep off the previous night's partying. It was so cold out, but as warm as fuck down there. We also worked in Iceland for a bit, packing stuff into freezers on the night shift. We worked in an office in London somewhere too; I can't remember what we were doing because we obviously weren't at a desk, maybe moving stuff or packing.

London was totally exciting to us – just the energy of the place, and so much fun after growing up in Knowle West. It was good to get out of there. Me and Whitley definitely didn't want to stay there. There was nothing there for us – just like in 'Ghost Town' by The Specials, everything had been closed down, no pubs, no clubs, nowhere to go, nothing to do. You'd literally just hang around outside chip shops and stuff. If you're into music, you just want to get out. So, looking back, coming to London was the obvious move.

I think my first job was for a scaffolding company in King's Cross, cleaning floors and putting up the scaffolding, getting about forty or fifty quid a day. When you're squatting, you're not paying rent, so it suddenly felt like I had decent money – no rent, no electricity, and you could party. It wasn't a poor life, certainly not to us anyway. Sometimes we were totally broke, because we'd party hard for a while, and then we'd have to go out and get work again.

Squatting is exciting, because it's total freedom. You're in one place, and then you could meet someone, they live in a different squat, and they're saying, 'Oh, this one is better,' and then you just move there. You get a bin liner, stuff in your clothes, and then you're living in another squat! You're talking about absolute, total freedom. You could meet someone, and the next day you could wake up living in a different area altogether. Or a different city! No paperwork, and no responsibilities whatsoever. And you work when you need to work, not because you feel like you have to work.

While we were there, me and Whitley would sometimes hang out with my 'cousin' Shaun Fray in East Ham. His mum, my auntie Iona, had been my mum's best mate, so we weren't actually blood relations. It was quite a schlep for us to go and see Shaun, but we would see him on weekends sometimes, and he'd take us out to clubs. Whitley noticed it before me, how he had an aura around him. People were wary of him. He wasn't much different in age to us, maybe early twenties, but he owned a house and two shops on Lonsdale Avenue in East Ham. I didn't know what he was about back then, but later on he did a security van robbery in London, for a few million quid I think, and then he went to prison for seven years. But this was before he did the job.

Whitley noticed this thing about him, how we went to a club once, and Shaun just walked straight in. He must've been a serious guy, and he'd done well for himself, probably by illicit means. In a way it was lucky that me and Whitley weren't into money in a big way – all we wanted money for was to go out – because if we'd have asked him if we could make some money with him, he probably wouldn't have been against that, and who knows where that may have led?

Every now and again, we'd go back down to Bristol on weekends, but hardly ever. London was so enthralling for us, coming from a small city like Bristol. Even getting on the Tube was exciting. So we kind of forgot about Bristol. I stayed very involved with my family, we're quite tight-knit like that, but they were happy for me, getting away to London.

And the whole rapping thing with Wild Bunch, and anybody else, I kind of left behind. When I say I never chased the music, it really is true. While I was in York Way Court, the Wild Bunch went to Japan to do some shows, and they ended up arguing loads and breaking up. It wasn't like my world was ending, just because they'd packed it in.

WHITLEY ALLEN: Going to London, it was like, 'Yeah, let's do it!' I'm sure he would have done it on his own, but he knew if he asked me, it would be, 'Let's go! Come on, then!' That's how we were, and we were stronger together.

Before we actually moved up, we'd gone up to London on an overnighter because Public Enemy, Eric B & Rakim and LL Cool J were playing at Hammersmith Odeon – a legendary run of gigs, which ended up featuring as crowd noise between the tracks on PE's *It Takes a Nation of Millions* album. I think Ade must have organised it: 'We're going!' 'Okay!'

In the daytime, we were in Kensington High Street, mucking about. We've gone into Kensington market – and remember, we are Knowle West guys. I'm thinking, 'Whoa! It's all a bit lacksadaisy up here on the security front!'

Meanwhile, he sees a pair of red brothel creepers, like the Teddy Boys used to wear, with the thick rubber sole.

'I've got to have them!' he beams.

'Shut up,' I say, 'we've only just arrived.'

He tries them on, puts the trainers he's been wearing in the box the brothel creepers came in, and just walks out of the shop with the box under his arm. So, he was wearing red brothel creepers that night at Public Enemy. Clothes-wise, we always made our own style.

We actually went with Shaun Fray to the gig, and he'd said he would take us out afterwards. We were sat around having a smoke, and it was like, 'Are we going out or what?' He was just sat there, chilled, and we were raring to go. Eventually he was like, 'Come on, then.' This was like midnight, and he took us uptown in his metallic-blue VW Beetle – the most gorgeous Herbie I've ever seen, kitted right out. That's when I began to realise he was different.

He was the same age as me, but he talked to me like an elder. We've gone in the first club, had a bit of music, then he was, 'Come on, we're going to another club.' Then we've gone into this next club, and we're just walking into these clubs, without paying. I twigged, like, hold on a minute …

We've gone into the last club, and the next minute, all the Public Enemy geezers we've just paid to see onstage turn up, and now they're doing the same routine as they've done onstage, but in the club. Like, holding DJ Houdini up while he's scratching on the decks. They've got all the security around them, they've got the chains, and we're like, 'What the hell?' but I clocked Shaun, and he's looking them all up and down. I'm thinking, 'What the hell is this guy on?' He's got a nice little gold chain on, not a fat one, but I'm looking at him different, like, these were big security guys, and the penny dropped – this dude is a known person, he's connected. He had some serious weight. He was a lovely guy, and I felt comfortable around him, but I felt like a kid, and he was the same age.

On the way home, Adrian was sick in the car, and he ended the night praying to the porcelain god. We had to take the door off the hinges to get him out, because he'd locked himself in, and I remember Shaun cleaning the car in the morning. I don't know what we were smoking, but it flipped us out, and he just reacted badly. When we got back to Bristol the next day, we must have gone home and then gone straight out again – Sunday night at the Inkerman. We never stopped.

By the time we were living in York Way Court, Michelle had a daughter with Claude from the Wild Bunch but, soon after, Michelle came up to London to visit, and we went clubbing. We had a load of acid in at the time, and me and Ade dropped some on the Tube going uptown. When we got to the club, the bouncer was like, 'Are they with you?' pointing to Michelle and this other girl with us. I said, 'Yeah!' He said, 'Then you're not coming in.' The guy was going to let me and Adrian in, because he had seen us before, but not them.

We ended up going to a gay club right in front of where we lived. We went in there, and Ade smokes a joint and I watched him wafting smoke towards this dude, and the guy just looks round … Oh my God! He had done it totally on purpose. I always used to watch him and say, in my head, 'Don't let him talk, you just need to hit him!' Because as soon as they let him talk, he wins, game over. People initially want to fight him because he's lairy and mouthy, but then he twists their words, and they end up mates. I would be like, 'You should have just hit him while you had the chance!'

I think that's why he ended up a rapper. He can captivate people. You've got to be careful because he's a likeable fellow when he's on his mission. He's complex. If he likes you, he likes you. If he don't, he will hate you forever. He's deep.

Living up in London, we had money and we were living the life. We were doing agency work, we were shoplifting, and I had this job in a warehouse. I used to get searched on the way out regularly, because they knew we were having stuff, so he used to turn up in this massive army-surplus coat, load up the pockets and disappear. When money started getting tight because we'd been partying too much, we'd get the *Evening Standard*, look in Situations Vacant, and end up on a building site.

He'd go back occasionally to do stuff with Wild Bunch, like St Paul's Carnival. He had a lyric about 'Trendy Wendy', because he was seeing this girl from Clifton/Redland – 'trendy Wendy rolling up her jeans'. That was a new lyric he did at the festival, and it just went off in the crowd big-time. People instantly reacted to it.

The Wild Bunch became the big sound that everyone went to at Carnival, because it wasn't just a reggae sound. Wild Bunch was already established by the time he was on the mic with them. He obviously had a connection because he grew up with a couple of them, and Claude was seeing Michelle, and had a kid with her.

We were Knowle West kids in our late teens, but we were getting around, like getting into the Dug Out, which wasn't easy. It closed down in '86, before he was actually old enough to get in legally, but he would, because he was with Michelle, or he'd call the sound system and get in that way. He saw a lot very young, with his wild family life as well, and that's why I think he evolved quicker than anyone else.

We were both strong, and we went out and did stuff. We were already being drawn into the serious side of music, because we were mixing with these heavy-duty people without knowing. Like Ray Mighty, from Smith & Mighty – he used to scare the hell out of me. We used to call him Medusa, with all his dreads hanging out. But I knew him through Nicky Tippett's family, because he was good friends with them, and I'd seen him around Knowle West going way back.

When we were in Bristol, me and Adrian started doing this thing with some other guys from Knowle West. Me and him were inseparable by now, and he was always, 'It's me and you – you DJ, and I'll MC.' But these other guys were all about themselves. They were in it for the wrong reasons, they just wanted to be famous, whereas we loved music, and that was the driving thing. I don't think Adrian thought he was going to be famous, he just wanted to rap.

It was all DJs and one MC, and these guys wanted both of us, but we would be with them, and as soon as they had to go home, we were off down to St Paul's or Easton. We were always together, and they weren't part of that, and it kept us outside of their clique. He was doing a lot of writing in his own room, but he freestyled a lot, probably on stuff he'd worked out before.

It was then that he got the name Tricky Kid. Up till then he'd always been known as Adrian Thaws, but we were supposed to be somewhere with this crew, and he didn't wanna go, and because he's got family all over the place, he just said he was in Manchester. But they were like Klingons, like, 'What's he doing?' We were leading them, and they were like sheep. They were like, 'You're tricky, you are – the Tricky Kid,' because he was never around when they wanted to find him.

We both realised at the same time that it wasn't for us and we wanted to leave it, and luckily we were able to get away to London. I always said to him that he's very advanced in his thinking. He's five years ahead of people. I don't know if it rubbed off on me, but at that point I was just chilled. If I don't want to do something, I ain't gonna do it, and we were getting away from a negative energy.

Towards the end of the two years in London, he was getting into doing music more seriously. He was spending more time in Bristol, and I was still spending more time in London, just going back to party on odd weekends. We were getting into different circles socially, but we'd always had a pact that if we were ever going to move back to Bristol, we'd do it together, so I rang him.

'You've moved back, Jack, haven't you?'

'I heard you had!' he goes.

We moved back, but he didn't tell me that he was as far along with music as he actually was. He'd been connecting with people, like we'd been walking back from Camden to York Way Court one night, and we bumped into Milo, and they'd started doing stuff again.

Back in Bristol, he started moving with Claude, doing a lot of MC-ing together. There was obviously a connection between them, but Claude is a nightmare – a major party animal, whereas Ade was more about dealing with the craft by then, taking it more serious.

MAXINE QUAYE, MY MUM

YOUNG ME

(CLOCKWISE) ARTHUR GODFREY WITH HIS FATHER, 'FARMER'; UNCLE MARTIN, AUNT OLIVE & MARTIN'S WIFE

UNCLE MARTIN & UNCLE TONY, 2012 (PHOTO © LEE JAFFE)

UNCLE MICHAEL

NANNY VIOLET

COUSIN MICHELLE & DAUGHTER
WITH HER MUM, MARLOW

UNCLE TONY & WIFE WITH MARLOW

MARLOW WITH HER KIDS, MARK & MICHELLE, AT BUTLINS, 1970S

ME AT BUTLINS

HANGING WITH MY COUSIN MICHELLE
& TREVOR & CLAUDE

COUSIN MARK & HIS SON RICKY

GREAT-GRANDMA MAGA

CHILDHOOD IN HARTCLIFFE

FARMER GODFREY & MAGA,
MY GREAT-GRANDPARENTS

HANGING OUT WITH FAMILY

RICKY & TASHA, MARK'S SON & MICHELLE'S DAUGHTER

UNCLE TONY, DICKIE EWING & UNCLE MICHAEL

AUNTIE MARLOW'S WEDDING. SOMEONE IN THE FAMILY LATER BLACKED OUT THE (EX-) HUSBAND

Before we headed up to London, I was just starting this thing we called Un Deux Trois, with a couple of mates from Totterdown. When we came back, I went to do that again, and me and Adrian kind of started drifting apart.

TRICKY: The Wild Bunch came back to life again for a short time when some record-company people in London contacted them, offering to put out a couple of singles. I never did any of that with them. I didn't know anything about going in the studio then. I was younger, and I was still knocking around with Whitley, and we had a totally different lifestyle to those guys. Those guys were part of a trendy, arty crowd in Bristol, and we were still hanging out in shitty little pubs.

When I rapped with Wild Bunch, I would go down there with Whitley; I'd rap, then me and him would go off and do our thing – probably go out to a bar, or go off and smoke a spliff and have a drink. If I'd been more focused on hanging out with them, perhaps I would have been on the records. In my head, it was just turn up, do a few vocals, then maybe go and get some food.

I had more time for people like Smith & Mighty. Those guys are one of the foundations of Bristol music. They are very ghetto, as in: they don't care that much. In the late '80s, they got a huge deal with FFRR Records, and they didn't go off to London, didn't change the way they dressed, didn't change their attitude, they just stayed the same – solid, solid people. They were solely about the music, and they did their own thing – they had their own sound, which was kind of dub, with breaks in there.

Rob Smith and Ray Mighty are the real deal, proper musicians, with no bullshit about them. They were retiring to the point where you were lucky if you could even get them out to DJ sometimes. They built a studio in the ghetto, right where they lived on City Road in St Paul's, and me and Whitley used to go down there and hang out and smoke.

RAY MIGHTY: In the early '80s, all you ever got told was, if you wanted to make it in the music business, you had to go to London. It was like, 'Oh, for fuck's sake!' because then obviously you had to breathe the London air, and you'd end up making stuff that played by their rules. Whereas we knew what would drop in our town, and just went for that. That's why it ended up sounding different to what was going on anywhere else, because it was made for Bristol.

Most people around us had exposure to reggae, and were used to hearing music really loud, so we all understood bass and sound systems and what works in that environment. The music from Bristol always has that vibe under it. When we started out, that swing/go-go thing was in fashion, and rare groove, with breaks. London is great, but at that time it did change styles really fast. Like, right, it's go-go time, everyone gets into it, let's all wear fucking Lycra shorts, then something else starts to take off and everyone fucking runs and follows that – rather than just mastering your art.

If you do anything long enough, you'll get good at it, so we stayed with our style, and learnt through experience what kind of sub-bass and drops and phrases would work in our town – take the bass out, take the bass in, drop the beat in certain places – and what samples to use to get everyone going. You just make it for local ears. You would take little bits from everything, like a little synth that you heard from a go-go track, always some dub in there somewhere along the line, and definitely something hip-hoppy – always hip-hop and reggae, with serious bass on a big system.

The local celebrity on our scene was Mark Stewart, because he'd been out there touring and releasing records with the Pop Group. After they split up in '81, he went to New York for a bit and started making these crazy electro-dub records. In Bristol, he was the one that everyone was looking to and influenced by – this punk-rocky indie sound with heavy dub effects and electronics. We had all seen him doing it, so we realised it was possible – you could get away with mixing up all these really over-the-top, brash effects. I've heard it said that he brought back loads of early hip-hop tracks on record and cassette, and turned a lot of people like the Wild Bunch crowd on to it all.

The Dug Out was the main place people went to. That was where you met and got to know everyone. You might see them out at different nights in bars here and there around town, but the Dug Out was the central place, in Park Row near the university. When that got shut down and turned into a Chinese restaurant, the next place was the Moon Club in Upper York Street, but it had more of a live-venue feel, with hard floors and a hard sound about it.

By then, hip-hop had been around a few years, and it was steeped in what people like the Wild Bunch and DJ groups like 2 Bad Crew were doing. That was what we would all go out and listen to, and Tricky was part of that scene. I always associated him with Wild Bunch and, as far as I was concerned, he was a part of that set-up. I would almost call him one of the Wild Bunch, but it turns out he wasn't. To me, he was around as much as Mushroom was, doing his little things on the mic, with Mushroom DJ-ing, and 3D – or 'Delj', as we call him – and Willy Wee on the mic too.

Most people in Knowle West were definitely not into what Tricky was into. Up there, he stood out for the fact that he wasn't fucking white, but also for the kind of music he was listening to, and the people he was hanging around with – not middle class exactly, but trendier kids, rather than the sort who would blatantly just go downtown, get pissed up, find a bird, have a fight, eat a kebab and go home. Because that is your average Knowle Wester.

If you don't know it, Knowle West just looks like a quiet, orangey-brick estate, but it's definitely the roughest place in Bristol. It's known as the white ghetto. You'll go into the pub there, and it's one of those places where, if you don't know someone there, someone is gonna call you out. It's not a place to hang if you don't know anybody.

Tricky definitely doesn't play the game, does he? I never saw him in drag, but I did hear of it. He was not a big guy, he was black, and he'd got a bit of an eczema thing going on – living in Knowle West with all that, every fucker would have picked on you, so you'd have to learn to fight. You'd have to be able to punch back. Knowle West toughens you up. You can't be a wanker around that area. They'll just call you out every day.

I came out of the Moon Club one night, and saw him fighting two guys, both bigger than him. These two guys were trying to beat him up, just as I stumbled out for some fresh air. He was up for it as well, and he tried having a go, so I just jumped in and grabbed one of them off, and left Tricky to the other one, but that one didn't want to know, so they both fucked off. But he was up for it!

The first time we played out as Smith & Mighty, it was just me and Rob Smith, at a little gathering that a friend of ours was putting on, called the Après-Ski Party – this was probably sometime in '86. We didn't even have any vocalists to start with, only a sequencer, some synths and a couple of drum machines. It was just instrumental tracks, with the sequencer playing, and us playing live over the top of it. Mark Stewart was in the crowd, with Tricky, because those two had been hanging out quite a bit. Mark was the celebrity of the day, so it was actually good for us that he was there to see us – Tricky we only knew from clubbing it, and seeing him as Tricky Kid with Wild Bunch.

There was a guy compèring the night, so there was a microphone onstage, and as we were playing our cover version of Erik Satie's 'Gymnopédie No. 1', Mark Stewart got up and shouted, 'This is fucking brilliant!' and pulled Tricky up there too. He started to chat over what we were doing, riding the sort of style you'd hear on early Massive Attack stuff – which instantly made us realise that we really needed vocals over what we were doing.

Apparently that was Tricky's first time up on a proper stage. The Wild Bunch used to put on odd things in different little places, and derelict buildings. We did that a couple of times, too, all of us as a group of people, so you had that cooperative, supportive element to what was going on.

St Paul's Carnival used to be the highlight of the Wild Bunch year. They always pulled the best crowd, and those were definitely the best gigs they played. They'd have a sound system going all day at the top of Campbell Street, which is near my family's home, and they'd fill out the whole street from the off. They'd get different MCs to come through, and it really was the best part of the festival. At that point, it was almost entirely a reggae festival. There was lots of good stuff going on all over, but then you'd have this one hip-hop, reggae, soul, funk thing going on in the middle of it.

One time, not when the festival was on, I ran into Tricky and Grant coming down Campbell Street, after they'd been stopped by the Old Bill. One of them had just bought some weed, I think, and the Old Bill were putting them in the back of the van. I went down and stood in front of the van and held it up. I said, 'This van is not going anywhere!' After a crowd had gathered and surrounded the van, I went around the back, opened the door and got them out of the van – then we all scarpered!

We helped each other on a personal level – it wasn't just music; it was day-to-day stuff as well.

TRICKY: Smith & Mighty used to play all over, and the Après-Ski was the first time I ever went on a *proper* stage – no rehearsal, no warning, just 'Get up here!' Before that, I'd always rapped on the floor, next to the turntables. I was out at this party with Mark, and he came up to me in the crowd and said, 'Are you going to get up and do a vocal?'

'Yeah, yeah, yeah!'

Mark's mad, though, so I didn't take him seriously. Then, all of a sudden, he's up onstage introducing me, so I have to get up there and I'm shitting myself. I'd always been next to the turntables where no one can really see you, with my back to the crowd.

Doing music, you don't know how serious to take it sometimes, but Ray's partner, Rob Smith, said to me once, 'Your voice makes the hairs on my arm stand up.' Little things like that made me think, 'You know what, I'm gonna do this!' Another time, he came up to me in the street and said, 'Universe – one verse!' He said a couple of things where, if you're not feeling confident, he's just encouraging you.

I was a kid, and these things have stayed with me all these years, from Wild Bunch days. At that age, you don't know if it's all just for fun or not. I liked doing it, but you never thought, 'I'm going to have a career out of this.' Those couple of things Rob said to me were like, 'Right – okay!'

Mark Stewart was a different animal – very intelligent, to the point of making him eccentric. He used to make albums splicing together pieces of cassette tape. He used to have people following him around in London, these weirdos who would find out where he was staying and then follow him around on the street. When I was living in York Way Court, he came to stay with me for a bit, and this guy actually had a record deal with Mute Records. Like, couldn't they put him up in a hotel?

One day, we went over to the record company, because they wanted to renew his deal, and the guy there obviously didn't have a clue who I was, because by that point I was Tricky, but I wasn't *Tricky* – I was just a guy living in a squat in London. So, Mark marches into the meeting with a brown paper bag and a Bible, and he goes, 'I want the money in this brown paper bag, and we're not signing a contract – you just have to swear on the Bible.' Mark was different, alright.

After the two years in London, I went back to squatting in Bristol, but it wasn't long before I moved into a rented bedsit in Saville Place in Clifton. My cousin Michelle had moved up there and, because she was like my sister and my mother rolled into one, I moved into this place right across the road from hers. After that I got a flat two minutes down a lane called the Fosseway.

I don't think I would have lived in Clifton if it wasn't for Michelle. There wouldn't have been reason for it. She'd moved up there for her daughter, because it had better schools than Hartcliffe. From Knowle West to Clifton, it was like two different worlds. You won't see many Knowle West guys drinking in pubs in Clifton, and you certainly ain't gonna see Clifton people hanging out in Knowle West.

After growing up in Bristol's poorer neighbourhoods, and then sampling London lowlife in King's Cross, I suppose I'd come to see Bristol as a great place to live. I can't think of anywhere I didn't like in Bristol, and you can walk everywhere – not like living in London. London is hard. At York Way Court, I knew that if I was skint and hungry, I could go out to see Shaun and auntie Iona in East Ham, and they'd feed me and lend me a tenner. But you can't walk to East Ham, so how do you get there, if you ain't got no money?

Bristol is an easy place to live. It makes you wonder why there's crime there, in a way. There's crime in Knowle West, and I can understand that, but it ain't like living in London. Crime makes more sense in London. I can understand why people are hustling and dealing drugs there. In Bristol, it makes less sense, because you can survive in Bristol a lot easier than you can in London.

MICRODOTS

Weed was a cultural thing. For me, in my teens, it was a part of the music, it heightened your sense of listening. You have a smoke, you listen to a cassette of Saxon sound system, and it's like you're there! With some good sensimilla, it's like you're in the place – sat there, stoned, you're actually in the place. That was my buzz.

When me and Whitley started smoking in the '80s, there was none of that skunk or hydroponic shit on the market. We had sensimilla, which we could only get every now and then. That was really strong weed, but a different kind of strong – it wasn't chemicals. Then we had Lebanese, and hashish, and the thing with all of these types was, we used to get the giggles, just laughing the whole time, and vibing on the music.

I've never seen weed as illegal. It was totally normal to me, just part of the culture, especially with my Jamaican background. Knowle West guys used to smoke it, too. It was just something you did, that you fell into at a very early age, and you probably dealt a bit as well.

I didn't see it as an illegal drug, maybe because my dad smoked. He was nothing to do with Rasta, but he used to sell it, too, at one time, and he would get some of the best weed in Bristol. Sometimes, once I was in my twenties, I used to go up to his house and get some. The best weed I've ever smoked in Bristol was from my dad, but he wouldn't give it to me for free – definitely not! I'd have to buy it.

Growing up in the reggae culture back then, alcohol and weed were fine, but if you took coke, you were a crackhead, so it really wasn't cool to take it. It ain't like now, where you get a young black kid dropping an E or taking coke, and it's accepted. It was in Jamaican lyrics that taking cocaine wasn't cool. In our circles, if you snorted cocaine, you were a dirtbag, so it was something you didn't do. We wouldn't have even known where to get it.

The strongest thing we ever got was microdots. I took a lot of acid. I would do it around Bristol, and at Glastonbury, and even in London. I would do it anywhere. I would do it in York Way Court, in Tube stations – fucking everywhere! I'd do it with friends, and also by myself – just drop a tab then wander off alone and sit around watching things. I wasn't big into it, like for any spiritual dimension or hippy nonsense. I would just take it. It was a thing I did. I used to like taking acid and going for a walk, standing around watching things – drop a microdot and walk around Bristol in the rain, with all the floor shiny underneath your feet.

Me and Whitley took a load of mushrooms out in the countryside near Swansea, and we did a load of microdots at Glastonbury, before it got corporate. I've had some bad trips as well – real bad trips.

One of my worst trips ever, though, was on weed. Me and Whitley went to this blues in St Paul's where my uncle Michael got murdered. It was only about two months after he'd died, and I was smoking a spliff, getting really stoned, thinking, 'I wonder where he got it? Fucking hell, what part of the room did it happen in?' We're talking about a small room maybe twenty-foot square, like the front room of the house. He didn't make it out of there, so he actually died on that floor somewhere. I'm smoking and paranoid and I'm looking around the place thinking, 'Where did he die?' I can remember being stoned and everything was alright, then I had a few more drinks and all of a sudden it got very dark and weird.

One time, me and 3D were walking in Bristol, and the guys who were supposed to have done it slowed down in a car and asked me if I wanted a lift. 3D goes to me, 'If you get in there, you won't get out again.' They definitely knew who I was, but I was too young for them to see me as a threat, I would've thought, because they were men. So why would they offer me a lift? It wasn't like they were going to get me in the car and warn me. I found that one really strange ...

CHAPTER SIX
DAYDREAMING

On one of my return visits to Bristol from York Way Court, I wandered into this pub, The Montpelier. It was a good old haunt, where you could smoke a spliff, play bar football and relax – not exactly a squat pub, or a hipster hangout, but a bit of a hippy place, and I knew it was somewhere that 3D would be, because he used to have an artist space there, where he worked on his graffiti.

I hadn't been into this pub for about a year and, sure enough, D was in there, so we got a drink and started catching up on what we'd both been up to. Nobody had seen me in there for a year or more, but after about fifteen or twenty minutes, the phone rang in the pub, and it was for me. While I was talking to whoever it was, I could see D just looking at me in disbelief. After I've hung up, he goes, 'You're an enigma, ain't you?' At the time, I didn't even know what that word meant.

As I was shuttling more and more between London and Bristol, I guess me and 3D got quite close, because we were the rappers, and to begin with we'd write together in a fairly off-the-cuff way. In those months it went very quickly from Wild Bunch into Massive Attack. To be very honest, I don't even remember the changeover, but I suppose that the two Fourth & Broadway singles had put Wild Bunch on the map, and after the name became Massive Attack, they were soon signed to this label Circa, which would soon become a part of Richard Branson's Virgin Records – the big time!

Right around the point where they signed, there was a falling out, and Miles decided to leave. Something happened. Then the name changed, and Nellee went off to do Soul II Soul. I don't think Nellee went because of any problems; it was Miles and D who had the problem with each other. I don't actually know what that was over. After all that unravelled, Mushroom, D and Grant stayed together, and it was them that got the deal.

I was getting paid a wage to be a 'member' of the band without being a part of the deal, and I was very happy with that, because it meant I had regular money. I didn't have to work in Iceland. I didn't have to do anything dodgy. Honestly, in those days, to me Massive Attack just meant I had cash in my pocket, where I could do the things I wanted. Those three were smart enough to be more business-minded than me, because they knew they wanted to be a band – to me it still felt like I was doing a hobby, not taking it seriously.

They'd also got themselves a manager called Cameron McVey. Back in the early '80s, he was the singer in a pop band called Bim, which also had the producer Stephen Street in it, so he was in that English pop thing. I think they released a couple of songs that didn't do anything. I noticed this a lot over the years, how you get guys who were trying to be singers or in a band, but it didn't work out and their careers didn't go that way, so they end up being managers or working in the business in some other capacity.

At the same time as Massive Attack, Cameron was also managing Neneh Cherry. He and Neneh later had two kids together, one of whom is now a musician called Mabel. Back then, a single B-side he'd made in his own pop duo was reworked into Neneh's first single, 'Buffalo Stance'. So in relation to the 'history' of Massive Attack, he was someone who had connections in the London music business, and I think he was the one who got them the Virgin contract, because he would've known those label people. After the deal, the organisation got bigger really quickly, and looking back, that was when I think I stopped enjoying it as much.

WHITLEY ALLEN: After Wild Bunch did those two singles on Fourth & Broadway, 'Tearing Down the Avenue' and 'Friends and Countrymen', it was on the decline – they were splitting because Nellee, who was one of the main dudes driving it, had already disappeared up to London to produce Soul II Soul's album. So they had the connection with that world, but that's also why they were falling apart.

Tricky was really only in at the tail-end of it, but that meant he moved seamlessly into Massive Attack. They only really had one MC, which was Delj [3D]. They would always have guest MCs, and Tricky became a guest MC who automatically became a full MC once the name changed, because he was just different. Just look at his lyrics – there's comedy, street things, political stuff. He's a complex individual, so you can see why they wanted to keep him in.

He was commuting backwards and forwards from London to do stuff with the Wild Bunch, but towards the end was when they were forming Massive Attack, because it was becoming something else without Nellee there. I was still on the phone to him, and he was like, 'Yeah, it's evolving.' Me and the Un Deux Trois guy had a sampler, and we started looping tracks and making beats around the same time, but they were obviously more advanced than us.

One time there was a big DJ sound-system thing – three or four different sounds, all playing in Temple Meads under the banner of Massive Attack. This was when we were still based in London, and he was working with Milo. Milo didn't like 3D. I don't think it was personal, but when Milo was cutting up at that event, it seemed like every time Delj was rapping, Milo would make a mistake. I can remember Delj looking at him, and Milo just had his head down. Then Tricks got on and Milo was perfect. So even though they were on the same sound, you would get that vibe.

That time, it was Wild Bunch, UD4, City Rockas, all these different crews on one stage. That was the only time it actually happened – this huge show. They have gigs there now, but back then it was unusual, brilliant – something new happening in Bristol.

During the early stages of Massive Attack, me and Adrian were talking, then we just sort of drifted. Mobiles weren't about then, obviously, and anyway Tricks is a nightmare, as a person. I always tell him: the best thing that's happened to him is having a manager. He knows it! He is the most disorganised dude. We used to go out, and I'd say, 'Okay, I'll look after your money,' but then we would argue, because people latch on to him, and I don't stay around him then.

He's getting people drinks, and he'll go to me, 'Get the drinks in with that money I gave you, yeah?'

'You've only got like a tenner left.'

'But I gave you sixty quid!'

'That was two hours ago … Actually, have your money, and fuck off!'

We would argue all the time about that stuff – always friends, but after a while it was, 'I'm not looking after your shit. Do it yourself!' He's a nightmare. Anyway, he was getting busier, and we kind of lost touch.

RAY MIGHTY: Originally, Massive Attack was an idea that Delj had for a British version of Afrika Bambaataa's Zulu Nation – not actually a group as such, or an artist, but a movement of like-minded people looking after each other against dodgy promoters and helping each other make records. That's what it was supposed to be when it was first talked about. That's how me and Rob [Smith] ended up working on that first self-released single under the Massive Attack name, 'Any Love', in 1988 – it was all according to this 'Massive Attack helping each other out' thing.

Because of their relative success in Bristol and beyond, Delj had all the connections and knew everybody, and on top of that he was DJ-ing and had the graffiti thing, so it was like bringing everybody in – artists, DJs, producers – and having a collective to watch out for each other. That was the idea that Massive Attack was started under. Tricky was jumping up and chatting with them, and hanging around with Delj, so he still seemed to be part of it.

Hip-hop and graffiti was a big part of their style. Even then, Delj was known as one of the top three or four graffiti artists in the country – there weren't that many around in Britain, obviously – it was him, Goldie, and a couple of others, representing the UK for graffiti. So that all tied in with the music. A couple of times, they would get New York graffiti artists coming over, putting exhibitions on at the Arnolfini gallery – the more famous ones at the time like Brim Fuentes and Bio [aka Wilfredo Feliciano] from New York – and Massive would be doing the music, hip-hop with heavy bass, which was very much Tricky's thing.

While all that was going on, there was a guy called Peter D, or Peter Davies, who was doing pre-production stuff for Massive before they actually got a deal. At that time, in 1988/9, he was the only one that had any equipment and could sequence shit together. He was doing pre-production on rough ideas that everyone had – Tricky, Mushroom, D – putting breaks together, using samples and moving those rough ideas forward. Because he had the gear, everyone was doing stuff with him.

Some of those tracks actually even made it onto their album, as well as the lyrics they were dropping. Because he was working with them, we were good friends with him, and we kind of consider him as part of Massive – and Tricky, too. After 'Any Love', they became a little clique which we didn't get involved in. We left them to it because it was their thing, and we had our own thing going.

At the same time as they got their deal with Virgin, we got a major deal, so we spent a good part of '89 commuting up and down to London, trying to get our record together, and they were probably doing much the same thing.

TRICKY: Massive Attack was never a thing where everybody made the music together. One person would bring their bit, another person would bring a bit – it was bits and bobs that people had done very separately, all put together to make an album, which became *Blue Lines*.

For instance, I know that Mushroom did the skeleton of 'Unfinished Sympathy', then someone worked on it, then maybe a string section was added, and so on. The one I did was 'Daydreaming', which ended up being the first single. I did the music in the studio by myself.

I was starting to toy around with sampling, but I didn't actually have any of the equipment, so I'd go around to these two blokes' house who had bought themselves an Akai S1000 sampler, and muck about with it. It wasn't even a proper recording studio. 'Daydreaming' was based around a sample from an old Indian song, just looped off a cassette tape of Bollywood music – for some reason I loved that kind of music at the time. I always listen to a bit of everything.

On the mic, I'd always voiced quietly, which was a confidence thing. I didn't think I was as good as Rakim or Chuck D. The quiet thing probably started from rapping live, when you've got people in front of you – still managing to do it, but not having that real confidence and presence. It was just because I'm shy by nature, so I'd do it soft – hiding, almost, and totally *not* aggressive, like most rappers were at the beginning. My lyrics were softer, too, less boasty.

That's something people may not know or understand: I'm a really shy person. Getting up on the mic was hard for me. I soon found it was something that I loved to do, but I was just always very quiet doing it. I never had the confidence to be in your face and loud.

It was a natural thing for me, to have that slower, more low-key thing going, but then once we started on Massive Attack, 3D noticed it, and he goes, 'Aha, that should be our style – the soft vocal.' To me at the time, it wasn't a style, it was just how I did it while I coped with my shyness. From my side, it was all accident. Me, I just fumble along and things happen. It's like with music and films, right? I never look for music, and I never look for films – everything I see or hear happens accidentally, I never go in search of it. But if something is good and I'm supposed to find it, I'll find it. Just fumbling along.

'Daydreaming', the track I produced, was the first single. Now, it ain't the best song they've released, I'm not saying that, but in some ways I helped to set a precedent for them – the gentler style of rapping, the English thing, not afraid to sound like you're from Bristol, rather than Brooklyn.

Blue Lines was mostly recorded in Bristol, and then them three – D, G and Mushroom – mostly mixed and finished off the tracks in London. I found it cool that they stayed living in Bristol, and then once they were a huge band, that they just stayed where they were. They're homeboys, D and G.

I only went to London with them once, while they were mixing. No disrespect to those guys, but we came from different worlds. We drove up there to work on a song, and I was a kid – I had no money. On the way back, we were at the services, and everybody got off the bus to go and eat – we had a tour bus for some reason but we were just on a studio trip. We walked into the service station, and it was £2.50 for sausage and chips, and I was starving. I said to G, 'Here, lend me two quid!' I was just a kid, but he wouldn't lend me the money.

That affected me a lot. That day was when I realised I would end up leaving Massive Attack, although it was way before I truly knew it or actually thought about leaving. When he wouldn't lend me two pounds to eat, that was the end of our relationship on a certain level. Like, you know, these people come from a different place to you. Where I grew up, they would steal that money so I could eat. That's when I knew that it was about business, about a band and a music career – and Massive wasn't even big at that point.

Once I'd done my part in it, I was off doing my own thing, just like I was with the Wild Bunch. They were Massive Attack, they were taking it seriously. Me? I was still hanging out with my friends, and more interested in going to clubs, and reggae gigs. What was important to me was when a sound system came to Bristol or was playing in London. If King Tubby's was playing in London, we'd get on the train, thumb a lift – however we could do it, to get there and see them. And I was so focused on that, that the potential for being more involved with Massive Attack didn't really sink in with me.

Going to see the best DJ, all the best reggae – that was my thing. Even something like going to Notting Hill Carnival – that was a big deal to me and my mates.

I just couldn't comprehend it as a business at that point. Certainly not like, 'Oh, I could actually make a living off this!' If I'd been a bit older, I'd have been wiser about the money, and made sure I was getting paid, because back then I didn't give a fuck. I just loved music, loved making it, and it went no further than that. It probably would've been better if I'd had a smarter head with money, but I've never been a money guy or cared about it. I'm not interested in a big house or a big car. I probably signed things that lost me money, and I also wasn't able to manage the money I earned – because I didn't come from money, I didn't know how to manage it.

I was on a wage, and then I got publishing income for the stuff I wrote, which was all done fair. Only thing was, I signed some of my publishing over to a mate, to help him out – this was Claude, who'd just had a kid with my cousin, Michelle, so my thing was, 'Okay, I'll sign some of my publishing over to you, so you have an income to help out your daughter in the future.'

This was just for lyrics I wrote on a couple of songs. I mean, if I was a millionaire at the time – okay! But I wasn't, so signing my publishing over to him was a bit crazy. I wanted to help him out, because he'd been involved longer than me, and otherwise he wasn't gonna make any money off the album. He was a mate, so, alright, you help a mate out. He still has it to this day, and he's still making money from it now. I'm not quite sure if he really sorted Michelle out, though.

When 'Daydreaming' was finally getting released, it was a weird feeling. You've done this music in the studio and, all of a sudden, you're doing a video to it. That's like, wow! When you're first writing stuff, you don't think of it coming out. So when we did the video for 'Daydreaming', and then saw the video, it was a really strange vibe. You've made a song in a little studio in someone's front room, and then they're playing it on MTV and it's being shown all around the world. It was hard to get a connection to it, like, it's not real. I didn't quite get the concept. I felt alienated from that public side of releasing music.

But the track really blew up. No one had heard music like that in England. It's hard to imagine today, but back then people in the UK didn't actually know what rap was, so *Blue Lines* brought a hip-hop feel to people who didn't know that hip-hop even existed. Saying that now, it sounds insane. Nowadays everybody on the planet knows what rap is, but back then people didn't know what it was unless they were actually into it.

So, 'Daydreaming' changed everything, and the next thing you know, it was videos, touring, interviews. It was a very fast transition, and I wasn't really into it as a lifestyle. Coming up to London for a meeting or doing a video – I could take it or leave it back then. It was just boring to me, so, day to day, I operated like I always had: I would work for a bit, get some money, and then they wouldn't see me for a while. I wasn't signed to their Virgin deal. They paid me as a hired hand, so I didn't feel like I had to turn up.

With a mature head, I can see that I had access to success, and I just didn't take it up. I would do the odd thing, and then I would disappear, and they wouldn't know where I was. I just wasn't around. What kid has a chance to be in music videos and doesn't turn up? That side of things immediately didn't appeal to me. I'd rather be doing something else, like going out to a party or a club, or smoking a spliff and listening to music at a mate's house. I saw a video as taking up my time. When you're young, you want your own time.

It went really quickly from the Wild Bunch – a very loosely affiliated meeting-up thing, doing live stuff, then disappearing for a while, and everybody can go and do their thing – to like, 'Okay, we've got to meet at twelve o'clock tomorrow in the studio and spend the whole day there till twelve o'clock at night.' I struggled with that transition. It became like a job, and one of the reasons I did music was because I didn't want to work. 'You have to be here at a certain time and do this and do that' – that just wasn't my vibe at all.

You know, I could be out the night before, so I don't know if I can be up at twelve o'clock. To be able to meet someone at a certain time, when you're a young kid – you're all over the place, aren't you? I could walk out of my house to get some breakfast, and then by teatime I could be up in Manchester for six weeks. Seriously, that's how my life works, so telling me where and when to be places was just not convenient for me back then.

I was living a different life to them. I was still knocking about the streets, still getting into little bits of trouble here and there. I wasn't like, 'I'm going to be famous!' I was notorious for not turning up to interviews, or to the studio, or for videos. If we were doing a video, I might just not be there – they'd eventually find out I was in Manchester with my family, or in London. It wasn't particularly that there was any separation or resentment, just that I'd rather be doing something else other than a video.

To start with, I think it amused them. They even made a short promo film to go with an early track they'd done called 'Just a Matter of Time', and they ended up titling the movie, *Where Is Tricky?* The whole thing was like, 'Where is he?!' like a shaggy dog story, so they must have thought it was funny.

I can see now that they must have been a bit frustrated at times, too. I think I was too young really to want success, while they were that bit older – G was almost ten years older – so they were more prepared to work hard to achieve it. G was actually quite a mellow guy, he would probably have been happy staying at the level of doing sound system stuff; it was really 3D who had that get-up-and-go, which I don't in any way mean as a criticism. It was him dealing with the management, and the label. I knew those people and I was cool with them, but it wasn't my band, or my future.

When I first got into it, I was used to writing by myself, like, 'Oh, St Paul's festival is coming up, I'd better get moving with some lyrics for that!' With Massive Attack it became, 'Let's meet at my house at twelve o'clock and sit there for six hours, trying to write lyrics.' When you're young, you don't want to do that – sitting there with the cassette going over the same lyrics, over and over again. I just go in and write the lyrics and put the vocals down. It's not a big deal. You write when you're inspired, not when you're told.

Doing the album just became a hassle to me as a kid. I can remember saying one afternoon, 'Why are we doing these vocals *again*? The vocals are fine.' Then we stayed until midnight and ended up using the original vocals anyway!

When we were doing 'Five Man Army', we had done our vocals, and I went back the next day, and the mix in the part where I voiced had changed, and certain things were dropped out so that, to me, I wasn't sounding as good as I had the day before. Maybe I was being paranoid, but I was thinking, 'Has this turned into a competition?' But I wouldn't say anything. I would just keep quiet about it, thinking, well, maybe I ain't gonna be with them much longer anyway.

■ ■ ■ ■ ■ ■ ■

The first time I ever went on a plane was to do a couple of Massive Attack shows in Europe – in France, I think. I would probably never have got a passport otherwise, because there would've been no real reason for me to have one. If it hadn't been for music, I might have never got on a plane, either – just like my nan. At most maybe I might've gone to Jamaica, because of my heritage – usually people with family ties in Jamaica visit there at one point or another.

I got myself a passport and started that part of my life's adventure full of optimism. I have very few positive memories associated with those trips, however, because Massive Attack was anything but an established live operation, and now we were expected to put on a show, a real live show. In the UK, it had been possible to stay true to our roots as a product of sound-system culture, throwing parties more than formal gigs, with DJ-ing instead of traditional instruments providing the music. There would be decks on the floor, down with the punters just as it had been in Wild Bunch days, but as *Blue Lines* started to take off at home, and gradually abroad as well, pressure mounted to put on some kind of show.

America was the place that really wouldn't allow us to stick to our preferred format. We were booked onto a club tour of six or eight dates, in a handful of major cities, playing up on a proper stage to 500 or 800 people, with a couple of turntables and us rappers. It just didn't work. For one thing, being onstage with a microphone means being a singer, and an entertainer, which neither me nor G nor D were prepared for, and there was no vibe whatsoever at the shows. It was horrible standing up there with people staring at you like fucking doughnuts.

Worse still, the album was only just taking off in America – America's a big place – so a couple of the shows weren't even that busy. At Prince's club in Minneapolis, they apparently pulled the plug on the gig before our set was even finished. It wasn't simply a problem of bringing hip-hop from England over to its country of origin, because it wasn't all hip-hop – both Shara Nelson and Horace Andy were on the tour, bringing soul and reggae vibes respectively.

I didn't get to know either of them that well, because I hadn't been around that much for the record, and on tour I kind of kept myself to myself. I didn't know America like I do now, and initially I didn't really like it. It was too much of a culture shock being in such a strange environment, when you've never been before. Back then I didn't understand it. I just wanted to come home.

I now know that it ain't going to be the greatest thing for any band, coming from England for your first US tour. New York and LA are going to be alright, but then the places in between will be tough. Now, I love Detroit, but back then I saw the place, and went, 'Fucking hell, where is this?' It was so strange. The others were ambitious for the group, so they were probably excited from that point of view.

While we were out there, we kept bumping into Happy Mondays, who were touring there at the same time – imagine them in America in 1992! It must have been chaos. I'm surprised they got back alive.

The only place I was really impressed with was New York. That was like, 'Woah, this city is crazy!' I think the show at Irving Plaza was okay, but I can remember getting off the plane at JFK airport and the energy went right through me from my feet to my head. That was so exciting. I knew one day I was going to live there.

When we got home, Massive Attack was in a state of flux. Shara was leaving to pursue a solo career. She was a nice girl, but I didn't know her that well because we weren't around at the same times until the US tour. One of her songs, 'Unfinished Sympathy', was the biggest hit, so it must've been a bit of a blow.

By that point, even before we'd finished promoting the first album, I knew I didn't want to be in it either. For me, it was too much like having a job. I did a couple of bits for the second album, *Protection*, which eventually came out in 1994. I left soon after, but I didn't leave thinking of doing anything in particular. I literally left and did nothing for a few months. There wasn't any plan whatsoever.

· ■ ■ ■ ■ ■ ·

It was a year earlier, around 1992/93, that I met Martina Topley-Bird. She was a boarder at a huge private school called Clifton College, which was right around the corner from my home in Fosseway. She was in the middle of her exams, and that day, she'd just finished school and happened to be sitting on the wall right outside my cousin Michelle's place, humming to herself, as I was walking past. We talked for a bit. 'Can you sing?' Boom! 'Let's get in the studio.'

I knew deep inside that I was going to do something of consequence musically, and even if I didn't fully know it at the time, there Martina was, my means of achieving it, hiding in plain sight a hundred yards from my own front door.

Today more than ever, I see artists who are chasing their dream, and obviously you have to work hard to get anywhere with music, but in all honesty, I never chased it. It just happened for me, so I almost feel a bit too lucky. People ask me, 'How do you break through? Can you give me any advice?' And I can't, because I never had that struggle. I had street struggle, but when you're young you don't notice being poor – you're just having fun.

By that stage, I'd been rapping for eight or ten years, and I noticed with rappers, they would always be with a producer, like Rakim with Eric B. Then I noticed that when the rapper and the producer split up, the rapper would have no career any more and just disappear – rappers didn't survive when their producers left. So that scared me. I thought, 'I don't want to have a career and then for it to end,' so I realised that if you want longevity in this game, you had to learn to produce music as well, or suffer the consequences.

Up until then, rapping was just fun for me. I wasn't making music at home. I was a music lover. I'd been writing words since I was five, so that part of being a rapper seemed to be the part that came naturally to me, the part that I was good at. Producing music was something I gradually forced myself into, because otherwise I thought I wouldn't survive as a vocalist.

This realisation set me on the path to try out sampling with the Akai S1000, because there was no proper instrument I could play. First, I came up with 'Daydreaming', and after that I took any opportunity that came my way to keep experimenting in that area.

Still, what's mad is, it wasn't exactly me who took the first step to making a track completely on my own. It all just happened to me. One day, around the time that I met Martina, I was in the squat in Totterdown and I ran into Mark Stewart. He goes to me, 'I've got a day's studio time booked and I can't be there – do you want it?' My first step was almost taken for me – I wasn't pushed into it exactly, but I obviously said, 'Yeah!'

It wasn't a proper studio, it was just a friend's home studio at a squat, but Mark obviously saw something in me where I might use that time productively. He thinks I'm a bit mad, but I think he's a bit mad as well. At one point, he had nowhere to live so he came and stayed at mine for a while. Still, it's a bit bizarre that he offered me the time – what was I gonna do with it? If he hadn't, I probably wouldn't be here now. I might just be doing the odd vocal for Massive Attack still.

By the appointed day, Martina had finished her exams, and she turned up with some mates, all pissed on cheap cider to celebrate that their exams were over. Why did I need her? I guess it was all about masking my own vocal inadequacies, because I didn't think I was that good a vocalist, so I obviously felt I needed someone else to carry it – like, 'Okay, let's have a girl come and be at the front.'

In my head, I had matched up a slowed-down break from an LL Cool J track with an old Marvin Gaye guitar riff, and I'd got some lyrics ready. When I heard Martina sing them, that was the most beautiful thing – to hear her female voice singing my words, it blew my mind. It wasn't just because I didn't like the way it sounded from me, but, because I was into words, I just saw it as such a compliment to hear a girl singing something I'd written so beautifully. Like, you wrote a *song*. If you rap, it's just a rap. But giving the lyrics to a girl made it something else altogether, and I'd sing in there too, softer, you might not even notice me, but it was always the two vocals over each other, and that would become my thing, and after that first try-out, I soon got addicted to it.

It's possible that we tried out two or three tracks that day, but there was only one that I kept, the Marvin Gaye/LL Cool J one called 'Aftermath', on a C60 cassette. Once everyone had recovered from the American tour debacle and there was talk of another Massive Attack album, I took my prized new track to 3D and offered it up for inclusion.

It was weird, because the first song they released was 'Daydreaming', which I produced, and that song blew them up. I'm not saying it's any better than the stuff they did – 'Unfinished Sympathy' is much better, and I didn't work on that – but it was the introduction where people said, 'What the fuck is this?' There was nothing like 'Daydreaming' out there, and I felt the same way about 'Aftermath'.

3D listens and says to me, 'Don't worry about that, focus on Massive Attack,' which I understand, because if I'm in Massive Attack, indeed being paid by Massive Attack, I should be focusing on that. But I was like, 'Come on, let's put this on the album!' and he just wasn't into it. I guess they'd just had a hit with 'Unfinished Sympathy', so they didn't need me to produce independently any more, just to be a part of the band, and write lyrics.

For the moment, there was nothing I could do with 'Aftermath', and I kept that cassette, and over the following months as I drifted away from Massive, I'd play it to people occasionally, but not in a hustling way to try and get a deal. It wasn't at all like I quit Massive so that I could go solo and release my 'overlooked masterpiece'. Most people would say, them not wanting to use 'Aftermath' – that's a good reason to leave. At the time, I didn't give a fuck: they just didn't want to use it, that's business. What was the end for me? When I couldn't borrow that £2.50 so I had to drive all the way back to Bristol feeling really hungry – that was it. I'm a funny guy like that.

After leaving Massive, I literally sat about partying and not doing much else for a few months. Occasionally, I'd play the cassette to people, but it was my cousin Michelle, who has nothing to do with the music business and generally doesn't talk music with me, who intervened.

'You've got to do something with that song,' she told me, in no uncertain terms.

'But I played it to Massive Attack,' I replied, 'and I don't think they want it.'

'Well,' Michelle reasoned, 'you should release it yourself, then.'

That sounded a great idea in principle, but I wasn't on a wage from Massive anymore, so how could I release it? After thinking it through for a couple of days, I remembered a weird encounter in The Montpelier, where this white hippy guy who used to sell weed in there came up and said to me, 'If you ever want to do anything, I'll give you some money.' At the time, I thought, 'That's strange, why is he choosing me?' But after thinking it over, it all started to make some sense, to me at least. That night, I went down to The Montpelier, found the guy, had a short talk with him, and got 500 quid off him.

With that money, I pressed up some white labels of 'Aftermath' on my own Nyeeve label. A bunch of copies I took to local record stores in Bristol; the rest I took up to London and dropped off at radio stations and record labels. Six weeks later, I had my own record contract with Chris Blackwell's iconic label, Island.

I often wonder what might've happened to me if Michelle hadn't given me a nudge at that crucial moment …

CHAPTER SEVEN
ISLAND RECORDS

My auntie Sandy used to do Tarot cards. She was my mum's brother Michael's wife, and she was just as much family to me as, say, my uncle Tony. I never really liked that Tarot stuff, it weirds me out, but she was my auntie and she used to say, 'Come down, I'll do you a reading.' Usually, I'd be like, 'Uh, oh, um, maybe …' but one day I finally went down to see her.

She was a white woman who lived on the verge of the black ghetto in the Montpelier/St Paul's area. She was quite well known with the students in Bristol, because she used to do readings for all of them, and she was well known by everybody for being spot on with the Tarot.

One day, I went down to her house and she did mine. She laid out my cards on the table and started looking at them. Eventually, she said, 'There's something to do with eyes that is going to make you successful.' I'm sat there thinking, 'What the fuck is she talking about?'

Years and years went by, to the point where I'd all but forgotten about Auntie Sandy's prediction that day. And it was only a good while after I'd circulated those white labels and started my solo career that I realised: the first line of the lyrics to 'Aftermath' go, 'Your eyes resemble mine', and that's the song that got me my record deal. Crazy, right?

The whole verse goes, 'Your eyes resemble mine, you'll see as no others can/Here, inherit my kingdom, speak of our people's plan.' If I had written those words in later life, you could say, 'Oh, he wrote that about his children,' but I had no kids at that point. So, that's my mum speaking. And as my auntie said, 'something with eyes'.

I usually remember writing my lyrics, but I can never remember where they come from. When I write, I'm not really thinking – they just come into my head. I always used to think Auntie Sandy was a bit different, even though Tarot was never really my thing, but when I thought about her reading, I began to think my mum had been speaking through me.

. . ▪ ▣ ▪ . .

The whole business of getting signed was more mundane. Me and the hippy geezer from The Montpelier pub drove to London in his car and dropped the white labels off at radio stations and label offices, and then everything went mad. It was getting played in clubs in London, and on the radio – just unreal.

Then me and this geezer had a disagreement. I got calls from four different labels, everybody wanting to sign me for that single, or more. Straight off, I wanted to sign to Island, because of their amazing history in music going back to the late '50s. This other guy wanted to wait and wait and wait. I don't know if in the back of his mind he wanted to start a record company himself or something, but I was like, 'Island Records is the one,' so I went with them.

Then it got a bit complicated, because I had another meeting there and it seemed like they weren't so sure. Basically, they were interested in 'Aftermath', but I didn't get a deal straight away, it was just a one-off deal for that single. Maybe they weren't totally convinced, like, 'Alright, you've got a good single – is there anything else?'

I may have recorded more tracks with Martina that day, but 'Aftermath' was the only one I kept on cassette, and so that was the only song I had. It's hard for me to say exactly how much time went by between that studio day and the day I got signed for 'Aftermath' – maybe as much as four years – but the one thing I do know is, I hadn't seen her in the meantime.

As a rapper in those days, you didn't take yourself so seriously. People didn't used to think of rappers as poets, or the new Shakespeare. It used to be just, 'Ugh, what's he doing?' Coming at it with that attitude, to hear someone sing your words was mind-blowing. The first time I heard it was with Shara Nelson on 'Daydreaming', but that was just the chorus. With it happening for the whole song, it was like, 'Wow!' It takes your lyrics somewhere else, and I knew Martina was the one to do it.

When I think back to me being my mum's ghost while I listened to Billie Holiday with my nan, and then one day coming out of my house and there's Martina, and I say to her, 'Can you sing?' and we do 'Aftermath' and she's like the new Billie Holiday – how the fuck did that happen? How do you come out of your house, and someone is sat on your wall, and they are the new Billie Holiday?

What's double weird is, Martina has a similar look to my mum. She doesn't look *like* my mum, but there are definite similarities there. Her vibe, and the big eyes. If you see old pictures of my mum and you see pictures of Martina, they aren't identical, but you can see the connection. And the vibe and the tone of her voice are definitely Billie Holiday. No English girl was sounding like Billie Holiday back then, they couldn't do it.

When I got my record deal, I thought, 'I've got to find this girl. She is the voice for my music!' How the fuck did I even find her again? It's ridiculous, I don't know how it happened. I didn't stay in touch with her, then all that time elapsed, and then I'm looking for her, and someone saw her on the street. Insane, right? It was meant to be.

That search had given me time to write 'Ponderosa', and the two of us duly went up to London to record it with this lovely Glaswegian guy called Howie B, who was engineering in the studio. When that one went mad as well, that's when Island properly wanted to know.

MARC MAROT: I'd been the managing director of Island for four years or so when we started our association with Tricky. I was a protégé of Chris

Blackwell, and I started out in music publishing with him. My introduction to the Bristol scene was that I signed a band called Startled Insects in 1985, who went on to work with Massive Attack on *Blue Lines* – and the last act I signed before I got the job as Island MD was Massive Attack.

I was well aware of this mysterious character called Tricky, when Dave Gilmour – not the Pink Floyd one, but one of the scouts at Island's dance subsidiary, Fourth & Broadway – excitedly brought the 'Aftermath' white label into an A&R meeting.

Island, as a major label, was supposed to be commercial but in that period we were the antithesis of commercial. We were trying to turn over stones that nobody else was. Chris had a fervent belief that it's the distance an artist stands from other artists that measures them, rather than the closeness and the similarities. We were always looking for things that were different, and there was something mysterious about 'Aftermath' that really turned everybody on – particularly Julian Palmer, the young guy who ran Fourth & Broadway.

Tricky was incredibly difficult to pin down, we found. Our opinion initially was that he didn't really believe in himself as an artist. He saw himself as a rapper and a producer, but that didn't necessarily mean fronting something was on his agenda. To him, he was just knocking out tracks, with the mindset of the sound-system background he came from. From Island's perspective, it was just like the early days of reggae before Bob Marley came along, where there were no artists per se, only records.

The Chris Blackwell philosophy was that you signed people who were auteurs, who had a vision for who they were, not just for their music. If you look at the people we signed under my tenure, like Trent Reznor from Nine Inch Nails, or PJ Harvey, or Jarvis Cocker, or Elbow's Guy Garvey, they didn't come to the record company to dress them, or tell them what to say, or get co-writers to write the songs for them – they came as a complete package.

We effectively bought the rights to the 'Aftermath' single, without entering into any major record deal, with a view to building trust. Chris

Blackwell very much took a personal interest in Tricky. Tricky absolutely fitted into that continuum of Island Records in Chris's head, and was nurtured by him as the perfect artist to carry it on.

The second single was 'Ponderosa', which everyone absolutely loved as well, but chart activity was slow to begin with. 'Aftermath' we got to No.69, and 'Ponderosa' we got to 77, so you might ask, why would a record company that is going backwards with an artist, as it were, feel like keeping on with the investment? Doubly so, bearing in mind that at this stage we still didn't have anything in writing – we were funding the recordings, and putting them out with absolutely no right to them, in some respects.

The more that came out of the studio, the more we realised he was growing into that role as an artist and beginning to feel a little more comfortable with it in terms of public persona and presentation, because of the critical reception that was building. We began to really get some traction, not from Radio One, just occasional John Peel-style plays, and exceptional press that made us feel like we needed to carry on. All the component parts were falling into place, but we still had no contract.

This is where Tricky could have become really tricky. He was being managed by Debbie Swainson and Caroline Killoury. They were in London, but I felt they didn't have a lot of experience, and where that showed is that they had little control over Tricky. No one did! Nobody has control over Tricky, other than Tricky. Even once his album was coming together and slated for release, we could not get the two managers to focus on closing the deal. You might suggest that it was actually a strategy, but I didn't ever think it was. I never thought that I was being played, I just thought it was their inability to get Tricky to focus on the business details of what putting a record out actually means.

It was almost a career ruination moment for me. I trusted Tricky. I looked him in the eye, and I asked him whether he was going to sign our record deal, and he said that he was. As such, I committed to the marketing spend, the videos, everything, even though I still didn't have a bloody contract.

TRICKY: Before I gave 'Ponderosa' to Island, I was planning to put out a white label myself – I guess I wanted to test the water, to see if people liked it – but Julian Palmer caught me at it. He calls me into the office and goes to me, 'No, no, no, you don't put it out, Tricks – we'll do that for you!'

I have to say, from that point on it was fucking easy for me to write my album. I never had no problem. I never thought about it. I moved up to London, to a flat up in Harlesden, and got down to it there. My manager found me the place, and at the time that was all I could afford, just renting. I had signed to Island, but it wasn't the full deal yet, so I didn't have lots of money. It was an apartment on the second floor of a normal house just off Harlesden high street. I went and looked at it, and said, 'Yeah, I'll take it.' I didn't need to take anything in there, all the furniture was already provided, so I just moved right in.

I used to hang out on the high street. It was ghetto as fuck, but obviously I didn't have no problems there, because I'm not from there. Sometimes you can have problems in an area, if you are involved in stuff. But no one knew me, and I wasn't involved in anything dodgy. You could still feel it was ghetto. You would hear gunshots sometimes, and the odd murder going on. But I wasn't involved in anything, so it was okay. It was a good place. I lived there for a year or so, and that was where I recorded my album.

I would sit on the floor in the living room, with a bunch of records and a turntable, looping up breaks and taking sounds and bits of music, all using the Akai S1000 sampler. That was a really good machine – the only piece of machinery I actually ever liked using. Pro Tools, Logic, and all that studio software – I hate them. You just spend all day staring at a screen. The S1000 was fun, real fun – very simple, and you could build a track in no time at all, once you'd heard it in your head.

My early stuff sounded so different from everything else because I didn't know how to make music. When I first did 'Aftermath', I had a guy playing the flute on it. At one point, he looked all flustered.

'That's two blues notes next to each other!' he goes.

'What do you mean?'

'You can't do that,' he says, 'it's not correct.'

Apparently, you're not allowed to put two blues notes next to each other. That's why my stuff was different: I had no rules. I've always had weird time signatures, not because I'm trying to do it – some artists use them to try and make their music weird. My music is weird because I don't know what I'm doing. You know, I kick with my left foot, and I write with my right hand. I *am* a weird time signature already!

While I was recording, Britpop was going on, and I just couldn't see any of that as being new. Everything I was seeing around me – there were new bands, but there was no new music. That's why I wrote 'Brand New, You're Retro', about all these bands coming along, like, 'This is the new shit.' My answer was, 'No, you sound like The Beatles, you sound like the Rolling Stones, you've even got the same haircut, you wear sunglasses in a nightclub – there's nothing new about you at all! You're just a retro band that's having some success.'

There were people doing soul music in the charts, straight up – like, why the fuck are you doing soul music? How are you new? It's like second-hand emotions, acting all traumatised on TV. It was like, 'You ain't Billie Holiday!' I just thought I'd heard it all before, and I wanted to be different, and turn it all upside down.

Some of what I was listening to came from Martina. She was a rock chick, and at the time she was listening to Soundgarden, Pearl Jam and Smashing Pumpkins, which is why there was a sample from Smashing Pumpkins' *Gish* album on my song 'Pumpkin'. She also got me into Polly Harvey, before all these people were as famous as they are now. She used to rock a pair of Dr Martens because she was into that music, so that's how I got into rock. Before that, all I knew about was reggae, hip-hop, and English pop like Marc Bolan.

You can hear that influence from Martina on our version of Public Enemy's 'Black Steel in the Hour of Chaos', too. That song was about not going into the army in the Vietnam War. Chuck D used to write stories. I don't know what the rappers are talking about anymore. I'm not saying it's not good, but back then Rakim and Chuck D were writing like a movie unfolding in front of you. It was like watching a movie or reading a book, and people like Chuck D and Rakim and Slick Rick were my poets, my Shakespeare. With them, you could smoke a spliff, close your eyes, and let your imagination go with it.

I used to get frustrated, because I was absorbing all kinds of music, but I knew for sure that most average people didn't know who Rakim was, and the same probably went for many of the people who might eventually listen to my music. Sampling or covering Chuck D or Rakim was my way of showing them the way.

Then, getting Martina to sing 'Black Steel' – that was gonna make someone know about Chuck D who didn't know about him already. Because if someone listens to that and then finds out where it comes from, they might go back and hear the original, and discover Public Enemy. I just wanted to take those heroes of mine to another crowd.

I felt like these artists deserved to be opened out to a wider audience. You can't just call Rakim a rapper. That guy is a genius. Some of his words are the most amazing poetry. It frustrated me when people said, 'Rakim, the rapper'. He isn't really, he's a poet who doesn't sing; instead he uses the avenue that is available to him. People called me a rapper, too – why? I find it weird; it puts you in a box – 'rapper'! I might have started off thinking I was a rapper, but even from when I first started, I have never been one really.

When Martina and I first met, there hadn't been any relationship between us. We only started seeing each other once we started making the album. She was five or six years younger than me, and it didn't work out. When we started seeing each other, she got pregnant straight away. Suddenly she was pregnant, so that changed the dynamic of the relationship, and I don't think there was supposed to be any relationship in the first place. We used to drive each other crazy.

She was a posh girl – very posh, but tough as well. She went to a very good school in Bristol, but she has family in Connecticut who are ghetto. She has black American ghetto in her background, and she's definitely got that in her. She used to go to rock clubs, her and her friends, and they would fight. Martina was a rucker, someone not to mess around with.

People might see her as serious, but she is a very funny person, too. She's got a good sense of humour. We make fun of each other. Still these days, when we talk about music we've made together, I'll say, 'You sound alright, your chorus sounds okay – but the track is about *me*,' and then she will say something sarcastic back. We make fun of each other. Harsh maybe, but funny. We just take the piss. It's always been like that.

Looking back at it now, I realise that we weren't supposed to be together – we were just supposed to have a baby together. We weren't boyfriend and girlfriend material. We met to make music and to have a kid, and that was it.

In a way, her getting pregnant was good because it took away from the career pressure. We were doing the album, and then the videos, and it took the pressure away. You're not just sitting there, thinking, 'Oh shit!' I think it would've been a lot harder, doing either of them on their own – sat in the house thinking, 'Oh God, we've got to get the pram, the nappies …' There was no time to worry or think.

Once I'd recorded most of the tracks in Harlesden, I finished the album off with an engineer in west London called Mark Saunders. This guy was just an engineer, but he later claimed in interviews that he'd created me, or something. He'd worked with The Cure, Neneh Cherry and a few other people before, and he is a great engineer – great at making things sound great – and a good mixer. But he's definitely one of those wannabe musicians. An upper-middle-class white kid who seems like he's got connections to record labels, and probably was in a band years ago, but it never went right. He's a corny old dude.

For instance, I would take a sample, then I would tell him, 'Put this on a keyboard.' I would do loops, add to it, write some lyrics for Martina, and then me and her would leave for the day. When we turned up in the studio the next day, there would be guitar parts all over what we recorded the night before. I'd hear it and think, 'What the fuck is this?' He was trying to inject himself into the music, and I would have to make him take it off. Maybe I might not have been gentle with him. Instead of saying, 'Oh, sorry, Mark, this doesn't work,' me and Martina would just laugh at him. Maybe I hurt his feelings, and this is why he still goes on about it today. Because he's engineered The Cure and a few other big bands, but he's never claimed to have made any of their records. So, I think his problem is with me.

The irony is that at the time, with songs like 'Strugglin'', you could see he just didn't get it. He just couldn't understand the music.

'Musically, you can't do that,' he'd moan.

'Listen, if I can hear it in my head, it can be done!'

The arguments would go on for hours, but luckily enough, it was my record and he didn't need to understand it. The guy is a proper doughnut.

The A&R guy from Island, Dave Gilmour, used to come down occasionally to see how things were progressing. One time in Harlesden, I think we'd done 'Overcome' and 'Black Steel' and I'd just written 'Strugglin''. He said, 'Can I have a listen?' I pressed play for him and went in the other room. I was sat there smoking a spliff, and soon Dave came back in the room, and his face was red.

That's when I first knew: fucking hell, my music is affecting people! He was red-faced and uncomfortable. He heard 'Strugglin'' and I could see in his face it was an experience he had never had before. To me it was normal – I don't see what the big deal is. That's what was in my head, but I could see in his face that it had fucked him up. He didn't know what the fuck was going on.

Anyway, I have Mark Saunders to thank for that. We should interview him and ask him how he did it.

When I cast my mind back to the day I looked into the open coffin of my deceased mother, as a small kid – that's definitely left a mark on me. You could say I was always gonna make dark music after that.

You've heard my family stories, and perhaps you realise how lucky I really am. Yeah, I lost my mum, but then when you look at what my uncles went through – they had such a hard life. They became criminals, not because they wanted to look cool or look good, they just didn't know any different. When you see that, it almost makes me look lucky.

My whole life went into that first album. It's like my soul laid bare, and it's the album that got me everything. Initially when I signed to Island, I was going to present myself as a band called Maxinquaye, which was effectively me and Martina, but Island persuaded me not to. It was written as one word, because if it had been written as Maxine Quaye, people might have thought that was Martina's name. Island were like, 'No, no, your name is out there already – stay Tricky!' and they convinced me.

At least then I had a name for the album, but I never actually planned to go under Tricky. All this was never planned by me! I wasn't going to be a top producer or a top artist. I can remember having meetings with Julian Palmer and saying to him, 'Are you sure that you want to sign me? I'm not a commercial vehicle.'

I was never a tough guy or a gangster either, but I grew up in that kind of world, so there was a moody atmosphere to the album because I'd had a dark life. I'd been in a blues smoking weed, shortly after my uncle got murdered, wondering where in the room he'd died. I have certainly seen some darkness.

A song like 'Hell Is Round the Corner' came about because I was living by the front line in St Paul's. I had no money, so I was staying in someone's basement there for a short time. One day I was sat around, talking with a mate about hell for some reason, and he goes, 'Hell? Hell is round the corner, mate!' Literally, the next street was where everyone was selling drugs on the ghetto frontline. So that became a song a few years later.

When I released 'Overcome' as a single, various people commented like, 'Oh, he's using the lyrics from Massive Attack's "Karmacoma".' Actually, those were my lyrics that I gave 3D to sing on their track, and I'd written 'Overcome' way before 'Karmacoma' ever happened. When 'Overcome' finally came out, people thought I was using the same lyrics again, but it wasn't like that. They are mine, so I'd given them to Martina, too.

Once I'd finished recording, there were things to think about, like the album cover. Island probably put a lot of thought into it. I wasn't concerned about having an image as such. It was just having fun, so if I had a photo shoot, I'd think of something, and do it on the spur of the moment. I didn't do any of the marketing meetings. I'd just turn up, ask for a make-up artist or some sort of clothing. It gets boring doing photo shoots, so I'd just try and make it into a laugh.

I was having fun with images, in the same way that I was writing dark lyrics for Martina to sing with her sweet voice. It was turning things upside down. That photo shoot for the *Maxinquaye* album artwork was done in London somewhere, with Island's art director, Cally Callomon. The idea was to have me and Martina dressed as a married couple, with her as the groom and me as the bride. Back in those days, you wouldn't have seen that kind of gender reversal from a 'rapper'.

Once the album was done, I didn't know what to do with myself. Often, I'd go down to Island's offices in Chiswick. I didn't use Island like a record company. I used to go in there just to hang out, because I didn't really know anybody in London. There were a few places I'd go to in Harlesden, but when you live somewhere, you ain't there all the time, are you? You've got to do other things, and in a way, the album had actually come from being isolated up there, with no distractions. I had my cousin Shaun, but he lived miles away over in East Ham, so I used to go into Island to kill some time, listen to music, and smoke a spliff. It wasn't that London felt alien, so much as I simply didn't know anybody.

That's how much of a loner I was, right? My album is done and dusted, I'm waiting for it to come out, and I go to hang out in the record company because I have nothing to do. There was a very comfy couch in their offices. I used to go in there, talk to people, maybe put on the latest Public Enemy release, or a PJ Harvey record, then I would just fall asleep on the couch for an hour or so. I never really had a life. I could smoke weed there, because it wasn't like a corporate vibe there back then.

Island Records was my hangout, and there was a point where I'd see Julian Palmer almost every day. He was a constant, and I quickly trusted him totally.

JULIAN PALMER: Fourth & Broadway was my label within Island. In the mid-80s, I was fortunate enough to find the Wild Bunch, which was Nellee Hooper, Daddy G, Mushroom, 3D, and Tricky was loosely involved, but really Nellee and 3D were driving it. We never met Tricky at the label offices at all in those days. It was always Nellee with his long fur coat, looking very rock 'n' roll.

Much like Tricky, when they came aboard, they had a punk ethic and weren't overly ambitious, certainly not in terms of making albums and being big recording artists. We put out what I thought was a brilliant record in 'Friends and Countrymen', which was so out of kilter with everything else that was going on. Everybody thought it needed to play at 45rpm, when it was cut at 33. It was just way too slow compared to everything else around – so different from the whole house thing, and commercial hip-hop, fusing reggae, funk, rare groove and early breaks.

When Wild Bunch split, to be honest I never thought anything would come of it, but obviously, Massive Attack were born out of the ashes of it. I knew Tricky was a fringe player there, and when I heard 'Aftermath', I thought, 'That's that little kid who used to do live stuff with Wild Bunch.'

That was sometime in 1994, and I was absolutely captivated by the white label he'd circulated. I knew it was heavily sampled because I'm a

Marvin Gaye obsessive, but like everything with Tricky, it was so fucked up, distorted and recontextualised, and so menacing, it felt really valid to me. That's what Tricky had to do in order to express himself. He was born out of this DIY sampling/hip-hop world, which we both thought was the new punk – kids sitting in their room, borrowing from anywhere and everywhere. As long as you were creating something new from all these pre-existing components, and doing it inventively, then great! It was open season, wasn't it?

Eventually I got him in the office, and he was like, 'I don't want to make an album. I just want to put tracks out. I don't want to tie myself down.' Some of the discussion we had was about how he might be compensated for the money that he wasn't going to be making anymore by being a bad boy. He thought he could make more money doing those little jobs outside of doing music.

I impressed on him that at Island it was all about making albums, pushing boundaries and being original. Singles were merely how artists were introduced to people. Island was known for reggae – beyond Bob Marley, there were core bands like Black Uhuru and Aswad – then increasingly hip-hop with NWA, Ice Cube, etc., and those artists would always be able to trigger the options in their contract to make more records, because there was a big enough audience, slightly under the mainstream, to justify continuing.

It took a while to convince him that that was the way to go, with singles as enticing moments from a bigger body of work, but once he had bought into the idea, he went off and experimented, and I kept encouraging him to experiment and delve deeper and deeper.

With Tricky, it was all-encompassing. He had to get it out. I think he knew that once he got into it, it would be a different kind of pain in the creation, not the kind of pain that most people would endure. It would take him to the very edge, which is the mark of real artistry.

I think Massive had been love–hate from the beginning with him, for the simple reason that he found it difficult to have anybody close to his own creative process. Everything was so personal, even down to the way that he mixed the record. Most of it he did at his tiny flat at Harlesden, on his headphones. To begin with, he'd be blasting it out through the speakers, which would fuck the neighbours off, so after that he used to do it all on headphones – him sat on the floor with a stack of records and a sampler. I remember even thinking at the time that some of the whispered voicing was just to keep the neighbours from complaining. All the initial mixes he did on headphones, at home, immersed in his own world.

Martina played a prominent role, and that was certainly part of the reason why it was a long process making the record. It was a fractious relationship – he didn't like people getting too close to him. Sometimes she was there, and then other times she wouldn't be. No one ever put any pressure on him about her from our side, other than saying how beautiful the two of them were together, sonically, whether they were in love, or out of love, or hating each other, or whatever it was. The friction was probably the thing that made it click.

He had this obsession, an anxiety about being seen as a radio artist, pandering to those fickle demands. The music industry has been hits-driven since day one, and I just assured him that we would quite literally shut the door so that no one would interfere or judge. I just said, 'Everything I say to you is true, and I will shut out the world, and it will be just you and me until you say to me, "We're done." Then we'll go to Mr Blackwell, and we will blow his mind!' That was perhaps dangerous territory, looking back, with such a raw talent, but I was young and I wanted to change the world as much as he did – and that was to succeed on his terms.

After 'Aftermath' came 'Ponderosa', another demo of his, and then all this stuff just flew out of him. The cover of Public Enemy's 'Black Steel' got recorded because Martina took him to a gig the night before and they'd got chatting to the support band called FTV afterwards, and I think it was maybe even the next day they came to the studio to provide the full-band backing. We loved it in the office – it didn't need to be all polished. It needed the rawness that the band added – pure ramshackle chaos and noise.

With some tracks, the rhythms and patterns and general dynamics were so off-beam. None of it was considered like traditional musicianship. It was abstract, uncompromising and at times hard on the ears. The soundscape was everything, and once he was done it just needed somebody to mix it and finish it off. We called in Mark Saunders, who was best known for his mix work on Neneh Cherry's *Raw Like Sushi* album.

He and Tricky worked at a studio in Westbourne Park, and he immediately said he had never delved into anything quite like it before. A great mixing engineer knows where everything should sit – to add the final flourishes that ensure things sit subtly in the right place, and, in this case, to achieve the dramatic effect Tricky was going for. It certainly wasn't creative input, like a producer, more helping Tricky arrange the songs slightly differently. The record was entirely Tricky's vision.

My favourite aspect of the process was sequencing *Maxinquaye* with Tricky. The one nod to the commercial world was: there used to be listening booths in record stores, where you could select a CD and give it a listen. The thing was, if you didn't capture people within the first four tracks, then you had lost a sale. The first four on there – 'Overcome', 'Ponderosa', 'Black Steel' and 'Hell Is Round the Corner' – were all singles. Then, as it got deeper into the record, things got darker and edgier with stuff like 'Strugglin'' and 'Feed Me', but once you had been drawn in, they would become just as important as the ones front-loading it. He was sort of commercial by default.

We sat there forever going through that, me saying, 'We can hoodwink people into thinking this is going to be a comfortable listen for them, Tricks, and then they have to live with it as a body of work, and it might disturb them in places.' He definitely liked that idea. 'Fuck 'em all, Jules!' All that menace that's in him came through. Hearing Tricky is like watching *The Exorcist* for the first time. It's something you've just never experienced before.

We were proud of it as a body of work, a story, something that came from a troubled place. I identified with that in him, and we partied a lot together in '94 and '95. The industry was totally drug-fuelled by then, so it wasn't just us. The biz wasn't the squeaky-clean place of the '70s, pre-punk, when I was a kid trying to get into it, working in clubs in Soho. Back then, record-company people stood out a mile, and they weren't let in – they were dinosaurs with piano ties and Cuban heels and long grey hair, and you just spotted them a mile off. They had no edge; it was a nine-to-five job to them.

It had all started to change by the mid-80s: the old guard were pushed away, as we younger recruits brought the whole club/drug sensibility with us. It was an opportunity, at the right label at the right time, to make that kind of stand, and in Tricky I had somebody that was as anarchistic about doing it as I was. I was just the right side of knowing the mechanics of how to do it, without glossing over the emotional trauma that fuelled the record.

How we went about marketing him was very much the alternative route. He was a trailblazer for British black music, but he wasn't representing the British black music psyche of that moment. That fraternity saw him as quirky, an outsider. British black music wasn't spawning artists like Tricky, so to go to the black music community and expect them to embrace him was unlikely. We were trying to cross over and break the mould. In multicultural Britain, Tricky grew up listening to a diverse range of music, and his references reflected that, and he was instantly embraced by the alternative scene – that is, the music press and indie radio.

The reaction to *Maxinquaye* came from all the places that we'd hoped: the most influential of all publications at the time – the *NME* – were totally sold on him and his warped, twisted vision of the world. Everybody in that London indie media world understood it immediately. He went on to be the first black artist to have the *NME* front cover twice in one calendar year.

There was no obvious home for it in America, because white music and black music are always separate on the mass scale over there. But you can't make records thinking about those boxes that you can squeeze into, and Tricky initially wasn't built to be a big glossy American Top 200 crossover thing.

Preparing the album for release, there was a tight little unit of people, including Cally Callomon, Island's art director, who played a massive part with the artwork, and everything about the presentation. The album cover keyed into the ancient, dilapidated look of higher-budget reggae reissues at the time.

Everything about that record was like a perfect storm. Then there was the photo shoot of Tricky and Martina as a cross-dressing wedding couple. At that point with British black music, there were rules, and it could often get very America Lite, but Tricky came out more like a black Bowie. When Bowie ended up recognising his work very enthusiastically, it was like, yeah! You couldn't hoodwink Bowie.

Release was delayed for three months while we got samples cleared. You weren't quite sure where things were coming from, and Tricky certainly wasn't taking notes. A famous one was the lift from Isaac Hayes's 'Ike's Rap II' on 'Hell Is Round the Corner', which Portishead used concurrently on their single 'Glory Box'. I absolutely stand behind Tricky, who maintained it was his idea to use it first. People behind Geoff Barrow from Portishead say the opposite, but Tricky's is the genius one, isn't it? It was a sample that was out there anyway, on the underground. I recall hearing it a few times.

It was the brave new world, wasn't it? Sampling to me was part and parcel of the work we were doing. I can probably say, there were some things that we maybe didn't declare, because he'd torn them apart and reversed them and turned them into such a decomposed state that you couldn't possibly recognise what they were. That method is integral to what he was. What came out the other side was either genius or lunacy, but often when we needed to find out the rights owner, he didn't even know what it was he was sampling.

While all that legal side was getting sorted, in early February '95 I wheeled him into the Brits in a wheelchair. He came around my house first, and we dyed his hair silver. He wasn't nominated at this early stage – those were the days when you just had to be spotted. Back then, the ceremony took place at Alexandra Palace, which had a big flight of steps leading up to the front doors. We were getting snapped by paparazzi as I wheeled him along, and then when we got to the bottom of the steps, he got up out of the chair and walked up with me. As an emerging artist, we certainly got him noticed!

Once we were inside, I was saying to him, 'We're gonna take this next year, Tricks, this will be us!' We had that single-mindedness, to get his art into that kind of mainstream place, without selling out, without it being a radio thing, without making all the concessions that made him uncomfortable. I think that stance made people buy into him more, because he rebelled against playing the game.

Here I had a man that could change the world, I knew that. I didn't know quite to what extent. Without having hit singles, we made a bit of history. When the album finally came out on 20 February 1995, it was absolutely huge. The 'trip hop' moniker that the press gave to him and all the Bristol scene – in spite of him not wanting to be associated with it – definitely helped. Call it a scene with a catchy name, and everybody buys into it. That first month or two, it was *the* album that all the people we didn't think we'd get to – coffee-table listeners, the middle classes – were chin-wagging about at dinner parties. They probably didn't know what they were listening to, but we infiltrated them!

MARC MAROT: It only bloody went in at No.3 and caught everybody by surprise! We knew something was there, but the entire industry – retail, the media, the rest of the record industry – nobody saw it coming. I would say that we probably thought we would have a sleeper hit album on our hands that might take a little while to get going, but it was a big success, straight out of the traps – and I still didn't have a record deal!

TRICKY: I was never interested in being famous or successful. Like everyone, I have bills to pay, so I have to make money, but I've never been interested in being the richest guy on the planet. Driving around in a Rolls-Royce or Bentley sports car does nothing for me whatsoever. Making *Maxinquaye*, my attitude was, 'I'm going to turn music upside down.' That was a bit of a competitive hip-hop thing, like, 'No one can fuck with me! I'm gonna make music that no one has ever heard before.' There was always a bit of that. But being the biggest artist – it doesn't bother me.

The only thing that came out in the '90s that was new, was my album. I'm not saying it was the best, I'm just saying it was the only new music. When *Maxinquaye* came out, there was nothing that came before it or sounded like it. Things have come after it and tried to sound like it, but when *Maxinquaye* came out, there had been nothing like it. And it wasn't because I'm a genius, it was because I don't know what I'm doing.

Still, I thought I was going to be an underground artist, making my own little weird music. Because I was coming from hip-hop, it was cool to be underground. I was going to be the background guy – the guy who was hardly ever seen. That was the plan. Then all of a sudden, I'm on the front of *Time* magazine, and on the front of *The Face*, and David Bowie's writing fictional stories about me in *Q* magazine and sending me letters.

That was *not* my plan, and everything I'd prepared for went out of the window. Maybe it would have been different if it had been my third album that I'd gained success with, but because it was my first album, it just went fucking nuts.

One time during those crazy days in February/March '95, I was in a minicab going to Heathrow and there was a motorbike stopped beside my window at the traffic lights. There was a massive billboard poster of me beside the road, and the biker looked at the poster, looked at me, did a double take at the poster again, looked back at me, and then we sped off. Life suddenly was as weird as fuck.

CHAPTER EIGHT
ANONYMITY

Losing your anonymity is the worst thing that can ever happen to you. This is what some people don't realise about being a musician: these days especially, they want to be famous and have the whole celebrity thing happen to them. Believe me, you don't want it.

For example: you know that first part of the day where you're just meditating? You go out for some air, sit down somewhere and you're just having a coffee, then someone will come over to you and say, 'Oh, are you Tricky?' They walk into your world, and take over your energy, and it's really not healthy for you.

If you're walking down the street, and two people walk past, and you hear them whispering, 'Look, it's Tricky!' that will change the way you walk, the way you feel, the way you think, for the rest of that day. You are in your own world, and that suddenly brings you out. It totally changes you, that day, and for always.

You start to think, 'Why do most people want to know me now I've got to a certain level of recognition?' It's because you're in the limelight, and people are attracted to that. It's like when they talk about vampires in old Jamaican records. They don't mean literal vampires; they mean people who suck your energy. And that's why people want to know you, because they want to suck your energy – it makes them feel good about themselves, because they 'know' someone famous. Pretty dark, right?

So, losing your anonymity is the worst thing, and I think my music shows that as well: I'm not trying to be the loudest voice. I see a lot of young people now who seem to think celebrity is the best part of the music. No, that's the price you have to pay for your success. That's the problem part. The perfect thing would be to do your music, and then disappear, but we've got into a pattern since the 1990s where celebrity is part of the job. And the part people dream of.

I fucking hated it. My first album went to No.3 in the charts, and my time was taken after that. My time wasn't my time anymore. I never even had a chance to do music, almost – to have the space to do it on my terms. That was it, I was kind of a celeb, and it was not comfortable for me. I could be in a queue somewhere, then someone would recognise me and I'd see them go whisper-whisper to their friend or whoever, then they're both looking … I'd have to say to people sometimes, 'What are you looking at?' It's just not a good vibe.

People said I looked unhappy, and that's because I wasn't into that side of things. I didn't see myself as a pop artist, a chart-topping guy. Some people want to get to the top of the charts. I didn't think like that. I just wanted to make the best music, I wanted to change music. Getting in the charts wasn't my thing. I was thinking of myself as an underground artist, then all of a sudden – what the fuck? I thought I would be underground, making my music, and the next thing I know, I've got Elton John talking about me on morning TV. I didn't envisage my career being like that. I thought I would be more like a blues artist – semi-known, but not really.

I was being written about as part of 'the Bristol scene', which made no sense to me. There was a lot of music being made in Bristol, but everybody kept to their own little corner. People saw each other in clubs, because it's a small city, but there weren't no scene. It ain't like Manchester, where you had all these different rock bands doing their thing – the Stone Roses are hanging out with the Happy Mondays, but the Stone Roses are one thing, and Happy Mondays are another. Portishead made music like they did because of Massive Attack. Geoff Barrow would never have been doing music like their *Dummy* album if he hadn't met us guys. He didn't come through hip-hop like we did. Some people even thought that Portishead came before me. How can that ever happen? Come on! I'm a hip-hop head!

People fell for this 'Bristol scene' shit. Here's another thing: Portishead are not even from Bristol. They're from Portishead. And when people started talking about the 'Bristol Sound', what they didn't realise was, I had recorded some stuff there, like my stuff on *Blue Lines*, but *Maxinquaye* was made in Harlesden. It came from being isolated up there, not knowing anyone.

Even when I was at No.3 in the charts I was by myself almost all the time. With my success, I was able to move from Harlesden into a little flat just off Kensington High Street. I didn't know anybody there either, but it was really convenient: there was food around there, and shops, and cafés. I lived in areas like that, just off the high street, so I could go and get a coffee somewhere and watch people walking around. In that way, living somewhere like Kensington, you are with people. For someone who spends their time by themself, you ain't gonna get so lonely.

I never really got friends as such. I don't know, I'm not very good at making firm friends. Well, it's not that I'm not very good, but I'd rather be by myself, to be honest. I can't imagine living with anybody. It wouldn't matter how big the house was, I just prefer to be by myself.

. . ▪ ▪ ▪ . .

After that nightmare American tour with Massive Attack, I had already decided that, when I did my album, I wasn't going to do any live shows. I was never going to tour again. I was used to the sound-system way of doing things, but I felt like that was over – standing onstage with turntables just didn't work for me.

When my manager, Debbie Swainson, asked about live work, I said, 'No, I'm not going out with turntables and a microphone, because I did that with Massive Attack, and it was fucking awful. You're standing onstage next to the turntables, with all that space around you and everyone staring up, trying to recreate songs from the album, and the DJ is actually just playing the album. There's no way I'm going out with me and Martina and someone on turntables. It's too boring. So, no, let's not do touring, I'll just do interviews and that.'

'Why don't you get a band?' says Debbie.

'What live band could ever play my music?' I replied, thinking of all the grief I'd had explaining my ideas to people who thought like conventional musicians.

'Yeah, yeah,' shrugged Debbie, 'just let me put a band together and we'll see if we can make it work.'

It was Debbie that got me wondering if maybe we could do it live. Thinking about it, I have no idea how I ended up with Debbie as my manager. Everything was done for me. I did that album with Island, I had a manager, I had an accountant, I had a lawyer. It was all sorted for me, and fuck knows who did it – maybe Chris Blackwell.

Debbie made some calls about fixing me up with a band. She spoke to a guy called Pete Briquette – he used to play bass in the Boomtown Rats – and Pete got some people together. They worked together for two weeks at a rehearsal studio, then I went down there to see how they were getting on. They played 'Overcome', and I couldn't believe it. I just couldn't understand: how the fuck were they doing that live? I was a studio artist, I wasn't a live artist at that stage, and I didn't actually know you could make my music come to life like that.

One thing I'd said to Debbie from the start was I didn't want a trendy band where everybody looked really good. I didn't want that image. I just wanted old men. Old chubby dudes! I wasn't into that thing of everybody looking cool. I didn't want to go and do TV shows where everybody has got the right haircut, and the right clothes on – so obviously it was more about the music, and what they could play, but just visually as well – I didn't want that hipster vibe.

True to that request, the band were all way older than me, and I had them a long time before Massive Attack, Portishead or any of those electronic bands had live bands. I was the first to have a live band out of all those people, and that's not me tooting my own horn – that's because of Debbie Swainson.

I can't remember any particular gigs from that year, because you don't remember them as mind-blowing yourself. I don't really think like that, remembering gigs. You just get through them. A good show is a good show, but once a few days and weeks go by, you forget about it – you're doing a new show, and then another new show. And someone has to organise it all, which I couldn't do, so I started working with Ben Winchester, and he's still my booking agent to this day.

BEN WINCHESTER: I'd approached Debbie Swainson on other business and ended up landing an account with Tricky. His live trajectory was unusual because he didn't start out by playing the club circuit – his first live shows were after *Maxinquaye* had been released. The album came out in February '95, and in March he went out on the road supporting PJ Harvey. Normally people will have hit that milestone long before their album materialises.

His first headline show was at the Clapham Grand, London, in May 1995. It was an unusual entry into live performing, but there were obvious positives: he was going in at a level where there was proper production, a proper PA, a light show. From the start, it was a very unusual show, and quite theatrical. Pete Briquette had put together a band of older session musicians, if I can put that politely, and they all stood onstage wearing dinner jackets, while Tricky was in the middle wearing a dress, with Martina at his side.

Playing with Polly was amazing because she had a fantastic show as well – maybe he'd seen her and thought, 'Okay, I need to do something here.' I'd heard him discussing how to present his album, with all of the atmosphere and the musical themes, and how that would translate visually.

I know that Tricky sometimes wore a dress and make-up. My feeling was that he had watched David Byrne in the Talking Heads videos. He was trying to make his performance into a slightly discordant spectacle. And you obviously had Martina, who was amazing, so he wasn't on his own out front.

The lighting was put together by Angus McPhail, The Cure's old lighting designer, who claims to have invented black as a colour. He was the guy that turned all the lights down when Tricky was playing – not in pitch darkness, as happened later on, but it still had a distinct atmosphere.

The shows got darker and louder and more intense as time went on, as he learnt what worked, and what worked for him. I don't think he knew at the beginning; he just did what people asked, or what he thought they expected. Later on, he thought he'd be better off doing his own thing.

PETE BRIQUETTE: When Tricky's record was taking off – or at that early stage after a couple of white labels, when it *looked* like it was taking off – it was decided to form a band around him, and I got the call from Debbie Swainson to do that. Even though he had done gigs with Massive Attack, he didn't know anything about being in a band as such, and obviously I'd been around the block before in the Boomtown Rats.

I was very fond of Tricky. We were both misfits. He was a working-class black guy from Bristol, and I was a very middle-class Irishman from Dublin, so there was no great connection on that level, but I just liked the guy from day one. Also: that record was great. I helped remix one or two tracks, and I played bass on one, 'Suffocated Love'. I was so excited – you know, for someone like me to work in that completely cutting-edge style of music!

I enjoyed my time with him. He is a very interesting guy – I'm always attracted to odd, interesting men – rather than someone like Tony Hadley, you know what I'm saying.

Tricky had said to me, 'I want a band of really old guys, in their seventies, if possible.' These guys weren't quite that old – the drummer was a lovely old East End jazzer called Les Serpa, and he was in his sixties. So was the guitarist, this oddball Frenchman, Patrice Chevalier. The piano player was a bit younger. The initial keyboard guy came from the Beautiful South, but he was a really good keyboard/sampling guy, so me and him programmed up all the samples together, but he quickly left because the gig just didn't suit him.

Les was the first drummer I'd come up against who had a tiny kit. Little bass drum, little snare, little everything, so he played like a jazz player and he got a beautiful sound out of it. Up to that point I'd only had rock drummers, with big showy kits like Roger Taylor in Queen, whereas Les's little kit really sang.

On the sampling side, it wasn't a question of pressing one button and all the samples would go off at the right time. They would all be triggered live, manually, and if the samples went a bit haywire, we had a good drummer who would go with it. There was a certain amount of leeway for interpretation and improvisation. We would gradually extend the tracks a little bit, to give them life, but then Tricky would randomly change things live onstage. It was nerve-wracking, but we would just about get away with it. A loop would be going, and he would go, 'Yeah, play more!'

'Er, ooooo-kaaaay,' and the guitar player would keep going, and he would keep rapping. Sometimes it worked, sometimes it was a mess. But because it was Tricky, and it was all dark with hardly any lights and you couldn't see anything anyway, it sounded right – a bit dangerous and on the edge.

Maxinquaye was really blowing people's minds, and Tricky was absolutely the hippest, coolest kid on the block. People were ringing me up looking for guest passes – people I hadn't heard from in years, so I was living in his reflected glory, where I became hip and cool for two minutes. Which was fine by me!

At Shepherd's Bush Empire, the guest list was stuffed. David Bowie went to that gig, and a whole lot of the current supermodels of the day.

Bob Geldof was there, and it was right in the middle of the whole scandal about Bob's wife, Paula Yates, two-timing with Michael Hutchence. Our accountant went along as well, and he too soon realised Hutchence was there, so he had to manoeuvre things to make sure that Geldof and Hutchence were in different parts of the building at all times!

At one point in the evening, I called the lift backstage and, when the door opened, there was Geldof, Bowie, Bowie's wife Iman, Jerry Hall, and two or three supermodels. Like, hello! At that time, there was no doubt that Tricky's was the gig to go to. Everybody was jumping over each other to be in the same room as him. I remember looking at all these people, and it was like a dream, you were trying to take it all in. It was overload. I can't even remember the actual gig itself.

We did *The Word*, that awful late-night TV show on Channel 4. Backstage, Tricky and Martina put on the wedding gear from the *Maxinquaye* sleeve, and it looked fucking great. He came to me and said, 'What do you think – should we wear this?' I said, 'Yeah, absolutely!' When it came to it, they didn't wear it, and he might have been right. He is very dangerous, but he is also very careful. He has a keen eye for doing things right, and he probably thought it might have come across as cheap and gimmicky in that setting.

Onstage, there was always a certain irritated tension between him and Martina, which was intriguing to people, and was part of the atmosphere of the music. It wasn't traditional show business, like Tom Jones and Cilla Black. It was a darker musical connection between them, very much bound up with their personal lives, so the two of them seemed very interlocked up there, through the music and their personal agenda together.

I think once Tricky discovered being in a band, and going on the road, he loved it. But there was no madness on the road. He didn't do a lot of the partying. When it came to women, he was quite shy – not the most confident of guys. Often, he wasn't aware that women were actually falling at his feet, so in that sense he wasn't a natural rocker. He wasn't in it to swig from a bottle of Jack Daniels and throw a TV out of the window. But he wanted to do *something*.

TRICKY: It was dark onstage because I was scared. When I first tried it, I was shaking going up there. That night, there were hardly any lights on, and I got called a genius because of it. There were articles saying, 'Genius show!' 'He doesn't compromise!' No, I was just fucking shitting myself!

At first, having no lights was fear, pure and simple, but as we went on, touring with PJ Harvey, I very quickly realised that I just couldn't do the bright lights stuff, and no lights was the comfortable way to do it for me, so I never changed it.

Have you ever watched a band, and they put the lights on the crowd? What happens is, they freeze. When you light up the crowd, at that moment they could be getting into it, having a good time, feeling relaxed, then all of a sudden the lighting guy puts the lights on them, and it kills everything. It's the same if you're up onstage: it takes all the vibe away. A lighting guy will put a bright light on me, and I just don't want to do anything.

When you're onstage, it's like a meditation. You're meditating, or it's like when you're having a massage, and you're really mellow, and then someone opens the curtains and there's sunlight coming in on you. It takes you out of your moment.

That meditation begins in the dressing room before the show. A lot of times, I'll piss in a bin in there, because to go to the bathroom you might have to go through other people or other bands, and I don't want to see people and have conversations and break from the meditation.

It's even hard walking to the stage sometimes because you've got people hanging out and people who are working and you're going straight out of real life and you know that people are just looking at you.

By the time Bowie came to that big show at Shepherd's Bush, I had been performing *Maxinquaye* for a while, and it wasn't just dim lighting – you couldn't see fuck all, it was pitch-black!

Afterwards he came and met me, and he seemed quite a shy guy. When we first came face to face, we kind of stared at each other, then he offered me a cigarette and we smiled at each other, then we hung out. Kylie Minogue was there and Naomi Campbell and that actress Nicole Kidman. She didn't say a lot, she just stood there. You've just come offstage, and those situations are weird.

ROB SMITH: As Smith & Mighty, we supported at that Shepherd's Bush show, and it was to a big audience. When Tricky came onstage, he asked the crowd, 'Who likes trip hop?' Some people cheered and shouted 'Yeah!' and Tricky replied, 'Well, fuck off home then!' It's really great to be recognised in any way, but artists in Bristol generally don't like the term 'trip hop'. It's a journalistic phrase.

RAY MIGHTY: For all the artists in Bristol, though, it seemed like the stars were aligning. Everyone was doing their own thing, and everyone was coming out with something good. You had Massive's second album, you had Portishead, you had Tricky – these three things all from one town, and all completely different to what everybody else was doing. We all felt proud of Bristol; at that moment it was musically the hottest place on the planet. You had tourists turning up, asking what was going on.

I don't so much remember the Shepherd's Bush show, just the after-shenanigans. Damon Albarn, amongst other big names, were backstage, then we went to a club called Brown's, which was really arsey. We were all supposed to meet down there, and Tricky said, 'You guys have got to come, or I'm not going.' We all met up outside, and the bouncers wouldn't let us in: 'Nah, mate, I don't care, we are not letting anybody in now.' Then Nellee Hooper came out and got the lot of us in!

MARC MAROT: Island had gone through the incredibly expensive process of bankrolling Tricky's live show, and once he was up and running with it, I took Roger Ames, the chairman of Polygram, to see this first major headline show at Shepherd's Bush Empire. Roger wanted to see what all the fuss was about. From the start, I was incredibly angry with Tricky because he had a doting, sold-out audience, but he wouldn't turn the fucking lights on. He played virtually in the dark, with just some tungsten lights and none of the coloured lights – all the stuff we had paid for, and it costs a lot of money! – and he performed the whole set with his back to the audience.

At the end, the place was going mad for an encore, but he waited until the house lights went up and 90 per cent of the audience had gone, and then he came out and did an encore. I'm there with my chairman, who I have already had to sit with and say, 'Don't worry, he is going to sign the contract!' Now I'm having to say, 'Oh well, that's Tricky being Tricky! It's all part of the legend!'

I don't think at all that it was him trying to be clever. I think it was anxiety, and I've read later interviews where he refers to his early anxiety onstage. He was significantly more anxious about being thrown into the limelight than we knew, and I think you have to look into his past for that. I don't think he had anything in his background that allowed for the success to come comfortably and naturally to him.

So that was the moment where the lightbulb went off for me. I was used to working with shy artists: when we first saw PJ Harvey play, she literally couldn't look the audience in the eye. She would perform looking down at her shoes. It's part of doing a decent job in a record company, to coax the success out of your artist, but I think with Tricky it was just a little bit too much of a shock, with not enough stability in his life to begin with. He went from nought to sixty really fast, so it was very difficult for him.

JULIAN PALMER: He never did talk about the trauma in his past. Some days he was angrier than others. We used to just have a laugh, and then when he was on his own, this stuff used to come out in the music. I wouldn't analyse it with him. I just used to spend all my time trying to protect him from the various pressures.

We both enjoyed a lot of what went on that year. He dressed as the devil on the cover of the *NME*, which was a fun day, but then sometimes we'd go out and he'd scare people – just staring at them or whatever. I always thought it was part and parcel of Tricky – that menace. I also thought it was a temporary, transient thing, that he just needed to get this out of his system, and then he would move on, but he seemed to stay in a dark place.

Some days he was angry, others he was dark, very rarely was he actually jovial. But he was always creative, and that was all we were worried about. Sometimes it was a struggle, and as soon as the album was out there, it was like he wanted to step away from being Tricky.

I don't remember him not being ambitious, but it was all about doing it on his terms. We weren't trying to make something that nobody would ever hear, but success does strange things to people. *Maxinquaye* was such a deeply personal record that it might've freaked him out a little bit having to explain it on such a broad, big scale – a much bigger scale than anticipated.

TRICKY: Most of the first touring I did was with Polly Harvey, who is a West Country girl, too. We went through England, Europe and America. Polly is lovely, and very chilled out. She ain't got none of that popstar bullshit about her. Just as real as they come.

I was lucky to tour with her at the beginning, because she's one of the best live artists you could ever see. Normally when I'm watching a live show, I get bored, not because the show is bad necessarily, or the person is bad, it's just that from this point on performing onstage became part of what I do for a living. It's not that I'm not impressed, or I don't like the songs, it's that thing of not eating chocolate if you work in a chocolate factory. Watching Polly, though, it's always been, 'Fucking hell, that is some power!'

Once, I left her a message at reception in the hotel we were staying at – a smiley face with an upside-down mouth, and tears running down it. I've long since forgotten why I may have done that. Then I saw her in the lobby the next day, and her cat had died. I left this message before it had happened, a sad face, and then her cat had died. I thought, 'Oh fuck, that's bad timing!'

As our shows got better and I was feeling the crowd more, I started really loving the live thing. Pete Briquette, my musical director for those first couple of years, is a really nice guy, salt of the earth. Again, just like a normal bloke, and very funny. But there was a part of touring I immediately found confusing. After the first show we ever did, I was sat backstage by myself, and Pete walked in.

'So, what the fuck's this about then?' I asked him, a bit bewildered. 'What do I do now?'

'Meet people, meet some girls, have fun!' he beams at me.

I'm like, 'Yeah, but we did the show … what the fuck do I do now?'

It's the same sequence, every night: you're out there with a crowd, then you finish the show, and then you're sat in the dressing room by yourself. Because Pete had been touring for years, I really was looking for answers.

So what happens now, then? Is that it? You do a show and then you sit in your dressing room?

He was like, 'Have a drink, meet some people, have a laugh!'

On that level, I couldn't see what it was all about. I didn't get it. It was so weird to me. You're onstage, and then it's all over.

Elvis Presley was The Guy, right? He sold millions of records, more records than anybody – a ridiculous amount, like a billion or something. The biggest artist, the first popstar. I watched this documentary once, about him doing these huge shows in Vegas. Then they showed him in the dressing room, and it was a *shit* dressing room. It just made me realise: it doesn't matter how big you are, you could be playing in front of 100,000 people, but you're still going to have a shit dressing room. I mean, I have experienced that, but you wouldn't think Elvis ever did.

Going back into that shitty room, you're returning to real life with an almighty crash. Even Elvis, who you don't consider being real, is there in this horrible little hole with graffiti all over the walls, where hundreds of other bands have been before, having to face real life. That's the reality of things.

. ▪ ▨ ▦ ▨ ▪ .

It was only through working in the music industry – making records, and touring – that I started taking cocaine, and drinking more. As I said before, when I was younger, when me and Whitley used to hang around, if you snorted cocaine, you were a crackhead. In the reggae culture, it was not cool. It was something you didn't do.

Then, pretty early on in my days in the music industry, I took cocaine. I admitted that 'I snort the cheap thrills' in the lyrics of 'Abbaon Fat Tracks', on *Maxinquaye*. I've certainly never been a cokehead, but I'd never have got into it if I'd not got a deal and been successful. Look at Whitley: he was doing music for a bit then, once I moved to London, he gave it up and he *never* took cocaine, and that was my best mate.

When I left and got successful, that's when I found all this shit like cocaine and alcohol: for me thus far, drinking was a casual thing, of going to a club and having a whisky and a spliff to help you get into the music. Then I got successful, and alcohol became a survival mechanism. When I was as tired as fuck on tour, and I didn't want to do a show, I'd have to have a drink just to be able to do my show, to push back the exhaustion. So drug culture came into things because of the music, because of the success.

Once you're no longer anonymous, or just a normal person, that's when mad things start happening to you. When I was off tour, back at the flat in Kensington High Street I was a total insomniac. I couldn't adjust my body clock from the night shift on the road, to daytime at home. I would stay up all night, and then in the morning, when the shop was open, I would walk over in my pyjamas, with just a coat on over the top, and I'd buy a packet of crisps, a Lucozade and a Twix. I would walk back, eat and drink all of that and then go to sleep.

One day, I walked into the shop, and there was a woman in there with a kid of about eight with a posh school uniform on – and the kid goes, 'Mum, it's Tricky!'

Around that time, I had a photograph done with this guy for the London listings magazine, *Time Out*. I did so many shoots in those months, I didn't really know what it was for. I thought it was just for some article and forgot all about it.

On Easter Sunday, I come out of my apartment on Kensington High Street, I go to the same shop where the kid said, 'Mum, it's Tricky!' – only this time, on the railings outside, I see this poster of me from the cover of *Time Out*, with me as Jesus, wearing a crown of thorns. I don't go in the shop – I just turn around and walk straight back inside the apartment.

That really fucked me up. I can't explain what the feeling was, but it was when things started going very, very wrong for me.

BOWIE

When I was young, living in the Porters' house in Hartcliffe, I would hear David Bowie playing while I was getting ready for bed. At weekends, Milo, Trevor Beckford and my cousin Mark, who were all older than me, would be having showers and getting dressed up ready to hit the town, and they would play all of Bowie's classic records as their 'going-out' tunes.

That's how I know his music. I can't say that I then went on to become a massive fan of David Bowie. I never exactly followed his stuff, but once *Maxinquaye* came out, David Bowie was *my* fan. He came to my show at Shepherd's Bush Empire and dropped by to say hello afterwards. And Kylie was there, too!

Bowie then wrote me a really beautiful letter, saying: 'Iman and I loved the show the other night – I've loved the album for some time.' Also in that package, he sent me a copy of Jean-Michel Basquiat's *The Notebooks*, because he said I reminded him of Basquiat. I don't know if Bowie had ever met him, but he told me it wasn't the way I look, just a similar energy that I had.

In the letter, he also warned me that he'd written a story about me for *Q* magazine. David Bowie never wrote about another artist ever! It was actually a mad six-page story, imagining a meeting with me before we'd actually met. That story is genius. It's like a stream-of-consciousness fantasy, where he sort of interviews me while we both climb up the side of a building.

Bowie had obviously been around a lot longer than me, but the way he wrote to me, and about me, you'd almost think that I'd had the thirty-year career before that, not him. In person, he was humble. He was a businessman, too. When we first met, he brought his own private photographer, but get past that and he was as humble as fuck.

What's crazy is, I didn't even reply to the letter. He signed off saying, 'I hope we get to meet again,' and I never answered. I met him a couple of times, and I didn't engage. I think about that a lot. I can't believe that kid from Knowle West with not much future has grown up into a guy David Bowie writes a letter to. I didn't try and meet him – he came to my concert to try and meet me. If that happened now, I'm old enough to think, 'You know what, I wanna meet this guy, and make a connection.'

Back then, I didn't give a shit. Like, 'Oh, alright, David Bowie wrote a story.' I didn't care about it at all, I didn't reach out, I didn't try to meet him, I was not interested, I didn't give a fuck. You know when you're younger, everything is moving fast, and right around that time, I was moving *way* too fast. Now I think, 'Why didn't I call him? Why didn't I send a letter back to him?' All that love he showed me … I didn't return it. I didn't even say thank you. Which is a bit shit, really, because he's dead now.

It's still weird, thinking that he is dead. I almost forget, almost like he would always be with us. But he went out like a soldier, didn't he? He knew he was dying, he made his final album, *Blackstar*, did videos, made all the arrangements for it. He went out like a soldier. Fucking hell, what a brave man!

CHAPTER NINE
NEARLY GOOD

For the British music industry, 1995 was a massive year. Britpop was peaking, CD sales were at an all-time high, and my album – whatever they wanted to call it – was right in the mix, too: loads of different music magazines (including the all-powerful *NME*) and radio shows would vote *Maxinquaye* as the best album of the year.

Amongst all the touring, interviews and general craziness, one quiet afternoon off I took Martina down to the Odeon at the far end of Kensington High Street to watch Quentin Tarantino's *Pulp Fiction* – the movie of the moment, according to those same commentators. I didn't end up taking away many recollections of the film itself, because my attention had been swallowed up during the preamble before it actually started, with one ghastly observation – all the fucking ads sounded like *Maxinquaye*!

That's when I knew: it was over. They had ruined *Maxinquaye* already. So many people liked it and embraced it and followed it, it had become what they call a coffee-table album – a horrible phrase, not a compliment.

When it initially came out, *Maxinquaye* was weird. That's what people have forgotten ever since: upon impact, it was different, dangerous, a serious head-fuck. It was hardcore, a militant album. When my A&R guy went in to hear 'Strugglin'', he turned into a beetroot. There was nothing like it, but that record became so successful that it wasn't different anymore. It very quickly became the norm – normal. My punk-minded album had suddenly gone mainstream, and everyone was ripping it off. There were lame imitations of my music everywhere, and even big American producers like Timbaland started copying me. Listen to the song he recorded with Aaliyah. It was like music had changed, to sound like me.

Luckily, I realised that that's not a good position to be in. If I'd made a second album that sounded just like *Maxinquaye*, then I wouldn't've been different anymore. I'd be the same, and then I'd be stuck. That's how artists get trapped by their own success. In a way this predicament was good because it told me where to go next. It forced my hand. I was like, 'Right, I've got to get somewhere else now.' I wanted to say to these coffee-table people, 'So, you like what I do? I'll test you – let's see if you really support me!' I felt that there was only one thing to do: give people something harder, less easy to listen to, almost challenging them to stay with me, so I could get away from all that fucking success.

Even though Island had released *Maxinquaye*, and it had got to No.3 in the charts, we still hadn't signed a proper contract. From their point of view, if you've got someone with that much buzz about them on your label, it becomes more urgent that you sign them. You don't want to let them go. I knew all that. There was one show in '95 where I spotted Dave Gilmour, my red-faced A&R, in the crowd, waving a contract in the air at me.

Island didn't A&R me as such, but if I'd already signed and then decided to change course to something less commercial, they could've said, 'Look, this isn't gonna do as well as *Maxinquaye*, so we don't want it.' Then you'd be in trouble. If I had signed that deal earlier, and had an album refused, I would've had to record another album more on the vibe they thought they could sell.

But because I hadn't inked the deal, I kind of had them by the short and curlies! I said to my manager, 'I want it stated in the contract that if Island don't accept a record for release, I can take it to any other label I choose, and they can release it.' I don't think any other artist has had a contract that said that before. What's mad is, thinking back now, I don't know why I would've stipulated that, because I didn't know enough about contracts and the politics of it. It must've been instinct, because through that I landed up in a position where they couldn't control my music, and I could release anything I fucking wanted.

· ■ ■ ■ ■ ■ ·

In rural Somerset in early '95, I had my first near-death experience. We were between tours, recording at a studio down that way, in Poole in Dorset. We were staying at Martina's family's house in the middle of nowhere, and one night there I had a serious asthma attack. Asthma can be controlled quite easily: there are certain things you're not supposed to be eating or doing, but of course I was just not looking after myself, eating badly and what have you. People often said I wasn't gonna live long, even that guy who wrote the book about Bristol – *if he makes it to twenty, he could be someone.*

Well, on this occasion, I really didn't think I would make it through the night. It was funny, though: Martina was eight months pregnant by that point, and she was freaking out. She was thinking that the child she was carrying wasn't gonna know its dad. As for the poor doctor! When he arrived, he couldn't do anything, because he didn't come with the right equipment. He wasn't prepared for how far gone I was, so he was shitting himself. I said to him, 'I'm gonna fucking die here! Do something!' and he just sank down into a chair, closed his eyes and basically gave up. It was mad seeing this guy's face. He'd thrown in the towel.

Finally the paramedics came, and they put those electrodes on my chest, where they shock you, and every time they hit me with it, the lights in this old country house all started flickering and going out, like in a horror movie. They were hooked up to the mains, and every time they hit me, the lights would go haywire – although I obviously didn't piece that together until much later. I was totally gone, so they hit me with it a couple of times, and all I remember is, it was weird – I saw shadows picking me up, and for some reason I thought they were aliens. Going out to the ambulance ... that looked like a spaceship to me because of the blue lights on top. I was absolutely convinced it was aliens taking me away on a spaceship.

I woke up the next day in hospital with my family around me and my auntie saying, 'You've got to change your life, boy!' They didn't tell me for a while that I'd had the electric shocks – they don't want to tell you because of post-traumatic stress and all that. It's really weird that I thought I was being taken off by aliens. Why aliens? Why not God?

It was only three or four weeks later that our daughter Mazy was born, and I've got to say the experience of being in a birthing room in Poole hospital while I became a father was very alien, too.

As any helpless onlooking dad will tell you, it's weird seeing a kid being born. I don't believe in aliens, but I used to love the TV shows and films about them. It used to fascinate me even though I don't believe in it at all. But when you see your kid being born, you think, 'Well, *we* are the aliens!' When their head pops out, and their eyes open and they look around the room – I don't think you get any more alien than that, do you?

PETE BRIQUETTE: I was helping out on that album, and Martina had come down, heavily pregnant, to do some vocals. After a while, she got tired, but she did one more take of the song 'Black Coffee' and then suddenly her waters broke, actually in the vocal booth. I don't think either of them had even set it up with the hospital that she was about to drop, so I'm pretty sure I had to ring for an ambulance, and then she got whisked off to have the baby.

There was a big chemistry between Tricky and Martina, onstage and off, but it was very complicated, interspersed as it was between the relationship ending, having the baby, her being barely out of her teens, and him being an older guy who wasn't ready to settle down. The thing is, Tricky was just finding his way in life as well, and it all happened maybe a bit early for them both. So the relationship was pushed forward at a quicker pace than it naturally should have been, because of making records together, and having the kind of success that neither of them could've bargained for. I doubt that either of them wanted a lifetime partner at that stage, and they'd come to that realisation in the very heightened situation of creatively having a great thing together, and being very successful with it.

As with all super-talented guys like him, there was an element of the control freak there – most great artists really want to control the creative output, as to what exactly happens. And Martina was the younger, wilder person who didn't want to be controlled, so there was tension there, too.

As a singer, Martina was very instinctive. She really did have a fabulous voice. She sings really quietly, just up close to a mic, so you get that intimacy. She would sit beside you at the control desk with the mic and sing so quietly and beautifully. I loved the way she sang.

What fascinated me about Tricky himself, was that he had no obvious traditional skills as a musician, insofar as he didn't sing, and he couldn't play an instrument. He just rapped, and it wasn't the same as American rapping, as it had become known. What he had was great ears. I used to call him Golden Ears. I like guys who have that sort of talent, and Tricky was one of those. We'd be in the studio, playing away for a while, and he would just pick one bar of everything you'd done, and that's all he would use. And he would usually be absolutely right – that was the best bit. He had great taste, and a great knowledge of what would and wouldn't work. And it was innate – a natural talent.

One day, we got a bass player into the studio who was currently playing with Roxy Music – Gary Tibbs, who was in Adam and the Ants. I got him to play on a track, and he went flying around it, noodling away, and was really pleased with himself at the end. I thought, 'Not bad, maybe a bit busy!' Then Tricky came along and listened for a couple of minutes, then he goes, 'There!' We stopped the tape, and he took three notes. He binned the rest, took those three notes, looped them up, and that became the basis for a track. I think the guy was a bit put out, like he had just done a great performance and all that was used was three notes. But that was the way Tricky worked.

I would put Tricky absolutely on a par with other great singers, even though he couldn't sing well technically – he was a great musician although he didn't have traditional musical skills.

TRICKY: I'd decided to have other singers on the record, because it was another way of getting away from *Maxinquaye*, which obviously had been just me and Martina.

I'd met Björk through Julian Palmer. He walked me into a party one night out in London, and he goes, 'Look, there's Björk … hi, Björk, this is Tricky – oh, you two should work together!' It was like a set-up: 'Oh, wow, what a coincidence – look who's here!' I'm not saying it was definitely that, but that's how it felt, looking back on it.

I was really impressed by her in the studio, because she was not at all scared. She has no fear. She's not one of these artists that's going to think about everything too much. I would just get some drums up, and she would try a vocal straight off. She wouldn't say, 'Oh, but that's out of time there.' She's got no fear when it comes to recording, just pure talent and instinct.

One time I was saying to her, 'I'm thinking about having singing lessons to see if I can sing better.'

'Don't do that!' she fired back, straight off the bat. She was adamant about it.

'Why not?' I said, wondering why she felt that so strongly.

'Because you've got weird metering,' she explained. 'They'll ruin that if you have singing lessons.'

She was kind of saying: It's not right, what you're doing, but it works for you. Björk is very smart like that, she knows about music on that level, too. Everyone knows how good she is, how she can write excellent songs, but she's also the sort of person who can go freestyle. She wouldn't be scared to just go and vibe on something, on the fly. A lot of artists can't do that. They'll say, 'Oh no, can I have something more like *Maxinquaye*,' but she wasn't fazed at all.

We ended up dating, and she was a really good girl, and was really good to me. I was just a fuck-up, and not a great boyfriend. I think she loved me at the time, so I reckon I hurt her. She said to me that I'm emotionally numb. Obviously I didn't see that about myself, but it makes sense, doesn't it? I didn't really know my dad, my mum committed suicide – you're going to be emotionally numb, aren't you? She sussed me out.

I have no idea how long we were together, maybe a few weeks. We didn't live together, our thing was more working together, just music. I really don't know if she was looking for a more long-term relationship. I can't say that, but obviously she wasn't looking for someone who was emotionally numb. When it ended, it wasn't *bad* bad, but I can't speak for how she felt. I just disappeared one day. One day I was there, the next day I wasn't.

I'd also met Terry Hall from The Specials, and it was like meeting a family member I hadn't seen for years. Before I even met Terry, I felt like I knew him. I grew up with him. The Specials were such a huge part of my life, and they never fell into that popstar shit. Those guys never had no ego. They kept it street, which also really influenced me, so when I met him, it felt like we were destined to meet – not at all awkward, like when I met Prince, say. It wasn't like we had to get to know each other. It reminds me of when I see my cousin from Manchester after I haven't seen him for years. We just clicked straight away, just natural, like family, and we hung out quite a bit, not just in the studio.

Down at the studio in Poole, Terry wrote his own stuff for my album, and he wasn't one of those artists that takes a long time to do it, either. He wrote the lyrics and the melody for 'Poems', which many people these days see as one of my classic songs. Terry is very instinctive. He just writes something and does it. He's not scared or precious. Some artists, even talented ones, triple-think themselves, but he was very similar to me – I just write something and throw it down. He certainly ain't the sort of guy who will say, 'Ooh, you know what, this tune is a bit weird.' He's a trier, and that's what he's got to be – a guy from a council flat in Coventry is going to be a trier.

TERRY HALL: I had a copy of *Maxinquaye*, with Martina on, and I really liked it. I'd heard Tricky was influenced by The Specials, and liked our first album, so I wanted to meet up, and we did. A PR guy at Island got us together. It was just to sit down and have a chat about it all, really – nothing more at that point.

I related to him on the level that he was from Bristol, and I was from Coventry, both of which are on the outside of what you would call the music business. If you get a band from Coventry that's really successful, you'll be the most successful band from Coventry, and the same goes for Bristol, and you can't really do that if you're from London. He told me he'd once done a DJ set which was just our album – he played side one the whole way through, and when it finished, he just turned it over, and that was it – so he obviously liked us! Either that, or it was the only record he had with him.

He was pretty militant against stardom, and I had a lot of respect for that. He'd tasted it on his first album. I remember his reaction to bad reviews: instead of just dismissing it, he would want to kill the journalist! People will either get it or they won't. It's when you try and conform to it that it all goes wrong, because you're not doing what you wanna do, you're doing what other people want you to do. That's the danger. You can do that, but you won't be happy with the results.

I'd started to write with different people, after being locked into three or four groups in a row, and that's how we thought about doing something together. We were hanging out quite a bit: I would go to his place in Kensington High Street, we'd have a coffee and talk about records and stuff. All he had at home was a couple of VHS cassettes and a few records, and then there was a tiny keyboard next to the bed – that was about it.

The recording thing happened in Dorset. Martina was there, and Alison Moyet, and we started trying things out. I found it really different, because I'd been conditioned into how you're 'supposed' to make a record. I'd always been in bands where you wrote a song with an acoustic guitar or a piano, and then get the group to play it. There's a format to it all, but with Tricky, you didn't follow that.

I noticed that the little shitty keyboard by his bed went into the studio, and that was what went down onto tape. It wasn't a question of, 'Okay, shall we orchestrate this?' It was just that keyboard, and that I really, really liked. Plus the fact that he took my head out of that verse-chorus-middle-eight thing. Again, I grew up with the Glitter Band – not literally, but you know what I mean? There was a way of doing things with pop songs, and you expect a chorus after sixteen bars or something. This was a totally fresh approach which I really enjoyed being part of.

I came in with words already written. I was waiting to see what he was doing with programming stuff. It was all quite new to me at that point, the idea of working on computers and programming. The only experience I'd had with it before was with The Colourfield, where we used a programmer, very rigid, and I hated it, but Tricky's approach was fresh, and there wasn't a boundary there. It didn't seem to matter how the song was constructed, which I found really appealing.

'Poems' was all about promises. I was on the verge of a divorce at that point, so it was about the promises you make to another person, and the promises they make to you, and how often they are broken, and you can't always figure out why. A great laugh! The other song I did, 'Bubbles', was really loose, created in the studio, whereas for 'Poems' there was a definite form in my head.

I found it liberating because Tricky wasn't a musician – he just had ideas. That was the most important thing, I think – the ideas. It was all like he used to do it in his bedroom, with the sampler and the keyboard and the headphones, except I think he took his headphones off – that was the development from the first album.

We talked a lot about Public Enemy, and how we fitted in with it all. We were from very similar backgrounds, that rough-arse small-city thing, and it was all about trying to be creative coming from that. Not having a voice, and people not expecting anything from you, and how the only things they expected were bad things. It was about trying to break away from that and create something.

During recording, he had an asthma attack, quite a heavy one, so I had to drive him to hospital in Bournemouth, and all I could think about on the way was, how fast do you drive with someone who's having an asthma attack? Do you speed up to get there quickly, do you stop at traffic lights, or do you just drive straight through? We went from the studio to A&E, sitting there at two in the morning. It's weird saying that was a fond memory, because he was going through an asthma attack, but it *is* a fond memory in a funny way. You know, the whole thing! It was a bizarre night.

TRICKY: For that album, which didn't have a title yet, I would take samples, and little bits of things, and if I can hear it in my head, there's no way it cannot work. I never had no rules. I'd sample beats, or it might just be a bass sound. I have no idea about theoretical stuff, or the timing being three-four, or Martina being out of pitch with a song, which someone said about one of the songs on this album. If I hear something and I think it's good, it's good. I ain't gonna question it.

Most problems artists have, it's questioning themselves. They do something, and then they think about it and think about it, and fucking think about it more. I don't do that. That's why I put out 'mistakes'. I put out more mistakes than any other artist. That's good sometimes, other times not so good. But it is good from the point of: I've never had writer's block in my life. I don't believe there is such a thing, because I don't control what I do. It's a natural thing. So how can I have writer's block, if I ain't in control of it? Writer's block – what is that? It should just be called 'thinking too much'.

The title of the album came from a writer. I went to do an interview, and the guy shook my hand and we sat down.

'So, what's it like being God?' he asked.

I looked at him a bit nonplussed.

'Or nearly God, I should say!' he said, correcting himself. He was one of the nice guys, he wasn't being nasty. He was joking about my success, because after *Maxinquaye* I was the guy who'd changed the face of music. He was just having a laugh about all the surrounding hysteria, but I thought, 'Aha, nearly God – that's my next album title right there!' So I had that in place before I even started recording it.

The music itself was all about leaving that success behind. Once I'd turned that corner in my mind, it removed all the pressure I might've felt, to sustain my level of success, to play by those rules. I did *Nearly God* deliberately intending and knowing that it was not going to get in the charts, and it wasn't going to get radio airplay. That way I left all the pressure way behind.

As well as the album title, I even managed to get it through Island that *Nearly God* was the artist name, not Tricky, to distance it – and me – even further from that sound, and that idea, which had been ruined for me.

Because of how we'd managed to get that extra clause in my contract with Island, I was totally free to do what I wanted. Island didn't really like what they were hearing – they doubtless would've been happier with something more like *Maxinquaye* – so I was like, 'Alright, if you don't want the album, I'll take it somewhere else.'

I started shopping the album around, and at one point I was talking to this guy Derek Birkett from Björk's label, One Little Indian, but then Island heard about it and went, 'No, no, we'll put it out!' Of course, no record company wants you going somewhere else when you're signed to them, so I was kind of forcing them to release things they didn't want to release. From there on, instead of me having to do another album that Island liked, it was, 'Here's the album, do you want it? No? Okay, I'll go to One Little Indian,' then they changed their minds.

All this put me in a great position, because it proved I could actually get away with it!

MARC MAROT: Tricky was dating Björk, and I heard from Tricky himself that she was whispering in his ear: 'Well, you could just go and sign to Warner Bros. now if you want to, or EMI, or anyone!' – even though they probably wouldn't've been able to get *Maxinquaye* back, he might get a million quid from Warner in America, to release the next record. I had to go to the Hammersmith office of my chairman, Roger Ames, and explain that he shouldn't worry, because I trusted Tricky, but there was massive scepticism.

I believe that Tricky is principled – even if sometimes they are strange principles. This was a moment where in absolute reality he could have completely shafted Island Records. We had a draft contract that everybody had agreed but it just hadn't physically been signed – in reality, funded by a rival, he could have easily sought to sign elsewhere and simply left us with the rights to *Maxinquaye*.

A lot of people criticised *Nearly God*, and the form it took, with a different artist name, but if you look at Island under my stewardship, there was a history of people doing side projects, from PJ Harvey to Jah Wobble to Julian Cope.

Nearly God was nearly good. I sided with a few of the critics, who basically said that if he had just kept his powder dry and had delivered that record with a bit more effort and energy into the production, it could have been an absolute classic follow-up to *Maxinquaye*. But he just needed to get it out of his system, and got it recorded in a month.

JULIAN PALMER: Chris Blackwell was okay with *Nearly God*. In amongst the humongous success Island was having with U2, PJ Harvey and The Cranberries on the white rock side, all of a sudden, it had what Island was really all about – the most inventive young black artist of that moment, and Chris was happier for the artist to dictate than any record mogul I have ever met. All Chris's friends, and all the artists who grew up here, like Grace Jones – everybody was saying to him how incredible Tricky was, and that carried more cachet to him than any chart placing. Tricky was dangerous at every turn, and a showman, and a chameleon – all the things that represented the best of Island Records. So Tricky's every twist and turn was cherished by everybody.

Tricky started to remind me so much of what Bowie did in the '70s, where you will get something completely different every time. With him it was, you're not even getting me as an artist anymore, you're getting this persona. We had to go with where his head was at, and how he felt about the world.

He always had that feeling that 'the world wants a piece of me, and everybody has got it in for me'. With real artists, it all comes out, and there has not been one moment in Tricky's career where it hasn't just been him pouring everything out, and that comes at a price. I don't think he's ever had a manager for longer than ten minutes. He would be the first to accept that that side of himself is unmanageable.

But with *Nearly God* he had some good influences around. There's no question that Terry Hall was a useful person for Tricky to talk to at that point, having been through meteoric success himself in the early '80s.

I introduced him to Björk at a party at Nellee Hooper's house-slash-studio in England's Lane in Belsize Park. Nellee was working with her and, of course, Kate Moss, Naomi Campbell and everybody had been going to Tricky's shows, because Tricky was the kid to go and see. Therefore, he started to receive the cooler party invites, so he and I were going out and about all the time.

At Nellee's, a day's recording session would blur into an evening's party, which then blurred into a day's session again. Nellee obviously looked at Tricky differently after *Maxinquaye*: they had known each other so long, from the early Wild Bunch days, and maybe there was a bit of love–hate.

I wanted Tricky to meet Björk – of course I did. I just thought they were like-minded, and there weren't many out there for him like that. PJ Harvey was obviously another, but Björk was maybe being cleaned up and prepared for pop stardom at that point, after the success of *Debut*.

Musically, I saw an umbilical cord between them. She was excited to meet him, and in that situation you just leave them to it, don't you, and hope they hit it off. They seemed to immediately, and it really felt like they were meant to be together creatively in some shape or form.

He met her at absolutely the right time for him, and they were an inseparable item for a short period of time, as tends to be the case with Tricks. Everything was so transient, but if you look at the two songs she had on *Nearly God*, she definitely wasn't scared to go into his darker side.

For quite a while, me and him were as bad as each other, encouraging each other to do all sorts of narcotics. He could walk into my office and shut the door, and we could do whatever we wanted, and the world could just fuck off. He used to bang on all the time, 'I'm not making a fucking radio record, Jules!' I'm like, 'No, you are not!' Nobody could tell us anything.

At the Brit Awards in February 1996, we were up for a few Brits, and I remember thinking, 'I'm not going to let Tricky know this, but I think we should be walking away with these.' I personally would've liked a Brit for him, more perhaps than he did for himself, but it was always a step too far for the establishment to recognise him. I think he would be recognised like a shot today, but who cares? It wasn't about winning Brits, we had already succeeded, on his terms.

We were in the loos at one point in the evening, and Liam Gallagher strolled in and came on a bit strong, and Tricky took umbrage. Liam is a fiery character, isn't he? And Tricky was beyond fiery, and menacing and dangerous – he was always up for it, switched on, and hyper, almost looking for trouble. For a moment, it got a little bit hairy, and I just said to Liam, 'Look, you really don't want to be fucking with this kid – you really don't, he is just gonna go fucking lunar!' Then suddenly it all just diffused. It was one of those Brits moments.

TRICKY: I was nominated for three Brits, and I was sitting there watching everybody get awards except me. I was sat there drinking with Shaun Ryder for a lot of the night. I can't remember if Shaun was actually nominated or not, but I was seeing all these Brits going to all these different people. I didn't give a fuck about winning one, I was just noticing.

'How come me and you don't win stuff like this?' I asked Shaun, once it was obvious we weren't going to.

'Because we're ugly, Tricky,' he goes.

'What are you talking about?' I said. We'd both had a lot of free drink.

'Because we're ugly *inside*,' he says.

Then I knew. I looked at all the people winning, all the shiny glossy people who were very good at being pop stars, and me and Shaun Ryder were a mess. Our demons showed. We weren't hiding our demons with make-up. You can't airbrush me and Shaun Ryder. I'd say we are 'wear your heart on your sleeve' kind of people.

Some people are just special, I believe that – when you meet someone like a Shaun Ryder, they have a psychic energy and they just feel a situation instantly. I can forget some of the biggest things I've done in my life, but the little things like that I'll never forget – 'because we're ugly inside'. He might not even remember it, but I remember it, and that's almost twenty-five years ago. Ugly on the inside. That kind of taught me about the industry. They don't want to give awards to people like me and Shaun. Too real.

Shaun is one of the best artists to come out of England. I've always wanted to work with him. I've talked to him about it, but it never happened. He's crazy, I'm crazy – it should work. I've always got on with him. I love that guy. He should be a legend like Bowie is a legend – that's how big he should be. I think he's been a gangster for real. I've never seen that side of him, but I've heard stories of him pulling guns out on people and shit. If he wasn't into the music, he would be properly naughty. Music saved him from the streets.

SHAUN RYDER: Me and Tricky got on really well. We was pretty similar sort of kids. I definitely identified with him coming from a shit place and making something good out of his life. He was a good kid, he was one of us, and I loved the music he was doing. I was always big into rap, and I liked the way he was doing his own thing with it. He wasn't trying to be American, was he, he was just being himself.

I know me and him hung around quite a bit, but I can't fucking remember. I'm under a specialist at the moment for my memory. I've also got to have both my hips replaced, all my fucking hair's fallen out all over my body, my thyroid is fucked, and my testosterone, and then I've got a bloody great lump on my testicle that's pressing on a nerve – and there's a load of problems with my fucking memory.

I think we spent quite a bit of time together at the Brits, which must've been 1996 – sat around smoking most of the time, probably staring at everyone else, muttering to each other, 'What a fucking bunch of middle-class cunts!' That's probably why we ended up talking to each other, because we couldn't get on with anyone else.

I'm pretty sure what happened that night was, I got up from our table, told him I'd be back in a minute, and then nipped out to get some gear – I was on the smack at the time. I went to this flat around the corner from there, but it turned out the police were watching the gaff. I go in, and then of course at that precise moment they decide to raid the fucking place, and I get nicked – all of this is when I'm supposed to be nipping out for ten minutes during these awards.

Somehow, I managed to blag my way out of it with a fucking bag of skag on me! I'm sat there telling them I'm at an awards show, and eventually they let me fuck off. So I walk back in, sit down: 'Sorry about that, Tricks, I got held up.'

It turned out that Tricky's relatives in Manchester knew some of my people. Me and this kid called Pat Ward grew up together. We used to say we were cousins, but we were really just pals. He's actually doing life now in prison – never going to get out, Pat. He's going to die in there. When I got in the music game, he came in and did all sorts for us. He basically used to do security for the Mondays. Tricky's Uncle Tony knew Pat's brother, Dave Ward, so his uncle ran with those kind of dudes!

At the time, Tricky was just getting into a bit of acting. He was just back from shooting his bits in *The Fifth Element*. He didn't enjoy it very much, but he made a better job of it than I did. I was in *The Avengers* in '98 and I fucked mine up big-time, didn't I? The worst you can do with a big Hollywood production is tell the truth and say it's a load of shit, so I never worked again. My co-star, Eddie Izzard, went to Hollywood afterwards, and I just fucking vanished.

TRICKY: After dating Björk, I'd be on the front page of the *Sun*, but I didn't win one fucking Brit. You know what was really nice, better than winning: one year, The Cure were getting a Q Inspiration award, and Robert Smith asked for me to present it to him, so I got up and did that. That's better than winning, for him to ask me.

After two visits, I'd worked out what the Brits were: they're just a pat on the shoulder, like, 'Oh, you've made a lot of money for the industry this year, well done!' It ain't what you've accomplished; it's because you've made the industry money. These people know what they're doing: 'Good boy, good girl, keep selling those records, then maybe you'll get one of these again next year.'

What is a Brit anyway? What does it mean? Is it the industry saying you've written the best songs this year? Or you've played the best guitar? Do you think these money guys sitting around at the ceremony actually care? The artists think they're getting them because they're talented. It amazes me! All these corporate fuckers who do this Brits shit, or the Oscars, it's just a pat on the back to say, 'Keep making money for us!' When artists get these awards, it boosts their egos through the roof. They should look where that award is coming from and ask, is it anybody you respect giving you that award?

Island were a little bit outside all of that. Someone told me once, 'U2 make big money, which enables Island to look for credible artists like you.' One of the reasons I signed to Island was because they had credible artists.

That's what they thought about artists then. These days, they don't give a fuck who you are. If that's the wrong record for the label, you ain't releasing it. Back then, there were no discussions about *Nearly God*, or with subsequent albums. It was just, 'This is the album!' 'Okay!' No discussion whatsoever, which I think was probably unusual, even then.

I bumped into Marc Marot a few years ago and he told me something, which I couldn't quite believe: he said I was signed to carry on the Bob Marley legacy. I just didn't get it. I don't sound like his music or nothing. But apparently that's what I was there for, which is kind of mind-blowing.

A weird thing happened: one time back then I was having dinner with Chris Blackwell, and Rita Marley, Bob's widow, was there. I was talking to her, and she goes to me – it really scared me – 'Oh, you remind me of Bob, you know!' It made me feel really fucking uncomfortable. It's a beautiful thing to say, but too scary. Bob Marley is mythical, isn't he? If that was now, I would've found out more from her, but that night I was so stunned I couldn't say anything, so I just went silent.

Chris always had these people around him. I met Rita, Cedella and Rohan Marley through him. I met the guy who started MTV, too, who was a really good guy. He said a mad thing to me. I had blown up with

Maxinquaye, I was all over MTV, but he said to me, 'Tricky, just because you're on MTV Europe, don't think that you've made it yet. I see a lot of artists like you who think they've conquered the world, but it's a big world out there!'

I thought, 'You know what, that's absolutely right – let's get to America.' Six months later, I was living in New York.

CHAPTER TEN
DURBAN POISON

My auntie Marlow says that my strongest asset is not my music-making or my lyric-writing; it's that I can move somewhere by myself and not know anybody there. I can just get up one day and decide I'm going to live in a foreign city and move there, and I don't care about being by myself. Marlow says that I can up sticks and go, with no friends or family there, and no plans, and that not a lot of people can do that by themselves.

Personally, I think I just don't like familiar – I like strange. I wouldn't describe myself as a confident guy, but I've always let life lead me wherever it goes.

In 1995/96, everything was moving very fast for me. Everyone's life goes fast anyway, you realise, but as a musician your life goes faster than average. It certainly all speeds up when you've got a record deal, with studio bookings, tour itineraries and promo schedules forcing you to plan months ahead. It feels like you're always ahead of yourself, wishing your life away, then you're off somewhere, and before you know it, all those months have actually gone by.

In amongst all of that, one minute I was living on Kensington High Street, the next minute I was living in New York City. London had been very different for a Bristol kid, but New York was like, 'Holy fuck!' and I think I definitely thrive on that strangeness.

I knew I was going to live there, right from the first time I touched down at JFK with Massive Attack, when I felt the energy rush from my feet up to my head. I moved there because of that energy, and because of the music. As well as The Specials, I'd grown up on American music, the sound of it, everything. When you were influenced by hip-hop in those days, New York was your Mecca, so it was almost like you've got to live in New York at one point in your life. That's your dream.

For a few weeks after I arrived there, I lived in an apartment on 34th Street in Manhattan, on the border of what used to be called Hell's Kitchen. Once, it was the old Irish gangster neighbourhood, but it wasn't like that when I lived there in 1996. It was as busy as fuck. I was about three or four flights up in this glass building, all glass outside, and it had glass ceilings so you could have a spliff and lie down on the sofa and see helicopters flying overhead. Mad!

One morning, I came out onto the street, and there was this little kid trundling along on a tiny three-wheel tricycle – he must have been only three or four years of age – and it just looked so weird, this little nipper surrounded by huge high-rise buildings. Just mind-blowing. It really was a different world. Another day, there was a taxi strike on, and it was crazy to see how quiet the streets were without the taxis working. Almost a bit haunting. It made you realise how manic it was the rest of the time.

Another reason for moving to New York was, they've got so many famous people there, they ain't gonna give a fuck about someone like me, know what I mean? In London, I'd had paparazzi after me, and it really fucks you up. You feel trapped. In New York, I went to restaurants where De Niro was also dining, and it wasn't even a big deal. No one was making a big fuss about him, so you can feel a bit more normal. If no one's making a big deal about seeing De Niro, they ain't gonna give a shit about seeing me! Moving from England to New York, you're like a speck of dust. There's the film industry there, the music industry, so many well-known people, and you can slip in there easily without being noticed, which suited me just fine.

Having said that, I loved going out to all the bars and clubs, and one night I was in this exclusive little place and Ben Stiller came up to me and

said, 'I love your music, da-da-da, do you want to come and sit down?'
So I went and sat down with him in this quiet section upstairs, and he
was with this girl, and the girl kept staring at me – staring and staring and
staring. I was thinking, 'This guy has been nice enough to invite me to sit
down and to buy me a drink, and this girl is staring at me!' I said to her,
'What are you looking at?' Then Ben Stiller said to me, a bit angrily, 'Hey,
that's my sister!'

After that, our quiet drink together was obviously over. I actually ran
into him outside the gym not long afterwards, and I tried to apologise to
him, but he just kind of brushed me off.

I embraced the New York nightlife with open arms. All these little bars
and clubs, which were open much later than London in those days – I
went to them all. Anything that was going on, I knew about it. I loved
living in Manhattan; it was such a great 24-hour vibe. To be honest, it's
a bit too busy for me these days, too hectic and cramped – I like slower
places now, which is what happens as you get older.

After the first place on 34th Street, I lived in a series of other apartments
– always nice ones, and usually pretty mad. I had one on Christopher
Street in the West Village, which is a cool neighbourhood, and there was
another in the financial district around Wall Street. I think that was the
one that had an elevator which took you from street level straight up into
your own apartment. As facilities go, that was pretty cool, but I found I
couldn't sleep very well because of it. There was no way anyone could get
out on my floor without the key, but every time I heard the elevator, I
always thought on some instinctive level that they might do, so I found it
hard to sleep in there. You know it's not possible, but it's hard to get that
out of your mind.

When I was in New York, and not touring or recording, my daughter
Mazy would live with me part-time. It was always cool with Martina,
arranging care for Mazy after we were separated, and one or other of us
would bring her to or from the UK. She was only one or two when I first

went there, and at the beginning it wasn't too bad being in such a crazy city. We used to walk around Christopher Street in the summer, Mazy with just her nappy on and her little shoes.

A really weird thing happened in Christopher Street. I was walking along with Mazy – who was about two years old at the time – and she let go of my hand and ran ahead, and there was this old woman maybe five paces in front of us. Mazy toddled up to her and grabbed the woman's hand, and she picked Mazy up. Suddenly, the woman started crying – just crying her eyes out. I obviously thought it over many times afterwards: perhaps the woman was someone with no family, and maybe Mazy felt that somehow. Otherwise, I don't know why she would leave me and go and run and hold this woman's hand – an old stranger that she had never met, who then started sobbing like fuck. At the time, I didn't understand what was going on. I wish I'd kept in contact with that woman, and maybe I would have taken Mazy to keep seeing her.

Over time, I began to feel that taking Mazy to the park in Manhattan was just weird. There might be a dodgy guy sitting around, and there'd be cars everywhere, so eventually I came to thinking: New York is just not good for a young kid. But for the time being, I loved living there.

· ■ ■ ■ ■ ·

I really had no time to think about being a dad. There was no thinking; I just *was* a dad. It was all instinct, and right from the start Martina and I decided to have Mazy on tour with us. She went on to spend much of her life on tour. If it had just been me, Martina and Mazy in a shitty tour van, that might've been more challenging to pull off, but I had money, so I would pay for various family members to accompany us on the road, to help with childcare. Over the years, my cousins Michelle or Mark, my auntie Marlow and my half-brothers have joined us to fill that role. I always liked family being involved, so my family and I have travelled the world together. Having the money to do that made parenting easy for us.

Mazy was only a few months old when we went to Australia and New Zealand on this touring festival called the Big Day Out, taking in Sydney, Melbourne, the Gold Coast and Auckland. It's a weird festival, a bit like their Glastonbury, except it moves around. On that trip, we flew out Martina's mother, CC, with us as well. Sometimes later on we had a nanny, but the best nanny is the real nanny, right?

CC used to travel with us a lot. CC and Mazy's grandad Drayton are both really good people. Me and her have not got on sometimes – because she's Martina's mother. On one occasion I riled her so badly she nearly glassed me. But she is a great woman, and she really helped with bringing up Mazy. I'm sure she had better things to do than tour with us. She ain't a woman who likes going to shows; she was coming to help out with the kid, which is amazing. An amazing lady, who's scared of nothing. She's had a life: she certainly hasn't lived in an ivory tower, or grown up privileged, but by nature she's actually more chilled out than Martina.

On the Gold Coast, we also had Porno for Pyros helping us babysit. We took her to this amazing waterpark called Sea World – me, Perry Farrell and the rest of the band, while Martina and her mother went off somewhere else. It wasn't a conventional childhood, you might say. Nor was Perry, who used to be the decadent shamanic frontman of '80s funk-metallers Jane's Addiction, exactly a textbook childminder, but my kid had him under control. She was in the pram, and would point and wave him over, and he would go straight over to her. It was quite funny; she had him on lock!

Going to Sea World was crazy. We got the train to the outskirts of town, with all of their band, and thinking back now, that was kind of mad – me with a pram on the train, not like in a bloody limo or anything! – but how cool was that for them to do that? These are really solid blokes – they don't want to be in a bloody waterpark in Australia on a day off from doing shows. To me, that is amazing.

Who's that English guy who does all the politics stuff? Billy Bragg! He was on the tour, too, a very funny guy. Me and him went out into the audience to watch Porno for Pyros at one of the shows. I hung out with Billy quite a few times. He's like some guy who works in a factory, or one of your family – dead normal. Me and him would bump into each other and go and walk around in the crowd. We had performed there already, and people didn't have a clue who we were, or else they just left us alone.

Anyway, Perry came onstage and Pornos started a song, and the crowd went fucking mental. I leaned over to Billy Bragg and said, 'Fuck me, look at this, it's like he's Jesus!' And Billy goes, 'Or the devil.' I was thinking, 'Does he really mean that?' I see Perry Farrell and it's like he's touching people's souls, but then, is that always a good thing? Billy Bragg is an intelligent man, who doesn't seem the type to say something he didn't mean, or that didn't have some sort of truth to it. We didn't say anything after that. We just stood there and watched him. I was thinking, 'Jesus or the devil? Fucking hell!'

So maybe there was a darkness about Perry, but I can always forgive someone when they've got a talent like his. He could do anything, because he has touched people's souls. For me, that is a get-out clause – I don't see any darkness in him at all. Maybe he was a heroin addict, and that might influence some young kids to take heroin, but for me he will always have that get-out clause.

PERRY FARRELL: Before we met on the Big Day Out, I knew of Tricky obviously, being a passionate devourer of great music, and I was very anxious to make his acquaintance out there. It was a classic Big Day Out, in that it had Tricky, Porno for Pyros, Nick Cave and Rage Against the Machine on the bill, amongst others. There was also those girls from Britain, Elastica. I was kind of in love with the guitar player, Donna. Everybody was! All the guys on the festival were kind of elephant-sealing around this girl – whenever she was around, they'd be lowing, like 'Uuuurrrgh!' and chasing each other away from her.

My guitar player in Porno, Peter DiStefano, is a zany practical joker. He's a California kid, but he's got touches of being Sicilian, with a little twinge of the Mafia, and they have these certain provocative manners and deliveries. So Tricky gets on this big bus that collects us all from the airport, and we get to meet each other for the first time. I go, 'Hey, Peter, this is the guy I've been telling you about – the guy from Bristol with that amazing album!' and Pete stands up and goes, 'Hey, Tricksy! Nice to meet you, Tricksy!'

Tricky goes, 'My name's Tricky!' But Pete goes on with it, calling him Tricksy, and he gave Pete a look like this was gonna be a problem. It got a little tense, but all of a sudden they gave each other a big hug, and basically Pete kept calling him Tricksy for the entire tour, but Tricky would let it go each time, because you could see he had a good heart.

He was travelling with an enormous martial arts instructor, and every morning we would see him doing a workout. I would say to Peter, 'You better quit calling him Tricksy, man, because he looks like he's about ready to kick your ass!' He'd be out there, shirtless, his body glistening and gleaming in the hot sun of Australia, throwing these combinations. He was real serious about it.

We loved his music, and it turns out he admired our music, too. His voice almost didn't match his body, how deep it was, way down there. His whole vibe called up Miles Davis to me. He invited us to a studio on a day off – 'Come on, we've gotta make some music together!' – and he had Pete recording guitar for him, line after line, doing thirty different takes, but we never heard any more about it. Whatever happened to that session? Didn't he like the music? Or maybe that was his way of paying Pete back for 'Tricksy' – making him work his ass off all day in the studio!

We had that great day at the waterpark, too: we walked around with a pram and I don't remember anything really bad happening to the baby, so I think we pulled it off. Martina, the mother of his child, was on that tour as well, and when Porno got back to the States, she sang backup with us, and we got to know her, and she is just a lovely, lovely person, too.

TRICKY: When I'm off tour, I don't hang out with other musicians. At home, I don't really hang out with anybody. My family call me a loner. I'm 95 per cent by myself. I see people when I tour. There are some musicians I get on with great, like Terry Hall, or Perry Farrell, or Maynard James Keenan from Tool, but a lot of musicians don't like me. On tour, I might get pissed up, and then have a joke with someone, and they'll take it the wrong way.

As you've probably twigged by now, I don't do the popstar thing. I ain't gonna hang out with you *like* a popstar. I'm quite fish and chips. Because I don't play that game, there are musicians who have got love for me, and others who I know hate me. Which is okay, I don't mind.

Our family say anything to each other; there's no boundaries. If you grow up and you've got your uncle saying you are a 'breed', I suppose that has an effect on how you communicate in later life. I think that's why some people don't like me, because I'll have a few drinks and sometimes I'll say something to someone, and I don't mean it in any way badly – because I've got a good heart really, and I don't want people to dislike me. But I might say something to a famous person, and you're not supposed to talk to them like that – you're supposed to respect them, and their celebrity, and I don't know about that stuff. Treating people with kid gloves, pampering them – I don't really do that.

Prince was one of them. He didn't like me, because I didn't go to his studio, but his engineer told me he used to soundcheck to my music all the time. He invited me to Paisley Park, but on the appointed day I had the flu and I couldn't go, and ever since then he didn't like me. One time, my name came up in an interview, and he claimed not to know who I was. If you soundcheck or get your studio ready to my music, then obviously you're a fan, and know who I am. Obviously his ego was bruised because I didn't go up there.

There was a similar thing with Madonna. She turned up in the lobby of my hotel in New York, and I had the worst hangover. She was with a film director – I can't remember which one – but I'd fallen asleep, and this director guy called up to my room, and I said, 'Mate, I can't now,' and I put the phone down. I was just fucked, so I didn't go and meet her, so that one was over and done with as well. It was a nice hotel, because in those days I was living large. They waited for ten minutes to see if I would materialise, but I'd just gone straight back to sleep again, so they must've fucked off after that.

I can't say whether I would have worked with her or not. Thinking about it after I'd woken up again, it was like, what could I have done for her? Madonna needs to get in the charts, right? I thought, 'What could I do for you? I could help you *not* get in the charts!' So I didn't follow it up.

Before I actually moved to New York, I used to stay in this really high-class hotel there called the Royalton, and I'd always bump into big stars who were staying there too. Bryan Adams was as funny as fuck. You know, I'm meant to be this street guy, who makes all this dark music, da-da-da, and Bryan Adams is supposed to be the corny one, right? Me and him are standing in the lift, and this old lady was hobbling up, just as the doors were closing, so he shouts at her, 'FUCK OFF!' pressing the 'close doors' button. As the doors shut on her, he laughed. Then he looked at me and went nonchalantly, 'Alright, Tricky, mate?'

I was just, like, open-mouthed. They used to call me the Prince of Darkness – I suppose that was because I'm black – but I was thinking, 'Who the fuck is the Prince of Darkness here in this lift?' It was a big shock, too, hearing someone like him say, 'Alright, Tricky, mate?'

I got the same thing off that legendary guitarist with the glasses – Eric Clapton. He said that to me once. I was out somewhere, and it really weirded me out. And the Rolling Stones guy, Mick Jagger! I was in this little party – there was hardly anyone there; maybe just ten people in someone's house in London, and Jagger walked over and said, 'Oh, hi, Tricky, alright?' You know, that's *Mick Jagger* saying hello to me. I'm from Knowle West, a tiny little council estate in Bristol, so how the fuck does Mick Jagger …

Some people might think that's an opportunity to hustle, but I was too busy thinking about it to work it. I was just like, 'Wow, that's weird.' These days, now I'm a bit wiser, maybe I would've thought, 'Ah, you know what, that's a hook-up. Let's do a song.' If I met Mick Jagger now, I would probably try and hustle: 'Hey, let's go in the studio!'

How does Mick Jagger know who I am? He's really small and he had leggings on, and he comes over and goes, 'Alright, Tricky?' It was bizarre.

· ▪ ▪ ▪ ▪ ▪ ·

Pre-Millennium Tension, the album Island were billing as my proper follow-up to *Maxinquaye*, was recorded in March–April '96, mostly at Grove Studios in Ocho Rios, a tropical resort on the north coast of Jamaica. One track was made back in New York, and we did the mixing in the summer somewhere in Spain, if I remember correctly, but the main sessions were for six weeks in Jamaica, and again I took Mazy along, which seemed natural to me. It was me, Mazy, CC, and an engineer from England called Ian Caple. We'd record at night, then I'd hang out by the sea with Mazy in the daytime.

Jamaica was great but it gets boring after a while. You get island fever if you spend too much time there, and you need to get out of there. Two weeks would probably have been enough for me. Six weeks in Jamaica is a long time, and after that I was like, 'Yeah, I'm done with this now.'

What I really loved was the food. Jamaican food is my favourite; it's the best food on the planet. Over there, you can get good food on the street, guys cook it up by the roadside. This guy called Sky used to cook up fish and rice on the street in Ocho Rios, and I would eat there every day, standing up on the street. He also had a little griddle for cooking chicken, and he'd sell sweets and stuff as well. It was just easy to eat on the go with him while I was walking around, so I would always stop by and eat there. I started talking to him, and eventually it was like, 'Come down to the studio!' I put him on the mic, and he just started talking off the top of his head about the realities of life in JA. He was just totally off on one, and that became the track 'Ghetto Youth' on the record – him chatting for six minutes halfway through the album.

I just did whatever I wanted, and again, Island were cool with that. You need that with artists, otherwise artists ain't gonna grow if you don't let them do whatever they want to do. If you can't take risks, and maybe make mistakes, you can't learn and adjust from those mistakes. That track might have been seen as a mistake, back then, and not a commercial vehicle, but Island stuck by my right to make it.

While I was in Ocho Rios, I heard from Chris Blackwell, who owns property and hotels on the island, that Bono from U2 wanted to hook up with me there. So I had a meeting with Bono and Chris in Ocho Rios, and he basically wanted me to produce their album, *Pop*. I was never a U2 fan, but there were tracks off *The Joshua Tree* which I thought were really great songs.

Bono played me the demos, and it was a really awkward situation.

'Look,' I said, 'you've got a great drummer there, and a great bass player, and some really great songs. I think this stuff is as good as *The Joshua Tree*, and it doesn't need anything doing to it.'

'No,' Bono grinned from behind his shades, 'but we want some more modern beats on it.'

'Mate, what can I do? All you've gotta do is mix it. You want me to put all this shit over it, and you're going to ruin it.'

And that's exactly what happened – they ruined it. I turned it down, because the demos were so good, I didn't see how I could help them, or make it any better than it was, so they got other people to do it instead.

I don't know if Bono thought I simply didn't want to do it, but it was nothing like that. I would have loved to. But I couldn't do anything to it. If I'd heard the demos, and felt I could make it sound better, I'd have done it, because it would have been fun, and I could have done it anywhere in the world I wanted to – Jamaica, fucking Miami, anywhere – because their budget is huge. I could have lived large for two months, and it would've been a great experience. I could've hired in any session musician, or even the London Philharmonic Orchestra, if I wanted. I definitely would've done it if I could have done something, but there was nothing I could do.

They should put out the demos they played me, but the version of *Pop* they released was unrecognisable from that. I was shocked by what I heard. I guess what I was supposed to do was just take the money, and the money would have been ridiculous. It would have been so easy, but I would have felt like a dick doing it. If I'd known then what I know now, maybe I would've done it, and I would be a multimillionaire still to this day. But money ain't my thing.

They weren't looking for better, they were 'chasing new', following fashion – 'Tricky, he's the man of the moment, da-da-da.' I could have done any old shit, and they would have liked it. Some artists want to be 'now', instead of just making a good album. If you want to be 'now', you're finished – that's when you become the past.

As Island prepared my own album for release, I began to see how cool they were as a label. I delivered the music, and then Julian Palmer helped me to sequence it as an album again, and to choose the singles. It was his idea to put out 'Tricky Kid' as a single. I didn't give a fuck what the single was: I had done the album. I'm just happy with the music I've made. I'm an artist – but I wouldn't have chosen that one, it seemed too crazy to me. Julian was like, 'That's the single!' 'Really?!'

That wasn't what you'd call traditional A&R, which is usually all about the charts, and radio, and trying to get the most out of an artist sales-wise – but 'Tricky Kid' was never getting on the radio. That is the weirdest fucking piece of music – what A&R guy would say, 'Release that as a single'? It was more than taking risks – Julian was a visionary. He was quite punk rock – not as in the genre of music, more the attitude. I remember calling him about something around that time, and he said, 'You're Tricky – you can do anything you want!' He always put that in my head, fuelled me with that idea that there were absolutely no limits to what I could do. Would a corporate company allow any of that nowadays? I doubt it.

When *Pre-Millennium Tension* came out, quite a lot of reviewers slated it for being too dark and claustrophobic, but now a lot of my fans prefer it to *Maxinquaye*. I've got kids who bring it to my shows, who weren't born when it came out, saying that it saved their life: 'I had depression, everything was going wrong, and that album got me through it!' Maybe it was just ahead of its time.

JULIAN PALMER: The only way to really shake the beast is to get in amongst it, so I thought it was a great idea for him to go to New York and become the *cause célèbre* there, that it would help the Americans understand who he was, but for him it was just an escape. London music gets very claustrophobic, and he needed to get away, a change of scenery. Tricky has always needed to move, from one tiny space to another, and never even contemplating making it feel like home by putting pictures up or whatever. He always lived a transient lifestyle.

Pre-Millennium Tension was absolute genius. It didn't matter where he was in the world – Jamaica, New York, wherever – it was him and his headphones in a little room. The music was always so deeply personal, and nothing really changed in that regard. He wasn't making polished American records, and he wasn't collaborating with Jamaican reggae artists – he was just Tricky.

Pre-Millennium was the last thing I did with him, and the pressures to deliver hits weren't there because he had sold a lot of records on *Maxinquaye* without having a hit single in the traditional sense. This time, 'Christiansands' was actually reasonably placed in the singles chart, but it wasn't about that. It was there to announce that Tricky had another body of work out.

'Tricky Kid' was just the business, though, wasn't it? I thought it was like an anthem; it was who he was. There was a little dig at Goldie in there, who was now dating Björk – 'the king of jungle, used to be humble'. I never thought it was a radio record, just one that you think people will connect with. It's the most basic and simplistic side of what he did, the hookiest side, but menacing!

With Martina, it was heading to a place where it couldn't survive – it had got too fractious, but then 'Makes Me Wanna Die' was so beautiful, and a large part of that was down to her, so the album had those moments, too.

His whole life went into *Maxinquaye*, and everything that followed on the second record had to be the journey he went on after that one had been successful – all the parties and the drugs and the self-loathing. Even though it didn't do as well in the UK, I thought it was the perfect follow-up. It might well have done a little bit better in America, with the US hip-hop samples, and of course it always takes two or three albums to get anywhere there.

Through him being the darling of the indie alternative media in the UK, he was always gonna be the darling of New York, LA, Miami and Chicago as well. That is the one thing about America: you may not hit the Midwest *ever*, but you are certainly going to be the go-to gig when you turn up in those places, and that certainly came to pass. His life got very rock 'n' roll.

I personally enjoyed the celebrity he had acquired. We certainly weren't doing it for him to become a celebrity of any sort, and *he* certainly wasn't, but that's what he had become, and all the right people wanted to know him, so we enjoyed ourselves a little bit too much. I certainly did – so much that I went off the rails and ended up in rehab, and left Island.

I was let go, because Polygram's corporate mindset was gradually taking over as Blackwell drifted out of the picture. Island was one of the last bastions of independence, but it couldn't last forever. U2 was becoming too big a thing to progress further without the might of a corporation behind it globally. Politically I was too much Blackwell's boy, and too mad, bad and dangerous to know. There was a night of the long knives, and I was one of the first people whom the accountants and lawyers muscled out.

God knows what dark spaces Tricky ended up inhabiting, but the mid-90s were a bit like that anyway. It was like one non-stop party. I don't regret any of it, I'm just glad that I experienced it. It almost felt as if we kind of had an obligation to go as far as we could in every single way.

He was working on a lot of the ideas for the next album while we were still together, and I got a name-check on this track, 'Demise': 'we'll disarm ya, ask Julian Palmer'. I'd said to him, 'Just keep the fuckers out, and don't let anybody stand in your way!' He had earned himself the right to have that autonomy as an artist, so that's what that lyric was saying, but by then it was very much fingers-in-the-air time, and I was on my bike.

TRICKY: Any time I was at home in New York, I'd be out at hip-hop clubs, living the way I'd always kind of dreamed of. Before Jay-Z was huge I used to see him in clubs. Even better, Puffy Combs was one of the first people over there to big up my name. We're not friends or anything, but he was one of the first people who was like, 'I want this guy to do a remix!' You can see why he did well in music: he's not a producer as such; he just had his ear to the ground.

Ghetto guys in America don't see Puffy as any kind of hip-hop bad boy. He is a powerful guy – so powerful that the FBI wanted to shut him down at one time. When you've got money, you can make things happen in America. So you could really say Puffy is just as gangsta as Suge Knight from Death Row Records – he just does his gangsta a bit different, because I know for a fact that Puffy could shut you down. He can blackball you. Puffy could say to certain radio stations, 'Don't play so-and-so,' and you mysteriously won't get played. Powerful guy.

So Puffy had me doing a remix of The Notorious B.I.G.'s 'Hypnotize', when no one over there knew me. It was just after Biggie had died, and I was doing it in one of the well-known hip-hop studios. All these young hip-hop guys were looking through the door, because Biggie had just been killed and yet they were hearing his voice.

Before I'd even moved to New York I'd done a few tracks for an EP with RZA, the producer behind the Wu-Tang Clan, along with this rap crew called Gravediggaz. Someone at Island had told me that he wasn't too keen on working with me initially because he'd seen me wearing a dress on the cover of *Maxinquaye*. I suppose he thought that wasn't right for a rapper, but then we did the EP together and he was totally cool. We did three or four tracks in one night, and there was no problem whatsoever.

Amani Vance is someone who was with me through all my time in New York. We were together for a few years there, and even lived together for a while, and I still talk to her all the time. She often used to babysit for Mazy, and she knows Chris Blackwell really well. I first met her while she was working at Island's New York office, where I used to go for meetings when I first went to the US to do promo and live shows. She is also the first person who got me weed in New York – she took me to Washington Park and we scored there.

Amani's dad, Jim Vance, was very famous as one of the first black newsreaders on prime-time TV in America. She grew up in Washington DC around a guy called Rayful Edmond, one of the biggest drug dealers in America, and his enforcer guy, Wayne Perry, who killed 500 people. But she's got her own interesting story, coming from Washington DC.

She's black American, through and through. Black America was certainly never my biggest market, but she is a black American who knows and understands my music. The fact that she, from her part of the world, knows me, from Knowle West, strikes me as pretty insane. I don't think there are many guys from Knowle West who would know somebody from Washington DC!

AMANI VANCE: My dad was a big-time TV news journalist for NBC here in the States, based in DC, which, as the nation's capital, is obviously the number-one news market. He wasn't the very first black TV journalist ever, but he was definitely one of the first and one of the biggest. He was known for being very honest: In the '80s, he had a really bad cocaine problem, and he announced it on air when he went into Betty Ford, which was a really big deal in the media. His ratings always surpassed CNN and all the others for his timeslot, and even though he revealed his own vulnerabilities, like his depression in later years, these things actually only seemed to spice up his popularity and make people love him more.

When he died a couple of years ago, he was the number-one trending story on Twitter for that day, and his obituary was on the front page of the *Washington Post*. His memorial service was held at the National Cathedral where Bush and McCain were recently buried – you have to be invited to have your memorial there. I can't possibly say how many times I've had brothers come up to me and say, 'Your dad showed me that you can fall down and get back up' – how many people he influenced as a black role model.

I grew up in the area of DC where Rayful Edmond was the big-time gangster. In the '80s and early '90s, DC was the murder capital of North America, and Rayful Edmond was the number-one gangster in town. Rayful had a lot of sides to him. He himself was not a killer. He was just a drug dealer, but there would be other dudes like Wayne 'Silk' Perry who did all the killing in DC. A lot of the characters in that TV series, *The Wire*, are based on real-life DC characters transposed to Baltimore, which is only an hour away from DC anyway.

It was the crack era, and the coke era, all that shit coming up from Colombia. Everyone in America had been doing coke, and then crack became the cheaper way, so it became huge and blew up in the poor communities and the black communities, because it cost a hundred dollars to buy a gram of cocaine, but five dollars to buy a hit of crack. DC became a major hub, and my theory is that it was because DC was America's only majority black city.

Rayful Edmond came to my house a couple of times, and he was a really nice guy – cultured and smart. He just happened to grow up where his grandmother and his parents and everyone in his family were in the drugs business. If he had grown up in a family that was like the Murdoch family, he'd be running a Fortune 500 company right now, because he was just a brilliant dude, and there are all these studies now about how he accomplished what he accomplished at such a high level.

Rayful was friends with my first ever boyfriend at high school, Matt, who was a white Italian-American dude who was always in the mix of things. He wasn't a drug dealer himself, but he was really turned on by the life. He worked for his family's construction business, but somehow worked his way into black city life. His family was generations-old DC too, but not rich DC. His family had moved to the suburbs in the '70s, but he just managed somehow to become friends with these dudes. He didn't do drugs, he didn't sell drugs, but somehow he made his way into the world.

Because my dad was a big deal in DC, Matt somehow mentioned to Rayful, like, 'Oh, I'm dating Jim Vance's daughter,' and then Rayful really wanted to meet him, because he was a smart guy – not like a dumb street guy. They met a couple of times, and he was so cool – a really good guy.

After high school, I came to New York to go to Parsons School of Design in Greenwich Village. It's really funny how I got close to Island Records: in my last year at Parsons in '93, this friendly weed dealer I knew called Max used to deliver to this woman Trish, who was high up at Island. I lived right down the street from Island, when the offices were on Lafayette, on this long block between West 4th and West 8th. I lived on 4th Avenue between 9th and 10th. One day this dealer guy was like, 'Can you do me a favour and drop off this bundle to Trish at Island, because it's near your house?' Because I was getting something for myself, I was like, 'Yeah, no problem.'

I walked into the offices for the first time, and I thought, 'Oh my God, I want to work here.' It was just so fly, with wooden walls, exposed brick, and palm trees everywhere – super-funky! Chris Blackwell's wife, Mary, had designed it all, with African fabric all over, so it looked like Goldeneye, or one of his properties.

From there, I talked myself into an internship with Trish, and because I'd gone to Parsons, a fashion school, Trish introduced me to Mary, Chris's wife, who had her Island Trading Company. I interviewed with Mary and Chris and landed my first job out of college there, because I just hit it off with them both. After a while, though, I was not loving the fashion side, so then I talked to Chris and was like, 'Is there any way I can move to the music side?'

So, I was working quite low down in marketing at Island in New York when Tricky was first signed for *Maxinquaye*, and Island was releasing the album in the US. I wasn't actually working the album, but by the time Tricky came to New York for promotion, Polygram/Def Jam had moved the label offices to this hideous corporate block at 825 8th Avenue, and the whole vibe had changed.

I met Tricky briefly there, and to be very honest I totally went after him. I found out where he was staying, and called him there, like, 'Do you want me to take you out around the city?' He thought I had been assigned to take him out on the town on Island's behalf. I got his hotel details through the people I worked with, so it was kind of true, but kind of not – maybe they didn't know quite why I was so keen to do it!

We immediately clicked. He got me right away, and vice versa, and we hung out the whole time for the week he was in New York. After he went back to London we stayed in touch, and then he moved here – right near Penn Station. It was a cool-ass apartment, like a duplex, but it's a weird neighbourhood.

He was kind of burnt by London, and he wanted to experience a new city. Back then New York really was an amazing place, especially if you'd grown up with New York hip-hop. You could drink up till 3am in regular clubs, but then after-hours clubs were everywhere. The all-nighter lifestyle and New York went hand-in-hand. Tricky probably even caught the tail-end of bottle service at tables, which was a big part of New York's original flavour in clubs.

He embraced New York like a duck to water – he went ape-shit wild. It was a lot of clubbing, always hip-hop. We just used to go out dancing. He loved to dance. He can really go and get lost in a club. If he wasn't dancing, he would be leaning against the wall kind of ingesting the music, really in another world, listening to the beats.

For a while, he was hanging out hard with Gang Starr, and they were tearing up the town, getting kicked out of places left and right. He and I lived together for a while at my place on 4th Avenue between 9th and 10th, a block from Astor Place, which is a great neighbourhood. Eventually Tricky moved out and got his own place in this building called the Archive, on Greenwich Avenue between Faro and Cristobel, but we were still very much in touch.

After *Pre-Millennium Tension* came out, he got offered a deal to start his own label through DreamWorks, not for his own music, but to sign other artists. DreamWorks had just been formed by Steven Spielberg, David Geffen and Jeffrey Katzenberg (a Walt Disney exec), and this guy Michael Goldstone was one of the first principals they hired. He was a big-time A&R guy, who'd signed Rage Against the Machine and Pearl Jam. It was him who offered Tricky the label deal. Tricky accepted, called it Durban Poison, and asked me to be the head of it. By that point, Chris Blackwell had moved me to be in charge of Island's world music division, so I had experience, and said yes.

Goldstone was very much a rock guy, so that was probably the kind of music he was hoping for, but Tricky was really into his hip-hop at that moment, fresh in New York, so he started signing all these local rappers, plus his Bristol mate, DJ Milo. None of them really stuck, though. They were all talented, but maybe Tricky was just thinking about great music, not from a marketing perspective. I think that is always how he's done his music, which is a big part of his success, but then also part of the thing that has stopped him from being even more successful, because he doesn't make music for anyone but himself. He likes it, and that's all that matters to him, and he doesn't care about money, which I also really liked. But then, that's also a double-edged sword: he probably should've cared more, and made more.

DreamWorks got us incredible office space actually in the Brill Building in Midtown – this iconic building where people like Carole King, Phil Spector and Neil Diamond all worked as songwriters. They did really well by us, and they certainly paid me and Tricky well, but then they didn't like any of the bands that he was signing, and then it became a bit of a testing match between him and Michael Goldstone. He and Tricky were never gonna get along.

When DreamWorks moved out of the Brill Building into offices downtown, in the interim Durban Poison worked out of Tricky's apartment – this huge duplex in the Wall Street/Tribeca area where the elevator opened into the apartment, and we just made the offices on the second floor. When the DreamWorks deal went down, I decided to go to business school back in DC, but Durban Poison still went on in a different form.

Tricky and I remained super-close, long after we weren't dating or working together anymore.

BRITISH AIRWAYS

I didn't experience what I consider real racism until I had money. You'd think I would've felt it growing up as a black kid in a white ghetto. Obviously I've had police in Bristol calling me a black bastard and chasing me around, but that's just street stuff. That's almost like football fans – just part of the street life – just normal.

I can remember me and my uncle Tony getting followed around by police in a car, just because we were black. We would laugh about it, like, 'Oh, come on, why are you pulling us over? You're so obvious!'

I had the same nonsense in London: I was running for a bus in Notting Hill, and an undercover police car screeched up.

'Why are you running? Where do you live?'

'I'm not telling you where I live.'

'What are you doing here?'

'I'm doing here what I wanna do here. I don't have to tell you anything. What do you want? You ain't gonna search me. It's just because I'm running and I'm black.'

Another time when I was living in Kensington High Street, I've been pulled over and taken out of a car. They made me take my shoes and socks off and sit on the kerb, then they searched me – and ten minutes down the road, there was a massive billboard of me, and their kids are probably listening to my music. That was around the time when *Time Out* had me as Jesus. In America they wouldn't release those photos because I was black, but I didn't find that out till much later.

The first time I experienced racism properly was when I started flying First Class on aeroplanes. One time, I was boarding a transatlantic flight with British Airways, and when I got to the entrance where the hostess directs you to your row, I turned left to go into First Class, and the woman came after me.

'Excuse me, sir,' she firmly stated, 'you're going the wrong way – Economy's that way!'

'But I haven't got an Economy ticket,' I replied, showing her my boarding card. She obviously thought that being black I couldn't possibly have a First Class ticket. I flipped out so bad they fell over themselves apologising to me, and even gave me a bottle of champagne to try and make me forget about it.

The way I see it, I never experienced racism in the same way that other people might've. I've seen racism against white people, where I'd go to a club with my white friends, and we couldn't get in – not because I'm black, but because they could tell we were from Knowle West. Maybe that's given me a different outlook on things, but I always thought that racism didn't go beyond those street hassles. I didn't think it affected things like music, where you'd expect people to be more open-minded.

I remember a meeting at Island where Julian Palmer was trying to explain to me why I had singles in the charts, and my album was at No.3, but I wasn't getting airplay on Radio One. The reason he gave shocked the fuck out of me.

'How come bands who sound like me,' I asked him, 'who are ripping off my music, are getting on Radio One, and I'm not?'

'Because you're black, Tricky, and they're white!' Julian replied.

I was dumbfounded. That really was an education for me. I should know about racism: I'm a black guy who grew up in a white ghetto, but it takes a white guy from London who went to a good school to tell me about racism. How does that make sense? Shouldn't I be teaching *him* about racism? I would never have thought in a million years that radio aren't gonna play someone because they're black. If you'd told me that before, I would've said you were absolutely nuts. You see, with my mixed-race background, I just don't think like that – because I never saw race in that way before.

I didn't believe Julian at first, but these wake-up moments, when I was starting to have success in the world, were the first times I found out about institutionalised racism. When it comes to things like First Class in aeroplanes and radio airplay, you've grown up assuming that society is more decent than that, that radio wouldn't discriminate against a record because it was made by a black person. Because I was a street kid, I didn't think it went that high. I didn't think it was that institutionalised.

It's when people make assumptions about you that you see how deep the racism runs. I had a vintage Rolex, and the strap was a special custom-made design. I think the whole thing had cost $25,000 altogether. When I was back visiting London, I walked into a Rolex store, and a black girl who worked there was following me around the store, giving me dirty looks, with a vibe like, 'What do *you* want?' So a black guy can even get racism off a black girl. It was like, 'I've got twenty-five grand on my wrist, and I could drop another fifty right now if I wanted to!'

That's one thing about LA that I like. You can go to a shop in LA, a jewellery shop, and they won't even look twice, because people who look like me might easily drop sixty grand on a piece of jewellery. We have this race system and this class system in England, and they're kind of tangled up together. It's funny how it's black people as well as white people who perpetuate it. I've even had an Indian man follow me around a 7–11 store, but then he let a white guy, who equally might be stealing something, walk around unsupervised. I went to an Asian store near Island's office in Chiswick to buy a packet of fags, and was followed around the store – and my album was No.3 in the charts.

At Paddington station around that time, I went to get a taxi: I've gone to the first one and he's left, gone to the second one and he's left – the third one, he leaves. Fourth, fifth … It was like, 'I've got money now!' Before, me and Whitley couldn't afford a taxi. Now that I could afford a taxi, I couldn't fucking get one!

With taxis on High Street Kensington, I used to do these little experiments. If I had dark clothes on, the taxi would go past me. If I had a white windbreaker on with brown trousers, the taxi would stop for me. If I've got nothing in my hands, and I'm wearing dark clothes – no taxi. If I've got dark clothes on and I'm carrying five shopping bags from Selfridge's, one'll stop for me straight away. As soon as they see those expensive bags – bang! But dark clothes and a Tesco bag, they'll go straight past me.

It's racism, or prejudice, but it goes beyond the colour of your skin. It's a class system, too. And do you know what's mad? A taxi driver will get a bigger tip from me than any white guy in a suit. I'll go, keep the tenner, mate! Rich people ain't giving a tenner to a taxi driver – just two quid or something. Dark clothes, no chance. Selfridge's bags, no problem. It's mind-blowing, but what's even more mind-blowing is that I played games like that. Pretty fucking twisted, right?

It's different in America, where money talks and there's more affluent black people about. Over there you know when you're seeing pure racism, but it's not class-system racism. In some ways, I've been more offended in England then I have in America. You know, a black girl following me around a Rolex store … Not that black people ain't got money in England, but … I don't know, it's just a different thing. I can't remember ever getting followed around a store in America. I've had Korean guys be rude to me in New York, but not followed around in a store like in England. Or taxis just driving off.

Having said that, one time quite recently I was on tour with my band and we were staying in this hotel in America, and I'm paying for everybody to stay in there – my band, my tour manager, everyone. I came down in the elevator and they were all sat there in the restaurant, and I go over and chat for a bit and then head off up to my room. A black waiter then went over to them and said, 'Who is that guy? Is he staying here? Is he bothering you?' He's a black guy, and I'm a black guy, and I'm staying there, and paying for seven people.

I think in America it's about cash, and if you look like you can afford to pay for stuff. In New York, I was walking past this really posh shop, and this African beaded chair caught my eye. I walked inside, and this white woman gave me a really dirty look through her spectacles, as if to say, 'You can't afford anything in here, are you thinking of robbing it?' I said to her, 'How much is that?' She goes, 'Five thousand dollars.' I go, 'I'll take it!'

I suppose we're all prejudiced in some way, whether you're black, white, Asian … I bought that chair just to show her that I could. I dropped five grand there and then, and she couldn't believe it. And when I gave her my address for it to be delivered, she couldn't believe that either.

And this chair for five grand – it has never been sat in. It's still in storage somewhere in New York, I think. I've never sat in it, no one has. It's just there.

CHAPTER ELEVEN
SPEAKING IN TONGUES

I don't have a fear of death. I'm not scared of stuff like that, because if you don't accept death, then you never accept life. Obviously I don't want to die, but I know it's coming, so I ain't scared of it. I've nearly died a couple of times from asthma attacks, like when I had the electrodes on my chest and the aliens came. Before I passed out it was scary, but once I went, I didn't feel nothing – no fear, no anything. Then I saw the lights on the ambulance that I thought was a spaceship. It's probably scary when you *are* going for real, but once you have stepped over, there ain't no fear then. That time, I guess I never actually stepped over. Nearly but not quite.

In New York, I had another near-death experience: I had someone put a gun in my face. First of all, it was a shock, then when you realise you have no control over it, it's like being so scared of something that your body shuts down and you just don't give a fuck anymore. The fear grips you so much, it starts affecting you physically, and then your body just says, 'Fuck it!'

This happened in the early hours of the morning at the Bowery Bar, after I'd just played a big sold-out show at the Irving Plaza in '97. I was with Amani, and her female friend Lee; a guy from Bristol called Andy Whittle who was my tour manager; this creative director called Earle Sebastian; and the owner of the bar, Serge Becker, who later became a well-known restaurateur. Serge had kept the bar open for us, so we were the only people in there at maybe two or three in the morning when these four guys came in and tried to rob it.

We were sitting in one of the round-tabled booths. There were people on my left and people on my right. They were all talking and laughing and drinking shots of whisky or tequila, and I was in the middle, rolling a spliff, not really listening. Then I looked up, and not far in front of us there was a guy with a balaclava on, waving a gun. There was another guy across the room, but nobody else had noticed them. I saw what was going on, and I carried on making the spliff. I didn't want to tell my friends, like, 'Oh, we've got guys pointing guns at us,' because I didn't really want to say anything. It was just, 'They ain't noticed it yet!' They were in their own world.

Then, one of them noticed, and one of the balaclava guys pulled the round table out and said, 'Get on the floor! Under the table!' I was laughing at him, like I thought it was a prank that maybe Serge had put on for us. One of the girls went down and then came back up again, and they threw some drink in her face. They beat up the owner and kicked him a few times in the head. Andy, who was sat next to me, went under the table, and Amani went under the table, but I didn't want to, because then I wouldn't be able to see anything.

I pretended like I didn't understand what the guy was talking about.

'Get under the table!'

'What do you mean?'

'Get – under – the – table!'

'Why? What's going on?'

Then, it was mad – the guy touched me, really nice. He had roughed up a couple of the other people and was aggressive towards them, but he put the gun in my face, and put his hand on my shoulder really nicely, and just slid me down. From that, I realised that he didn't want to kill me. He was there for the money. I remember the gun had a stag, or a horse, on the butt. He slid me down really slow, and then they went off to get the money. Apparently the other two guys were trying to get Serge to open the safe, and he was like, 'I don't know the combo!' so they found a bar manager who was still there out the back, and he opened the safe.

Talking about it afterwards, we reckoned it was an inside job, because they knew who Serge was, to ask him to open the safe, but I don't think they got much, because their timing was wrong – the till had already been emptied.

What interested me was that a couple of the guys were really traumatised, whereas the girls handled it better. Earle, the director, had problems – he wasn't very well – and one of the other guys, he doesn't really want to talk about it. People will stereotype, but the women weren't affected as badly. Everyone was scared at the time, but I talked to the two girls about it when I was in New York, and Amani was even laughing about it. The guys were not the same.

I would say that women are stronger than men. A man gets sent off to war, and they're all shooting each other across the field or whatever, but the woman is usually at home looking after the kids, watching them starve. I'd say the women have the worse job, having to listen to their kid cry because it's hungry. That would be scarier to me. I'm a dad myself, and hearing your baby cry is one of the worst things you can experience. You will have issues about that. So I'd say women have to be tougher.

When you watch two men fight, even though it'll be fairly vicious, they'll still want to look good. When two women fight, there's no looking good about it, it's as vicious as fuck! Because they ain't got the ego that men have. A man don't wanna lose a fight, not just because he doesn't want to get hurt – it's because he doesn't want to be embarrassed and have his ego dented. When two women fight, they don't give a fuck about any of that. It's not an ego thing, it's a rival thing, and they go at it, no holding back.

It's hard for me not to see women as tough, because I've seen women in my family have actual fistfights. But not many women become all-out gangsters, which is interesting. I think it's to do with men having more ego and women being more down-to-earth. And they are usually the ones taking care of the children. You can't be a full-time criminal and totally take care of your kid. Women are just more realistic.

· ▪ ■ ■ ■ ▪ ·

After I'd been in New York about a year and a half, I was having a look around the Bronx, when I started talking to this Jamaican guy on the street, called Rick, an immigration lawyer by trade. I asked him, 'Where can I get Jamaican food?' He took me to this place, and there I met a bunch of guys who became firm friends. I'd go there now and again to have a smoke and listen to music.

Coincidentally, my dad's younger brother was living in exactly the same area, and I got to meet him all because of that. He'd never been to London; he'd gone straight from Jamaica to New York. I learnt also that my dad's other brother lives in Miami, because there's a big Jamaican community there, too.

On one of my American tours after that, I brought my dad over for a few dates, and at the end he came and stayed with me in New York for a while. I would get him a car to see his brother for a couple of days, then he would come back and his brother would come up to my house with his sons. I'm sure he must have liked that.

These Jamaican guys from the Bronx that I started hanging around with were all very naughty boys. At the time, I thought they were just regular Jamaican G's, street guys, but I later found out from Rick that they were a bit more serious than that. They all had motorbikes, cars, guns, money – you knew something was going on. But in the few years we were knocking about, I never knew the full extent.

The positive thing about it for me was that I was hanging out with people who were not involved in the music industry. It was like I was slotting back into life as I used to live it. We were going to reggae nights together and I slotted back into a thing where people wouldn't recognise me. There used to be about twenty of us sometimes, and I was just one of those people. I was definitely on the run from celebrity, and from Bristol. It was almost like I was running away from the success, and Bristol was a part of that success. It was just getting away from everything.

For all that, after a while it was getting to the point where I was feeling I had to get out of Manhattan. I wanted to get away from the city, mainly for my daughter Mazy. Being in the middle of Manhattan with a kid is too difficult. Going to a play area is just chaos there, with millions of cars everywhere, which is always stressful for a dad. Just walking around in Manhattan with a two- or three-year-old kid was horrendous. It was traumatising; you're worried all the time.

I decided to move right out to rural New Jersey, and bought a four-bedroom house with two acres of land in this wooded area in Llewellyn Park, NJ. It was absolutely fucking beautiful out there, with deer everywhere that roamed into the garden after dark. In the summer, you could sit outside and the deer would come up, almost right in front of you.

At night, it was as dark as fuck. You couldn't see anything. There were no proper streetlights, just a few lamps around the property. There really was nothing there, apart from these houses every couple of miles. Mine was like one of those old colonial country houses made out of wood.

It was a totally different pace of life, and I was sort of ready for it, sort of not. I moved there for Mazy, and once she was going to reception class in school in England, she would come over mostly in the school holidays. It was lovely for her out there: she could run around to her heart's content, and I didn't have to worry about cars or anything, so I found it much more relaxing being with her there.

During term time I still went into Manhattan, because even though it was such a totally remote environment, you could be in the heart of the action in forty minutes, if the traffic wasn't too bad. So I would go out partying quite regularly when Mazy wasn't there. I also built a recording studio in there, so I was making music the whole time.

I liked it when my family were there – Mazy, and sometimes Martina and CC would come out and stay for the school vacation. During those times, it was amazing. But when I was on my own in a four-bedroom house with two acres of land around, and it took twenty minutes to get to any local shops to get coffee – and I still didn't drive – well, then I didn't enjoy it so much.

To beat the isolation, I was driving into Manhattan more and more often, and running up a considerable tab with a car service in the process. It's different from an actual chauffeur that you employ, you just make bookings when you need them, but you have to be careful to remember when you've booked them. I would have the driver take me out to a club, wait outside the club, and then take me all the way back to New Jersey. If I had to do something back there the next morning, the driver would come in and sleep on the couch, I would go to bed, and then the following day he would take me into Manhattan again.

Other times, we'd drive into town on a Friday or Saturday night, then I'd leave the club completely forgetting the driver was outside somewhere, party for a couple of days, only to be reminded of my existing car-service booking when I called them to drive me home again on Sunday or Monday. How we wasted money, pre-mobile phones!

Once you start relying on a car service, your bill can mount up. By the time I moved from New Jersey, I was spending $200,000 a year on it.

That probably sounds outrageous in today's world, but in the mid-90s, there was so much money around, it didn't seem to matter. Back then, I could get paid fifty grand just to do a remix. On my 28th birthday, I did two remixes on the same day, one for Stevie Wonder and the other for Yoko Ono. I can't remember which way round it was, but I got forty grand for one of them and fifty grand for the other. It was my birthday, and my cousin Mark was in town, so I didn't want to hang around: I took some of Stevie Wonder's music and put it under Yoko's voice, and put some of Yoko's music under Stevie Wonder – a few hours' work, job done! Then we went clubbing in the West End and got fucked up on the proceeds.

Ninety grand in one day – you really could make that kind of cash. I was earning *so much money*. In that period, I must've been through five million, easy. On one of the American tours, I got the flu, and by the time we got to New York, we were staying in this really top hotel, the Four Seasons, and I couldn't go on. I called Julian Palmer back in England and said, 'I'm sick, I can't move!' He just said, 'Stay in the hotel then!' I was there for a couple of weeks, and at their prices it ended up costing $20,000. Twenty grand because I had the flu!

Julian Palmer must have spent a lot of industry money, and so must I! If I was in a hotel and it ended up costing twenty grand, it wouldn't even enter my mind to consider who was paying the bill. It just would get sorted somehow.

I spent a lot of my own money, too. I would spend thirty grand in a club, no problem. I'd drop twenty grand here, twenty grand there. I would charter planes to go from New York to Miami and back again, then oversleep and not go, so twenty-five grand went for nothing. I could spend 200 grand, and literally make it back in a weekend. Oops, I spent 200 grand on a car service – never mind!

There was so much money around, and everybody spent it. In the music business, nobody thought twice about it. There was no saving or financial strategy going on whatsoever. It wasn't because you didn't have good people around you; it was just there was so much money, people didn't think like that. Nobody thought it would ever end. It wasn't like I didn't have good advisers. I had good managers, good accountants. There was so much money, it was like nobody *needed* to advise you.

．■ ■ ■ ■ ．

Many people have said, then and now, that my live shows got more and more challenging in the late '90s. It would be dark onstage, and we definitely weren't 'playing the hits'. I've toured with bands where they do the same songs every night, and it's the most boring fucking thing. I think live is where you can experiment. It turns into something else, and you've got to follow your instincts.

Sometimes I feel uncomfortable onstage, but it's either feel uncomfortable, or do what everybody expects and be safe and bored as fuck – because then it's a routine: come out, do this, do that, boring. I don't want to be doing the same fucking show every night, with people clapping at the right parts.

When people see my show, especially back then, they say, 'It's crazy energy – what is that? Is it anger?' My answer is, it's anger, because I'm so shy. I want to give a hundred per cent, but I can't sing and I can't dance. People don't think artists are shy, they would never consider a musician or an actor to be shy, but I'm really a shy person.

When someone comes to see your show – not a critic thing, I'm talking when someone will spend their time and money to come and see you – you owe them a hundred per cent of your soul, and I feel like I can't do that, because I'm shy, and because I can't sing. So that is a rage people are seeing – me trying to give everything.

After several years on the road, the show was getting more and more intense, and so was life behind the scenes, especially with Martina. It was a long time since we'd been a couple – we would travel as mum and dad, always with Mazy, but we weren't together anymore. She was my singer and the mother of my kid, but we still used to argue about stuff, even though we weren't together.

From the beginning, I knew that Mazy definitely was special. Being on the road so young made her who she was. Now I think about it, London to Australia was a long way to go with a baby on a plane, but she had her mum, her dad and her grandmother with her all the way, and she was no problem. She never had any issue with travelling whatsoever. When me and Martina were onstage, she would be in bed on the tour bus with CC, or asleep in the dressing room, or back at the hotel.

When she was about three or four, there was an extraordinary moment during an average humdrum soundcheck at a festival somewhere in Europe. Mazy walked onstage, grabbed the mic from her mum, went to the front of the stage and started speaking in tongues to the empty field in front of her. Martina was petrified, but you knew that this kid was somebody – even back then.

Mazy couldn't even talk at that point. She had made noises before obviously, but here she was talking, only not in real words, and to a crowd that wasn't there – there was no one there out front, but it was like she was having a conversation with someone.

One time at another festival, she hung out and played with Kylie Minogue! When I wasn't touring, I would take her into Island Records, and she would be climbing all over me while I was doing interviews. The first time she ever walked was backstage at an English TV show. Unfortunately, Martina missed it because she was in another room, but Mazy walked from her nan CC over to me.

I think the music life gave her a fun childhood. I'm glad it happened, because that's what made her what she was. She was a born musician. Like Floyd Mayweather is a born boxer, one of the best boxers who ever lived, because he was going into a gym with his dad at two or three years of age, because his dad was a boxer. Mazy was a born musician – the real deal.

As a parent, I think it's more stressful if you've got to get up and be at work at nine o'clock in the morning, worrying that you've got a kid and have to arrange childcare. I would wake up on the tour bus, or in a hotel room, and Mazy would be there too. We didn't have that pressure of money, either. We didn't have to worry about borrowing clothes for the kid and all that. Nothing mattered. I think we had it easier than most parents.

With Martina and I separated but together as parents and performers, I can see now that it was a very strange situation, but at the time it was just normal. It just about worked, but looking back, it was weird. Now, I wouldn't want to do that – it sounds like a nightmare! – but at the time it was totally natural, even though Martina and I still used to fight loads.

BEN WINCHESTER: Tricky was on the road pretty much solidly for four years, from 1995 to 1998. Though he didn't play his first full headline UK tour until November 1996, he had been around the world – loads of European dates in autumn/winter 1995, then Australia in January 1996, and maybe three tours of America. There was a lot going on.

As it went on into '97 and beyond, the show changed significantly. It progressively became more intense and confrontational and atmospheric. It was much more traditional and theatrical to start with, then it got darker and louder as it went on.

The Pete Briquette band lasted for the first two years, then there was a very competent band of younger session musicians centred on a drummer called Perry Melius. By then Martina had left the crew, so it was just him at the front, and that is when it got really dark. It was much more than either a live show or a club show. It was a very intense and absorbing evening.

Tricky had a knack of attracting very interesting and unusual people wherever he played. At that first Shepherd's Bush Empire show, I walked in the dressing room, and Kylie Minogue and David Bowie were in there before me – and he already seemed to know both of them – *and* Nicole Kidman was there with Kylie as well. But then the next night, you would meet somebody back there who had been on the run from the French Foreign Legion for three years, or the Mayor of Paris. It was very varied, the people who were attracted to him, and that he hung out with – from all walks of life.

PETE BRIQUETTE: Tricky and Martina were always in a state of chaos on the road. It used to drive me mad. Lobby call in the morning would be for 11am and there would be no Tricky and no Martina. You'd go upstairs, and the rooms would be like a bomb had hit them, and they would just be getting up.

The only time I got pissed off was back here in the UK. We had a TV show in Europe somewhere. We had our itinerary to go to Heathrow at

11am, and at 9am I get a call from management saying Tricky's in bed and he's refusing to move – could I go and persuade him to get up? I went around to his flat, and he'd obviously been partying non-stop for two days. He just wouldn't budge. That was the only time he reneged on his responsibilities. I think by then he was just exhausted, burnt out.

I did quite a few tours with Tricky and Martina, but then the two of them fell out irreparably, and Alison Goldfrapp, who had sung on 'Pumpkin' on *Maxinquaye*, came in to replace her in the middle of a tour. She had a great voice which really suited Tricky's music.

The shows were definitely getting darker, and as Tricky learnt how to do the gig, he relied on me less and I kind of naturally left once he didn't need me anymore. I'd gradually put together a new band line-up for him, but then I got a call from him, 'Please come back!' He hated the bass player, so I came in halfway through the tour. I was the only white guy on the bus, and they'd be playing NWA all day at full blast. That would kind of wear me down. Aged forty-odd, I was probably a little too long in the tooth. They treated me great, but I was outside the loop. When people are cracking jokes that you don't get, your time has come to move on.

I was involved in the beginning of the next record, though, when we went down to Kingsway studio in New Orleans, a homely place in the French Quarter belonging to Daniel Lanois, where U2, REM and Bob Dylan had all recorded. It should've been fabulous, but technically it was quite stressful. Then I had family issues myself at that point, so I bailed about two thirds of the way through.

TRICKY: When I got to New Orleans I had my leg in a cast because I'd broken my foot in a fight in a club in New York. I moved into this old church with a recording studio in it to recoup, and to record stuff with this full marching band I'd seen out on the street. I also had Trombone Shorty in there, before anybody knew who he was. That must've been some pretty great music, but none of it made it onto *Angels with Dirty Faces*, or ever got released.

I loved New Orleans. It's a great place, with great restaurants, great food and great music. Back then, it really felt like New Orleans, but it's become too touristy now. At Daniel Lanois' place, we had a black drummer called Gloria McElrath, a really cool girl, but I don't think too much stuff worked out there either.

Everybody always asks whether the city I record in is important, but nowhere really has an impact on my music. It doesn't happen like that with me. Where I live is just a place to record, and it doesn't really affect the music I'm going to make.

In the end, most of *Angels with Dirty Faces* was done in New York, with members of my live band, and a few guests, like this guitarist Marc Ribot, who plays with Tom Waits.

There's a track on there called 'Peyote Sings', and I was actually taking peyote all through the New York sessions. It's this hallucinogenic cactus that mostly grows in Mexico, but you can get anything in New York, can't you? It's like a lighter form of acid – acid can be quite tough, but this is more natural, and not as aggressive. What's mad is, I was taking peyote, and the guy who mastered it was a big-time cokehead. Mastering is just tweaking sounds, not mixing, and you can hear in the mastering that he was a cokehead. You've got the edgy, trippy thing that I was bringing to it, and then you've got the high-treble tweaky thing from the guy with his coke binges.

I was just on a mission at that point. I was fucked, and I think that is when mental health issues started to develop with me. A lot of the lyrics are pretty nightmarish and on-the-edge. An English writer once said about me that I'm an aerial – an aerial to what's going on, picking up the frequencies – and I guess at that time I was receiving some pretty dark messages. On 'Tear Out My Eyes', there's this line, 'I wanna blow my head off in Seattle', referring to Kurt Cobain's suicide a couple of years earlier.

On another song, 'Record Companies', it goes, 'Corporate companies love when them kill themselves, it boost up the record sales'. It was talking about rap, and how record companies love all that beef shit, with people like Biggie and Tupac getting shot, because it seems so obvious to me that the only people who benefit from rappers having those beefs are the record companies.

In summer '97, I did Lollapalooza, and at the LA show there were a couple of big hip-hop artists on the bill, and when I came offstage there was a bit of an atmosphere, apparently about that lyric. All the wives and girlfriends were looking at me, as if to say, 'Yeah, too right, mate ...'

I suppose I was noticing the exploitation in the entertainment industry I was now a part of. Around that time, I did an interview for a black culture magazine in America, and I was talking about how black music had turned into minstrels again. It must've registered, because Spike Lee basically made a movie called *Bamboozled* out of that idea.

The album title, *Angels with Dirty Faces*, was from the James Cagney movie – I grew up on that stuff with my nan. The funny thing is, this pop band called Sugababes called their album that a few years later. A lot of critics at the time said my album was too difficult, like a wrong move, but again nowadays it's seen as a classic album in my catalogue by a lot of my fans.

Martina was on a few tracks, but it wasn't like I felt I had to replace her, and certainly Island never asked me to do that. It was just time to go on. I'm not the sort of person who is going to do the things that people want.

I did 'Broken Homes' with PJ Harvey, and what people don't realise is that I wrote that song – the lyrics and the melody – for her, so it was just doing different things with different people. We did that song together on *Late Show with David Letterman* in New York. I had my band with us, and a gospel choir from Harlem or the Bronx. I've always had freedom like that.

Chris Blackwell and whoever was at Island always egged me on. Even though sometimes they didn't agree, they understood me and let me do what I wanted. Like, 'U2 can make the money for Island, so I don't have to so much.'

MARC MAROT: It was on *Angels* ... that I got much more involved day-to-day. Chris and Tricky really trusted each other, whereas I was like the straight colonel.

I don't recall *Angels* ... being difficult or unpleasant, I just wish it had been more rewarding. I thought it was a really good record, but it was difficult to make. We had allowed Tricky to become himself so deeply that he was quite entrenched, and actually getting him to listen to advice was really difficult. It was his way or the highway. I'm not saying he was more difficult than anyone else, but by this stage he may not have listened to constructive criticism.

He was getting further away from commercial potential, which I did flag up to him. The way record companies work is, it's all reflected in the bottom line. With someone like Tricky, what happened was a very silent erosion of budgets. *Angels* ... was well marketed, and we had some good videos, but we were not spending the kind of money that he would have wanted by then.

We always had an eye on breaking America with him, but his move there was also about opening his musical vistas, and thereafter Tricky's interests started to lean very heavily towards hip-hop.

Towards the end of that album, there were concerns about his weed consumption and his mental health. He was getting lost in it. It was becoming too big an influence, and paranoia was beginning to creep in that was uncomfortable to work around. That paranoia actually becomes a corrosive erosion of trust, and I think that's what began to happen with Tricky.

I don't want it to seem like the Island–Tricky relationship ended with me as the schoolmaster expelling him, because that is not what happened. The record didn't sell very well, and at that stage in the contract, carrying on would have been very expensive, because typically recording contracts in those days only got bigger in terms of the advance pay-out, not smaller. Also, around that time, Island, MCA and Universal were merging into a giant organisation. Chris Blackwell was gone, so I'm sure Tricky began to feel abandoned.

During that contractual limbo period of the reorganisation of the label, Tricky got very excited by this idea of doing a spoken-word record with well-known criminals telling their stories of violence and dodgy dealings. Through his uncle Tony's contacts, he got some of the most badass criminals in the country to assemble in a pub back-room in London – the people with scars right across their faces; we're talking armed robbery not just selling a bit of dope – along with Darcus Beese, who was an Island A&R at the time, but who went on to become the president of Island America. Darcus was the only black guy in the room other than Tricky, and then Tricky fucked off and left him there, in a room full of thoroughly malevolent people! Some tracks were completed, but we didn't end up releasing that one.

TRICKY: Weed was a big part of the creative process for me, and I've always had a tendency to think too much. Sitting around at home, I'd smoke a spliff and, instead of just listening to music like the average person, I'd get obsessive. Martina used to say this, when we lived together: I would play the same song over and over, like twenty or thirty times. In my mind, the weed would help me to chill. It might not have seemed that way from the outside.

In the late '90s, the weed changed. From about 1996 to 1998, skunk was all you could get, and it was a big change. It wasn't around when we were growing up. When me and Whitley started smoking, you had sensimilla, which was really strong but a different kind of strong – it wasn't chemicals. The shit they do to make skunk, it's just ridiculous.

After a certain point, skunk and all that hydroponic shit was all that was on the market, and it was way, way heavier. None of the giggles and good feelings you got from sensi.

When I was doing *Maxinquaye*, it hadn't quite come in yet. I was still smoking normal weed at that point. Lebanese was as mellow as fuck, and there were none of the crystals in there – I never saw that when I was growing up. That only came in with skunk, and it was *strong*.

Everything was still going so fast in my life, moving from London to New York to New Jersey. It was like a whirlwind, and I still wasn't enjoying being in the public eye, not having my anonymity. On top of that, I've had terrible insomnia most of my life, ever since I can remember. My asthma was another complication, which certainly didn't help. I guess I was self-medicating for all of the stress and upheaval with skunk, booze and other narcotics.

Through the '90s I'd been feeling progressively worse and worse, to the point where I thought I had mental health problems. I'd been depressed every now and then, like any normal person – you get moody and you don't feel good – but this was different. I really felt sick, and I went to every doctor to try and sort it out, but I couldn't get past it. I felt like I was going crazy. Your mind goes through some mad shit when you don't know what's wrong with you, and it was getting so bad by 1998/99, I wanted to jump out of a window.

One day, I sat on a window ledge a few flights up in Manhattan and mulled it over.

'I'm either gonna hurt myself,' I thought, 'or I'm going to hurt someone, like a cry for help.'

I didn't know how to get help, though. When you are fucked, that can be your way of thinking. I've never been suicidal at any other time in my life. I don't think I actually wanted to kill myself, just break my legs or something.

'Okay,' I pondered, according to my twisted logic in that moment, 'if I break my legs then I could find out what's going on. Or if I get arrested … Maybe I could stab someone, then I'll get the help I need.'

That was where I was coming to – get myself committed to psychiatric hospital so I can figure out what's going on. When you don't know what's wrong, you can't think of it as a regular illness.

Finally the day arrived that changed my life for the better. I'd seen so many different doctors and medical people, but then my friend Amani put me on to this guy, and the irony was, he was just walking distance from the old Wall Street apartment with the elevator. I walked into the surgery, and explained to the doctor how I was feeling, and he said, 'Stick out your tongue – oh, you've got candida!' It was that simple – diagnosed in five seconds. The doctor gave me this detox stuff, and within six weeks I was feeling so much better. Just knowing what is wrong with you makes a big difference, too.

You should read up on candida, it's absolutely nuts. It's basically thrush of the stomach, so a lot of it is about changing your diet and feeling better in yourself in that respect. But candida seriously affects your state of mind. The doctor told me this scary statistic that something like eight out of ten people who have candida are misdiagnosed with schizophrenia or other mental health problems. The problem is, many doctors either don't know about it, or don't accept it as a real illness.

This is where it gets into conspiracy theory territory, because I think it's a bit of a money thing, right? To treat yourself for candida, the main thing is to watch what you eat. Now, if everybody knew that this was all it would take to cure them, the pharmaceutical industry would be losing all these lucrative courses of steroids and antibiotics and sleeping pills.

Some doubting physicians say it's not fully proven to exist, but I think that just suits big business. If you stop giving people steroids and antibiotics and sleeping pills and just tell them to eat properly instead, that's gonna cost the industry billions of dollars worldwide. I don't think doctors are totally ignorant. They must know, but they have a vested interest in prescribing antidepressants, so you are never actually curing it, and then you end up in a mental institution.

How candida affects you mentally is very weird. To this day, if I drink too much it can be a problem. You know with some people, they get really drunk, but they still have some sense about them? With candida, you drink too much and suddenly you have no self-control.

In social situations, you might say something you don't want to say, or do something you don't really want to do, but something makes you cross that line. There is no actual physical pain. You can get stomach pains, but there's no real physical component to it. It's just mental stuff – what they now politely term 'mental health issues'. It goes from depression to actually wanting to hurt yourself. Or someone else. That was my choice in New York – hurt myself or hurt someone. Stab or shoot someone, and I will get help.

From that day of my diagnosis onwards, my entire diet had to change: suddenly it was no bread, no sugar, no milk. I had to give up everything; it was extreme and very hard to adhere to. I couldn't even have ketchup or almond milk or fruit – because almost everything has sugar in it.

I was just about to start a tour, and I had to employ a chef, who came out and cooked for me on the road – not a gourmet chef, just someone who prepared food for me without the things I shouldn't be eating. Mostly, it was brown rice with chicken and vegetables, with a bit of sea salt – no sauce, nothing fun or fancy, for six weeks.

If I hadn't had a guy cooking for me, I couldn't have done it, because he wasn't just cooking, he was watching me. He'd go everywhere with me, so I couldn't just nip into a shop and buy some chocolate because I was craving sugar. He was watching me everywhere. I couldn't get room service in the hotel, any of that stuff. No tea, no coffee.

For the first couple of weeks, I was puking up, then after six weeks, I walked into a convenience store somewhere in America and, after a month and a half without sugar in absolutely anything, I could smell the sugar through the candy-bar wrappers, and I nearly fainted and had to leave the shop. That meant I had fully detoxed. It was a good sign.

Once the tour was over, I had acupuncture, and loads of other treatments, because once I'd done the detox, I had to get the good lining back in my stomach.

The doctors who believe in candida think it's caused by things like antibiotics and steroids, which can destroy the lining and kill the good bacteria in your stomach. My doctor reckoned I'd contracted it from all the pharmaceuticals doctors had given me for my asthma. Whenever you have an asthma attack in England, the first thing they give you is loads of steroids. If you have a chest infection as an asthmatic, you get a course of antibiotics, because all the phlegm on the chest could lead to an asthma attack. Then after I'd had an asthma attack, they'd give me a steroid course – four or five times a year I'd be on steroids, because it's a quick and easy way to control asthma, when really all I needed to do was have some allergy tests, because no bread and no dairy would have helped the asthma immeasurably. Instead they just give out drugs like sweets, so I grew up on all that stuff.

I still struggle with candida now, but at least I know what's going on. It's like, 'Okay, I've let the regime slip a bit. I need to stop drinking, need to start eating the right stuff again.' Problems arise when you're superbusy and you can't look after it. In my case, that happens when I'm going around the world on tour, and everything is really fast, and you're not eating the right stuff, because it can be hard to source under time pressure abroad, when you're not getting regular sleep.

Then you see how it takes all your self-control away. One time much later, in the 2000s, I was in my apartment and I had a pump-action shotgun under my bed. My two friends came over, we partied, and they slept on my couch. I got up, and I was like, 'Why is my gun here? Have you gone into my room, and taken the gun out?' And they were like, 'No, it's because you were dancing around with it last night, drunk!' That's candida – that ain't just drink! When I've been well, I've been as drunk as fuck, but I've still known what I'm doing. But when I haven't been well, I could dance around with a loaded shotgun – not on safety, pump-action, dancing around in my boxer shorts with loud music on. Why would anybody in their right mind do that? You've got to be unwell to get to that place.

Apart from lapses like that one, it's actually relatively easy to manage. I don't do bread, I don't do milk. You can cheat with a bit of brown sugar, but if I stick to the regime I'm fine. I've been doing it for so long now, and things have changed with substitute foods on the market. Back in the day it was hard. When I started, you couldn't get good alternative bread. The stuff they had was like concrete. Now you can get very good gluten-free bread. A lot of places even have chickpea bread, but not too long ago you had no chance going into a café in Hackney and asking for chickpea bread. Now they have gluten-free waffles as well. As the years have gone by, it has got a whole lot easier.

Better still, changing my diet dramatically improved my asthma. Just not drinking milk stopped me having major asthma attacks – it clogs up your passages, and if you get a cold in the winter, milk turns to phlegm on your chest, and you're more prone to an attack. Not eating bread may have had something to do with it too. I didn't know that I was lactose intolerant, so that was also causing me all kinds of problems. Now, if I smell milk, I want to vomit.

A lot of people die from asthma, but when you've had it for so long, you learn your way around it. I could go and train for an hour and a half in the gym, and you couldn't keep up with me. Asthma doesn't make a difference to me anymore.

AMANI VANCE: Tricky and Martina used to fight really bad. Touring life is insanely hard. Even when you have money and are staying in nice hotels, it can be disorientating. It fucks up your system, so you're already in a bad mood. Then it turns out Tricky has a really sensitive system, with food allergies he wasn't even aware of, which do really fuck you up.

I was watching this interview with Eminem the other day: he was saying how he was addicted to all these pills, and he was depressed, and he was like, 'I was always walking around so angry, like, why the fuck am I so angry? I'm successful!' He only realised when he started eating well how much what you eat can affect your mood and behaviour. And that is exactly what happened with Tricky: he was exasperated. When he was in a foul mood on tour, which is already a situation that makes you drink more and do more drugs – all the things that make you feel worse – he would take it out on the person closest to him, who was Martina.

I remember him saying how insanely smart Martina is, like, 'She knows what clouds are made of,' kind of smart. She's got an IQ that is through the roof. Because she is a beautiful woman with a phenomenal voice, she started getting a lot of attention, because she was singing the songs. There was a point where a lot of people were saying, 'Oh, it's really Martina's thing,' and then Tricky felt the need to be like, 'Well, no, it's my lyrics, it's my music – she is singing but I'm directing.'

The Jersey place was a lovely, lovely house – huge but not mini-mansion huge. Mazy had her own room, and Martina even had her own room for when she came, too. It was in this really dope gated community, with tons of character.

It was perfect, but it was making him unhappy too. It was just a little far out for him. Without traffic it could be as little as a 35-minute commute into Manhattan, but with traffic it would be two hours, which was a real pain in the ass. I know he really liked it out there, but then I started to think that he felt a little isolated, because there were not a lot of people around.

TRICKY: In the beginning, I felt like the whole New York area was my home. Then the vibe started to change for me. I was with Island still, but none of the people I started with in England were there anymore, and I hardly knew anybody. Chris Blackwell was gone, and it was a big shock to me. Up till then, it didn't matter what I did – if I did *Angels* ... or

Pre-Millennium … or anything else that people didn't understand – I still always had my home at Island. It was like having a home and then all of a sudden you've got to move out. I was like, 'What the fuck do I do now?' I was in this total limbo. I wasn't even interested in doing music. It was like, 'Okay, my time is over now.'

At some point around this time, I did some recording with Grace Jones, but only one track really came out of it, called 'Clandestine Affair', which I ended up putting out myself as a white label. I took control of it – I used to do things like that! – probably because I didn't think it was good enough for proper release. Not because of her, though, and we got on great.

I did another 12-inch called 'Divine Comedy', which was inspired by this statement I'd heard from one of the Universal-Polygram conglomerate's top brass, Eric Kronfeld. He said, 'If the music industry refused to employ blacks with criminal records, the music industry would employ no blacks at all.' I don't think I ever met the guy, but the chorus went 'It's who I am Polygram – fuck you, niggers', because I didn't think he should be allowed to get away with making such a racist statement. Coming from Knowle West, I have always had that 'them and us' stance, and I suppose by then I knew what record companies were all about. The funny thing is, Polygram actually had to press it for me as a 12-inch!

Chris Blackwell loved that record. I played it to him in the studio. He thought it was really funny. Island was fucked after Chris went. I remember him saying to me, 'The internet is really gonna change things, Tricky.' At the time I hadn't got a clue what he was talking about, but he saw it all coming. All the big labels went through the '90s getting fatter and fatter, thinking everything was gonna stay the same, but Chris knew otherwise and bailed before it was too late.

After Chris went, however, Island was merged with Def Jam, the New York hip-hop label, and so, without my real agreement, I veered over onto 'Island Black Music' or something stupid like that. Now I was dealing with Def Jam's MD, Lyor Cohen, who is a good guy, although some people will say he isn't. He was always cool with me, but we weren't on the same page at all.

'We've got to build up your black fan base,' he'd declare.

'I don't think like that,' I'd reply. 'Whoever finds my music, finds my music. I don't care about black, white, any of that.'

He was basically trying to market me into the hip-hop world, which I was never into. It was almost like they were trying to make me fit with Def Jam, and that was never gonna work, because for starters I'm not a black American. Hip-hop radio has never played my music, so I'm just not a Def Jam artist. To escape this ridiculous mismatch, I did a final album, *Juxtapose*, for Island really quickly just in order to get off the label, and then I left because I didn't want to stay with them under those terms.

People don't understand: success has got nothing to do with happiness. It's two different things. I was still successful, but I wasn't happy. At the beginning, suddenly I was comfortably off. The only thing I had to think about was, when am I going to do my next record? Or, when is the next tour? That's the most I ever had to think about. When Chris sold Island, he sold my house almost. I didn't really know where to go or what to do.

I was thrown into further confusion one night when the phone rang at 2am while I was trying to get to sleep in my house in New Jersey. It was my cousin Michelle on the line.

'Hello, Moo?' I said – I never call her by her name, always Moo, but I was wondering why she would call at this strange hour.

'Adrian, I've got bad news,' she said.

'What's wrong?'

'Shaun Fray is dead.'

'What are you talking about?'

I couldn't compute: my 'cousin' Shaun – son of my mum's best friend who I visited in east London when I first arrived in the capital, and with whom I'd seen Public Enemy at the Hammersmith Odeon – had been shot in the back of the head with a shotgun, in his house in Lonsdale Avenue, East Ham.

In the weeks ahead, the story was all over the British newspapers: Shaun had taken part in a security van robbery in 1990 and served three years in prison for his involvement. However, apparently 150 grand was unaccounted for, and when one of his accomplices was released from a longer sentence in 2001, this guy, Merrick Brown, tracked down Shaun, who had started a hi-fi business in the interim, and shot him dead. Brown fled to Florida, but was eventually extradited and imprisoned for thirty-three years.

Shaun's murder, aged thirty-six, shocked me deeply. At his funeral, Nigel Benn, the boxer, was in attendance, amongst other East End notables. Shaun was a well-known guy.

After Michelle's call, I unplugged the phone and put it away in a cupboard, and I've never had a house phone connected since that day.

INK WORK

People often ask where I got my tattoos done, and what they symbolise. I'm lucky to have travelled so widely, and to have seen so much of the world, and my 'full-sleeve' tattoos were something that came from going to play in Japan in '99. As soon as I saw them over there on people, I just had to have them myself, because I'd never seen anything like them in my life. I'd had a few done before I went there, but these were totally unique – at that time, at least. Nobody in the West had them. The only people who had them were not musicians, or footballers, or trendy people – it was only people who were properly into tattoos.

On a day off in Tokyo, I went into a parlour, and said what I wanted, and the artist wasn't sure about doing it. The ones I wanted were basically traditional Japanese Mafia tattoos, for the Yakuza over there. There's a dragon in there, for protection, and cherry blossom, which symbolises the fleeting nature of life. These were traditional sleeves – so mind-blowing, literally thousands of years old.

I had to sit in the parlour for hours, then the guy chucked me out at the end of the day without any inkwork having been done, so I went back the next day and sat there again. Now and then he would look at me, and that went on until he knew that I really did want it done. Then he said, 'Okay, come tomorrow when we are closed.'

When I went back, the guy was cool and started the work. It was funny, that day: there were a couple of Japanese gangsters in there, and one of these Yakuza guys came over and went, 'Hurt?' If I'd lied and pretended

I was a tough guy – well, he has just had the same thing, so he knows it hurts – it might've started something. So I said, 'Yeah, hurt.'

Once we'd played our show there, we had to leave, but soon after I went back to Japan for three weeks by myself, just to continue the work I wanted done. It was literally – hotel, tattoo, hotel, tattoo, every day, nothing else, then back to England. Over the years since, if I had a show out there, I would go out maybe five days before, to have things added. Even in the daytime before a show, I've had stuff done. The sessions were sometimes six or seven hours, because I didn't have time to do two or three hours one day, and then come back.

Much of it was done by a guy called Horiyoshi III, who is very famous. You have to have an appointment with him, because he is like The Don of tattoos. I can't remember if I ever actually did this myself, but with some of the tattoo artists out there, you have to sign a contract saying that, when you die, they can take your skin and put it on display in a museum, because it's artwork and they are so renowned. Then, if they've done a back piece, say, they can take that and put it in a museum. It's like, if Picasso drew on you, someone would want to pay for something like that, right? It's art, and it might be worth a lot of money. If it was Picasso, you would want that to live forever. You wouldn't want that to get buried with the rest of you. We are just canvas at the end of the day, ain't we? Canvas with living organs.

I soon found out that, because of the Yakuza associations in what I'd had done, I can't go into a gym in Japan and be sleeveless, because someone will come over and say, 'Sorry, Mr Tricky, can you put your top on?' It's traditionally saying you're a criminal, so I can't just strip down and go on the exercise bike in the hotel – they'll tell me to put my clothes on.

In New York, I'd get Japanese guys checking me out. If I went into a Japanese restaurant there, say, with a vest on and parts of the tattoos showing, I might notice the waiter or the chef checking it out. That doesn't happen so much these days, because the cherry blossom is more common, and a lot of sportsmen and hipsters have gone full-sleeve.

When I first went to New York, the only people who had any tattoos at all were street guys, but there were no black guys who were sleeved down like me. I can remember running into the rapper 50 Cent, and him saying, 'Yo, I love your tattoos!' At that time, when I met him, he only had a couple of regular ones, but he soon got sleeved down. I was sleeved down before any of them. I can't think of any black guys who were sleeved down at that time.

Tattoos are very addictive. I keep adding stuff and having more done, and you just want more and more and more. It's not anything to do with me as an artist – it's not something I did to look good in videos or picture shoots. You don't need tattoos to have a good photo. It's about who you are. It's for me.

CHAPTER TWELVE
BROWN PUNK

People were saying I'd changed the face of British music, but now I couldn't get a record deal. It was only four years since *Maxinquaye*, which was about to be celebrated all over again across the media as one of the top five albums of the 1990s. Yet, as I put myself about trying to find a new home now that Island was over, no major UK label would sign me. They would sign a band that was ripping me off, but they wouldn't sign *me*. There were only two or three conglomerate companies left, and none of the fuckers would go near me! America was difficult, too. Isn't that crazy?

I had a meeting at Warner Bros., down a little alleyway off High Street Kensington, with a really nice A&R guy there. He wanted to do business. I played him some rough demos – usually I don't do that, a label either wants to sign me or they don't, and they'll release whatever finished music I give them. But he was a nice guy, so I played him some demos.

'Wow!' he says, beaming with excitement. 'With a middle-eight, that is a hit record!'

'Alright, thanks, mate!' I said, walking out, and I never called him again. It's not that I was or wasn't going to put a middle-eight in; it's just that it wasn't finished yet. If I say that it's not finished yet, that's exactly what it means – keep your mouth shut!

In the US, meanwhile, I was speaking to this really old-school geezer called Bob Cavallo at Hollywood Records, but I didn't like his Prince talk. I went into his office in LA and we were going to do a deal. He was sat back in this big chair, and he started giving me stories, like, 'When Prince was doing his album, I said, "Yeah, we need one more song," and that's when he wrote "1999"!' He was trying to take credit for Prince, almost.

I thought he was a bit of a cock, giving it large as the big exec. I said to him, 'Listen, I don't give a fuck about Prince, he's had his time – it's my time now!' I didn't really mean it like that; I was just trying to show him I didn't give a fuck what he'd done. Like, 'Mate, you are not the talent in the room, so leave your ego at home! Prince would have happened with or without you. There could be a thousand Bob Cavallos and Prince would have been here anyway.'

After that, I knew I was going to have trouble with him, so I called Chris Blackwell and said, 'Can you pretend to be my manager and help me deal with this dick?' Chris was living in New York, because his wife Mary was very ill and needed top treatment which was only available there. Chris said yes, so I called Bob Cavallo, saying, 'You know what? Talk to Blackwell, he is my manager.'

Chris had Cavallo fly over to New York for a meeting at Chris's offices. When he arrived, Chris took him into the stairwell. The guy was crawling all over Chris. 'Oh, Chris, you've had so many artists – Bob Marley and so-and-so ...' and Chris went, 'Well, you've got one of them right here, right now!' and he pointed to me. Then he says, 'Anyway, I've got to go.' He never even invited Cavallo in to sit down, so it was a ten-minute meeting in the fire escape! Cavallo left, and that was it – I was good, then. I had my deal, and Cavallo didn't give me any of the big-exec talk after that.

For Europe, Chris hooked me up with a guy called Heine, who used to be a director at his publishing company, but was now in Amsterdam, running the European part of ANTI-Records, this cool American punk-rock label that had been releasing records by another of his old artists, Tom Waits.

With deals for America and Europe sorted out, I was partying hard. I'd hooked up with a Jamaican MC called Hawkman and his cousin. First, we were clubbing in New York, and then we'd go to Miami for a week or two, smoking weed and going to clubs and hanging out, and then eventually I brought him out to Los Angeles, where I was starting an album for Hollywood Records.

At that time, LA felt like this massive sprawling place with no real music scene. The record business was all in New York, and most of the labels only had sub-divisions there. Hollywood Records, though, was an LA operation, because it came out of the movie biz – it was a sub-division of Disney. So I was signed to Walt Disney – I never saw that one coming!

Their idea was to get a load of big collaborations on the record. Of the ones that came off, there weren't really any people that I would've approached by choice, but I had this lovely woman called Jenny Price as my A&R. She really looked after me there – the only connection I had. That guy Bob Cavallo was from a totally different planet to me, so it was Jenny who would talk me into things. She would say, 'Why not work with so-and-so?' and she was so nice about it, I'd say, 'Okay!'

That's how I ended up with two songs with the Red Hot Chili Peppers on there. I've got to say, they're really not my thing. It was all done very quickly in the studio, and I never saw them again – same with Cyndi Lauper. There was a good guy called Ed Kowalcyk from the band Live, who used to carry a gun around with him – a little silver .38. It wasn't a gangster thing – he is a Christian! I quickly began to realise that guns really are part of the culture on the West Coast.

The only 'feature' on the album I would've chosen myself was Alanis Morissette. She was a very nice girl. In the mid-90s, Alanis sold something like 30 million albums with *Jagged Little Pill*, but I was quite impressed by how she didn't show the pressure. She just seemed to be totally normal. In the studio, she was very quick, and she would try anything. People might say her stuff is pop, but I could play her the strangest thing, and she'd jump on and try to sing to it off the top of her head, which I really hadn't expected. Very brave.

Afterwards, I went to a party at her house. It was really weird; me and her were dancing to some clubby house tune, and I said to her, 'It's kind of mad how you dance!' I'd always viewed her as an 'alternative pop' girl, but she was really having a proper dance to a club track. She said, 'What, did you think I would be moping in the corner?'

. ▪ ■ ▪ .

I'd been working in LA for a few months and the album, called *Blowback*, was mid-campaign when, on 11 September 2001, I awoke to the news that had already shaken much of the world. The World Trade Center, which towered in duplicate just a few blocks from my old duplex apartment in New York's financial district, had been felled by al-Qaeda, and now lay in ruins, leaving several thousand people dead.

Like everyone, I was stunned initially, glued to the TV news in my room. As the days went by, I kind of got trapped in LA. Friends were saying, 'Don't come back to New York yet – the vibe is fucked.' The label had put me in a hotel called Le Parc Suite in West Hollywood, but I'd been in there for nigh-on eight months. My manager said, 'Listen, you're wasting money on this hotel – if you don't want to go back to New York, then rent an apartment.' I found a temporary place, and I just never returned.

I never meant to move to LA. I didn't move there for the sunshine, like most people. It was an accident. I just got stuck there. Blame 9/11.

That terrorist act changed the world. Apart from anything else, when you think back to the way security was conducted in airports, things have got so much more complicated since then. It affected so much in international relations and politics, but from a personal perspective, it also affected my album campaign.

I went into the record company sometime in October, and everyone was going on about the lyrics of one song, 'Excess', which went, 'I believe in people flying, I believe in people dying'. People were looking at me weirdly, like I'd been talking about 9/11 before it even happened.

I soon found out that the album title, *Blowback*, could also be construed to mean more than just a fun way of smoking weed. Apparently, in military reporting, when a country goes to war, the blowback is what happens to it in return. It could mean literally a blowback from a gun, or if, say, America goes and shoots people in a faraway country, and then people from that country come and blow up the Twin Towers – that's blowback.

Everyone was agreed that the album itself – the music – was the most commercial and catchy stuff I'd done since *Maxinquaye*, if not ever, but the connotations with 9/11 destroyed the vibe of the whole record. FM stations across America certainly weren't gonna parade 'Excess' on the airwaves right after the Twin Towers, know what I mean?

I toured the album. It was my first jaunt for eighteen months, with all the upheaval changing labels. It was refreshing to get out on the road after all that, but, while critics on both sides of the Atlantic were hailing my latest offering as a return to form, *Blowback* was never going to take off in America, whatever I did to promote it.

One good thing was that I'd got my uncle Tony back as my security on the road. He was watching my back, but in a way it was just about having one of my family with me while I'm travelling around. He'd started coming out with us for Lollapalooza in '97, but right around this time he was unexpectedly detained elsewhere.

TONY GUEST: My job was to make sure nobody mithered Adrian. He rang me up, and then I toured with him all over North America. I knocked a fella out in Minehead, and at Glastonbury. He gets himself in trouble, with his mouth. I told him, 'The smoking, that wacky baccy – fucking hell, you wanna leave that alone!' I suppose it's difficult because it's part of the game, isn't it? He has a smoke first, but then he wouldn't say anything onstage, and he has his back to them!

I was in the crowd one day, and they were all peering at the stage in darkness, going, 'We can't even see him!' I was circling around to make sure everything was alright, and I went to the lighting man, Angus, and I said, 'If it's any darker they'll be walking into each other!'

I haven't got a lot of music myself, but Elvis is my favourite. I like Bob Dylan, but I don't like this rap. I said to him when I first got on tour with him, 'God almighty, you can't even sing!' He said, 'But they come to see me, Uncle Tone.' I've seen loads of shows since, and I'll tell you something: I don't know about his records, but he is a great stage performer. He moves his head about, and he really gets you – and you don't know what you're getting.

I was with him for about three years on the road, but then I went to prison. We was going to Japan for Fuji Rock Festival in '99, but I had to go to court, and I thought I was gonna get off. The tour manager, Sullivan, called me and said, 'Okay, I'll leave the tickets at the station and all you've got to do is go there and pick them up, and then meet us in Japan.' But I didn't meet them in Japan because I was in fucking Strangeways!

I was in for stun-gunning a couple of guys. We had an argument because they were trying to take over one of the clubs that we ran in Manchester. This fellow, Barry, was trying to take it over for protection money, and the owners of the club came and asked us to put a stop to it. They said there was a fat fella there on the sofa with a reputation and they didn't want him in there no more. So he came in with his minders, this Barry.

'You're finished, Barry,' I said. 'Your protection is finishing right now – I'm stopping it.'

'What do you mean, finished?' he goes.

'This is our club now!'

It was quite a fight – I got my thumb bitten off that night.

I was in Strangeways for six months, but they shipped me to Walton in Liverpool after that, and I finished my two years there. I've seen that fucking Bronson in there – the big fella who took his name off that film star, Charles Bronson. They've never let him out.

Adrian came up to see me in Walton, and after I got out I joined him on tour in Canada.

Everyone in the family was proud of him. If it wasn't for that, I don't know what he would have been, to tell you the truth. You know, he went to Horfield for bloody forged notes. Christ knows what he'd be up to if it wasn't for music.

TRICKY: I'm an observer and, for some reason, people always look after me. This is what happened with Cesar Aceituno in LA. I met him right at the beginning, when I first arrived in LA, at a pool party on a hotel roof with these stripper girls. Which was kind of crazy because I'd never been to anything like that before. It was a totally different culture, even to New York. Since that day we met, me and Cesar haven't left each other.

He's an ex-gangbanger, but now he's legit, and he's got his own gun company. Him and his partner make rifles, for the Sheriff Department, the army and people like that – like legal gun-running, I suppose. They make sniper rifles, suppressors and silencers for sniper rifles. He goes for weekends training people to shoot. I used to go with him sometimes, and he showed me, so I can shoot 800 yards with a sniper rifle, even 850, no problem.

LA was very hard to get my head around to start with, but with Cesar to guide me, I started having a lot of fun there. We would get in the car, the two of us, and drive to San Francisco, just for a night out. Or we'd go to Vegas for the boxing. Or we'd stay in LA and hang out at Oscars after-parties. Just living really large, going to all the top parties and top restaurants, and – unknown to me – hanging with ghetto legends.

Cesar wasn't a gangbanger when he met me, but his dad did say to me once, 'Thank you for looking after Cesar.' I thought, 'What does he mean by that?' What it was: when Cesar met me, it changed his life a little bit. A lot of his friends are either dead or doing life. So his dad thanked me, because when he was hanging out with me, he wasn't going to certain places anymore. We were in Oscars parties instead – and those are good parties, some of them! The Oscars I don't give a shit about, but some of the parties – gorgeous women, drink, total fun.

It would be a serious mix of people in the clubs. Britney Spears could be there, and on the next table it could be drug dealers. That's just the way it is in LA – gangbangers next to Britney Spears – because if the gangsters have got a lot of money, they can afford to go to the same places as Britney. It just mixes.

One night, we were out at this really small club with a tiny dancefloor and there was nobody in there. Occasionally you'd see people like Puffy in there, probably because it was never busy. Cesar was on one side of the club, and I was on the other at the bar getting drinks. After I'd paid up, I went to walk through the dancefloor, and this bouncer stopped me and said, 'You'll have to walk around – Prince is dancing.' It turned out that this was his own security, so I was like, 'That's not gonna happen!' and I just walked straight on through. Prince was there on his own – doing all these dance moves, like he was performing for himself. Like he was doing a show, but there was no one in there. Weird.

Me and Cesar went to a lot of boxing. One of the times we went to Vegas was to see Mike Tyson. While we were walking through the casino, we bumped into this fighter, Terry Norris – one of the best boxers that ever lived – and I got my picture taken with him. He was a handful, that guy. He used to do this thing at the beginning of a fight, just look at his opponent, almost like a Roman thing. Boxers try and do it now, some of them, but it don't work.

Aside from music, the only other thing I would love to have been was a boxer. A champion boxer. The only autograph I ever got off anyone was that of another boxer called Johnny Tapia – another of the best boxers that ever lived. His mum got killed – stabbed eleven times. He had such a hard life – he went into boxing because he had anger issues, and then he became world champion in the mid-90s. You would really have to know about boxing to know him. He ain't like Anthony Joshua, getting OBEs from the Queen – he was a boxing fan's boxer. I've only watched one Joshua fight, but I still watch Johnny Tapia's fights now. He was the only person I've ever asked to sign an autograph.

As I said before, around the time of making *Blowback*, I was in this hotel. Then 9/11 happened and I ended up staying and moving into this little ghetto place, with a girl. I said to her, 'I've got no money, I need to come and live with you.' She went, 'Okay,' and I went and moved all my stuff into her tiny ghetto apartment.

I can move from right up at the top, and go right down to the bottom. I've got no problem with that. My life didn't change. I was still going to all the clubs, but if I have to go and live rough, I would still be doing the same stuff. I would live out of my suitcase, as I always do anyway.

This girl lived in a really ghetto area – a Hispanic gangbanging area, apparently, and I was the only black person there. One time, I saw a car going by, then it stopped, reversed, the window wound down, and the black driver, shouted, 'Yo, homie, you live here? What's *that* like?' For me, ignorance was bliss: I was just living there. I had no idea that black people wouldn't be living there. I didn't think, 'There ain't no one who looks like me.' My head doesn't think like that. I don't have that concept.

From there, I eventually moved into my own place in Venice Beach – a very expensive apartment that cost $5,000 a month rent, but in a ghetto area. Dennis Hopper lived not far away, because it's right there by the ocean, but it was kind of a black neighbourhood, and I guess it was a long way from gentrified at that point. It was five minutes good, five minutes ghetto, but the apartment was amazing, with this huge window you could open and have the sun coming in. I'd have people round there, and we would hang out in the sun, smoking weed. Good times!

On the street outside, they used to call me Crazy Boy because I had a massive mohican, and after a while when they tried to start a conversation with me, it would be, 'Yo! Give me work, man, give me work!' They'd seen nice cars pulling up outside my place, and they obviously thought I was a drug dealer. I'd actually bought one of those brand-new BMWs myself – even though I didn't have a licence – and that was always parked out front. I would try and tell these kids, 'No, I'm a musician!' but these young black kids didn't have a clue who the fuck I was. Maybe I was being too paranoid, but I started thinking, 'They don't believe me, and I can't give them work like they're thinking – dodgy work – so it's only a matter of time before they come in to get the work.' The thing was, the apartment was a loft and there was only one entrance, so if someone broke in, there was no way out. Like, 'If they come in here one day, what the fuck am I gonna do?'

That's how I got into buying guns. Over in LA, once you've been there for a while, you get so used to people you know packing, guns stop feeling like such a big deal to you. Even my manager at the time, a wonderful lady called Caresse Henry, had guns, as did her husband. She managed Madonna up to about 2004, and also took care of Ricky Martin, Joss Stone and Paula Abdul. She was a very successful lady, and she'd got into that whole gun culture, not to be badass, but because everybody had one. In 2010, I'm afraid she used one of them to shoot herself in the head – but back when I was around her, seeing my rich and respectable manager with two 9mms in her house, it was kind of inevitable that I'd start to think, 'Well, I better get one as well.'

I ended up with three guns – an Uzi, a pump-action, and a 9mm just under the bed. I wasn't actually carrying anything outside of the house all the time, but sometimes I felt I had to take one with me, to be sure. I don't want people reading this thinking I'm a gangster or a gunman or a bad man – I'm not. I used to carry a weapon just in case anyone had a problem with me.

One time, I was out in this Chinese supermarket, where you could get Jamaican food – plantain, yam, stuff like that. I had an Uzi in my trousers, and the clip tucked in the other side of my trousers, but while I was walking around the supermarket, somehow the clip slipped down and came out of the bottom of the trouser leg, just as I got to the checkout. The Chinese woman behind the counter looked at the clip and carried on. Instead of just picking up the clip and tucking it back in, for some reason I decided to feed it back up through the inside of the trouser leg, which took ages, then I paid and left. The Chinese lady almost pretended she hadn't seen, minding her own business and counting out my change.

What's funny is: with all the trouble in America with black people getting stopped and searched, in sixteen-odd years over there I only got stopped twice. I was driving for about eight months illegally, with no insurance, not registered, so it's lucky I didn't get stopped then. You would think it would have happened more, right?

I've had some lucky breaks with cops in America. I had one of the guys from London Posse on one of my albums, this guy Bionic, so I flew him to New York. We were in this place called The Bank and a fight broke out. I'm fighting with this guy, and he's fucked – he's fighting the doorman, and me! We go through the exit fighting, and the guy is hitting both of us, and we're hitting him, then he fell and smashed his head – blood everywhere. Suddenly loads of cops came in, and they pulled me to the side, and this guy is covered in blood, and I thought, 'Oh dear, I'm arrested here!'

This black officer comes over and looks at me.

'Yo – Tricky, right?'

This cop had a tongue ring, which was kind of weird for a New York cop.

'Yeah?' I reply.

'Just go away,' he says. 'Go away!'

. . ■ ■ . .

Back in LA, I don't know why, but I bought this BMW, and I've never had a licence. You've got to want to have a car to get a licence, and I never wanted one. People get scared when I drive, because I've got no sense of speed. One time, I crashed into a palm tree in LA, and broke my hand. I was doing about sixty miles an hour, and people thought I must be dead. Actually, that one wasn't even my car, and we hadn't got the insurance, so we had to get out of the car and run. We got into my apartment, and I had to put a bag of peas on my hand, because the knuckle was up here. I waited until the morning, then I called Cesar and said, 'I broke my hand, take me to the hospital!' Which he did.

You really do need a car in LA, but in that period where I was driving, I was taking corners at ninety miles an hour – stupid, I have no sense. Cesar is a good guy, but he drives mad as well. He used to have this little black car – a Trans Am, I think. It was close to the ground and he used to drive like a fucking maniac. So really, he shouldn't ever be complaining about my driving. I've had some very hairy times with him at the wheel.

If I had problems over there, though, Cesar would come and handle it for me. He's got some amazing stories, about his background, and some situations that happened to me that he remembers better than I do.

CESAR ACEITUNO: When my friend Chani comes down from Atlanta to LA, we'll usually party together. One Saturday in '01 she gives me a call, and she wants me to meet somebody. I'm like, 'Okay.' I went over to this hotel, went up to the pool and saw Chani and her friend swimming topless, and all the other guests from the hotel were stripping down. I'm like, 'Hmm, this is interesting!'

That's how I met Tricky, and we immediately connected, talking about boxing. I told him that two of my friends where I grew up in Sun Valley were the world boxing champions, Rafael and Gabriel Ruelas – Rafael eventually lost his title to Oscar de la Hoya, while Gabriel actually killed a Colombian fighter in the ring, in Vegas, which really screwed with his head. That night, me, Tricky and the girls went out to the Standard Hotel, and after that me and him became kind of inseparable.

I'm of Mexican and Guatemalan ethnicity, and when I was a teenager in the '80s in Sun Valley, out in San Fernando Valley, there was a crack epidemic. LA was infested with gangs and violence, like in those movies, *Colors* and *Scarface*. Where I grew up there were a lot of football players that would meet in parks, but a lot of those turned into gangs because it was getting rough, and I was involved in one of those, the Vineland Boys. By the '90s, organised crime was trying to tax all the gangs. Big gangs like 17th Street, which had 7,000 guys in it, said 'no' at first, but ended up paying. Vineland Boys was one of the two gangs that did not pay taxes for six years. That meant there was a green light, where if you went to jail, or they caught you on the street, all the other gangs would come after you.

When one of our guys shot and killed a cop during a break-in, we were tagged by the police. In 2002, another cop got shot, and another paralysed, and the officer that died's father was a big guy in the LAPD, so the Feds got involved, and came after our people. A lot of them had connections in Mexico, and were running in drugs, so there was a two-year investigation. In 2005, they launched Operation Silent Night, using 200 police officers, four helicopters, and a bunch of armoured trucks, and they took about 200 people. There were forty-seven guys charged: in a normal case, some would've got ten or twelve years, but they got life; others got double life; eighteen to twenty years was the standard for what they were giving out.

In late 2018, they cracked down on the new-generation Vineland Boys that's come up, and took in thirty-seven guys, but luckily I'm now pretty much a born-again good citizen! In the beginning when I met Tricky, I was in it, but he did get me on a different bat: when all that was going down in '02 to '05, me and Tricky were just partying our asses off, so I wasn't hanging around with my guys as much. I lost a lot of them being killed or imprisoned, so it was a godsend meeting Tricky. Otherwise, I'd either be in prison, or I'd be dead. When my dad was saying thanks to him, though, Tricky was like, 'What the fuck? Me taking care of *him*?'

I was like Tricky's protector over here. LA is very devious, deceptive. It's nice and sunny with all the palm trees, very beautiful, but it's a very dangerous place. Now it's not as much as it was back then, but the element of danger has always been in the shadows, and it would come out a lot.

After Le Parc Suite, Tricky lived in that Hispanic neighbourhood, then Venice Beach, but that was still quite a gang-infested area with the Venice Crips, and some Mexican gangs floating around too. When he moved there, it was just starting to get where people were building these beautiful apartments, but across the street they were still selling drugs. After his run-ins there, he moved to a place on Doheney and Sunset, right by the Strip, and that's where he spent the majority of his time in LA. Towards the end, he moved into a beautiful building in mid-Wilshire – it was about eight or nine years that he was here.

Tricky had a really hard upbringing, and I think his music career had been a bit of a mind-fuck, so we definitely had some fun out here! He did tell me that he thinks he kind of self-sabotaged his career – subconsciously did a lot of stuff that wouldn't be beneficial – because he didn't know if he could take the fame. He was stuck in a very surreal area – he had his family background, and then all that was going on with Martina and having a baby – it was pretty challenging I'm sure. Then he was living in the middle of nowhere in New Jersey with Mazy, so once he got out here to LA it was like he was ready to party.

Most of the time we were in LA – Santa Monica and West Hollywood. We'd go to this upscale sushi bar on Sunset called Katana's quite a lot, right across from the Mondrian Hotel, but we went to San Diego a couple of times, and San Francisco. We went there when we first met, to this party called The Wet Party at this arty hotel, the Phoenix hotel, which has a back courtyard with a pool – the best party you've ever been to, a great vibe, beautiful girls. People would fly from all over the world to be there. We'd go to Vegas too, but one time we got kicked out. We got banned from the Venetian Hotel – for life – for having two guns, a load of weed and a bag of sniff.

In LA, we would be going out three or four times a week, to the best parties, with the most beautiful girls. It was a really good time. We were going to Oscar parties, and Grammy parties. The only thing I can recall from the Grammys is that I was really hammered, and I was driving Linda Perry, the songwriter. There was one time where we were dressed up in suits, and we were like, 'Man, we look pretty good! We gotta keep these clean so we can use them again, right?' We were drinking, we got to this club, and all of a sudden I'm on the floor fighting this guy – starting some shit with him on the floor, and before you know it both our suits are all torn up.

There was a point where, just because we were going out drinking so much, we ended up in fights. We had problems with this Mexican gang, and it ended up on the tabloid news website, *TMZ*. This gang were with a pretty famous rapper, but something turned with him and they hit him up at this club called Joseph's where all the celebrities would go on Monday night. There were about ten of them, and somehow it turned into a stand-off with us. I went to go get my gun in the car – I didn't want to say, 'We ain't fucking going, fuck these motherfuckers!' So we're outside by a hotdog stand eating hotdogs, and these guys are just tripping out why we didn't leave.

A bit later, we were at this club in Hollywood with a French name, maybe Les Deux, with my friend Isaac. This big Mexican dude comes in and starts talking to Tricky, and all of a sudden, the guy socks Tricky – and I mean, *hard*. Tricky has a chin, because he didn't go down. This guy was three times his size, probably 200 pounds. I ran over there – 'Hey, motherfucker!' – and I started fighting him, and suddenly we got jumped by maybe ten guys, against the three of us. Tricky hit this one guy with this big skull diamond ring he had, which cut the big dude's face open. What we didn't know was that they were filming it, and it ended up on *TMZ*. I was getting phone calls from friends in New York, saying, 'Hey, we saw you fighting on fuckin' *TMZ*!'

Tricky loves talking about gang shit. We call him the Inspector Clouseau of crime. One time we were walking down the street, and he had his hand in his pocket, as he was carrying a taser, and he accidentally tasered himself! Total Clouseau!

When he had that problem in Venice Beach, I gave him an Uzi and had him load it up with some gloves on – like, 'Just keep this at your house, and if you go somewhere, it's up to you if you take it or not.' A week or two after that, we went to eat lunch in this really beautiful area called Sunset Plaza, and then his neighbour called, saying that a round went through the wall connecting his apartment with Tricky's. We thought he might be joking, but we started heading back, then we saw all these cop cars blocking off the road. We just snuck through, and we were still joking, 'Hey, that's for us!'

Literally, it *was* for us! We parked at his apartment, and we go up there. What happened was: the maid was there, and she'd brought her kid; he went through Tricky's drawers, found the Uzi and shot a round through the wall. We actually became best friends with his neighbour afterwards, but the neighbour's brother was there, and the round went really close to his head.

We told the maid to leave, because we didn't want her to get in trouble. We were waiting there, and the door was kind of open, so I said, 'Hey, Tricks, go close the door!' As soon as he closed the door, he said, 'Hey, I see shadows when I look through the peephole.' He opened the door a little bit, and all of a sudden, all these lasers were on him. The door was in an L-shaped hallway, so there were cops on the left, and cops on the right, and they told him to come out. He came out, and one on the right told him to go right, and another guy was telling him to turn round, so he started doing a dance, but then they were screaming at him, so he got on his knees.

They grabbed me, handcuffed me, and took me outside, and they kept him inside. He called his lawyer, but all these white cops who looked like total rednecks ended up being the nicest guys. They questioned us and we were like, 'Hey, we weren't even here!' Then this black cop comes in, a motorcycle cop with a shotgun. They sent investigators to the restaurant to see if they could prove that we were there.

Everything was cool in the end, and this white guy went, 'Yeah, you know what, things happen – I almost shot my wife!'

Like, 'Shit happens!'

'Yeah, doesn't it!'

That black cop was a nightmare, though. At one point, he came in, put his leg on the chair, put the shotgun across his knee, and went, 'You guys are *fucked*!' After that, the guy would just harass us, putting his hand like a pistol, acting like he was shooting us. Tricky said, 'Man, this motherfucker is a psycho!'

A few weeks afterwards, we bumped into this cop at a restaurant. He was all built, so Tricky was like, 'Man, how come you are in such good shape?' After that, the guy was Tricky's best buddy, gives him his car: 'If you need anything, I mean anything – like you need somebody to get beat up, arrested, whatever – you call me!'

I took Tricky to shooting practice, because I'm a qualified instructor. The first time I took him, I had him shooting with a sniper rifle at 880 yards, which is half a mile, and he was hitting man-sized targets at that range on the first time out. He definitely does have a knack for it.

For shooting, yes, but not for driving! I've never been so scared until I saw him drive, or try to drive. Because he has never driven, I don't think he knows what the cars are capable, or not capable, of doing. He'll try and do a turn at fifty miles an hour. If he ever says, 'Oh, I'll drive,' be afraid. In LA, he always got around okay, because girls would drive him around. He's gone out with some real beautiful girls, famous girls, and somehow they'd always be his chauffeurs, too. So he never really needed a car, which is pretty crazy in LA – especially back then, before Uber and Lyft.

When I first met Tricky, these guys from the Gambino crime family were trying to force him to make them his manager. Me and my business partner Mike – both sides of his family are really mobbed up back East – went over there to their office, and one of these guys is smoking a cigar, and he goes to Mike, 'Who are you with?' I waited till he had a puff on his cigar, then I told him, 'My buddy Tricky's uncle considers Mike family.' Then I went up to his ear and I whispered, 'Tony Guest!' and he literally coughed on his cigar. After that, they never tried to move in on Tricky again.

Through all the partying, Tricky always remained fit. He practised Brazilian Ju-Jitsu out here, and he does have a thing of self-preservation. He will party for a while, but then he's real healthy for a good stretch. A lot of musicians and actors go overboard and destroy their health – like, everything in excess. Tricky has a really good balance, walking that tightrope. His life could have gone so different, with his family and uncles being top-notch gangsters, and he has had tons of temptations to go down that route, but he has stayed focused to keep his career going.

He was still making music out here. He had this manager who was a lawyer for Linkin Park, and the guy would get him work for TV shows. He was dating a girl from one of the biggest black sitcoms out here, *Girlfriends*, and he ended up acting in two or three episodes.

TRICKY: I'd been around long enough by then doing music that I didn't really need a record company. I was already established. Hollywood Records, to me, was just distribution and getting money. I did another album for them in '03 called *Vulnerable*, which was less about collaborations, more just songs with my live band and a couple of new singers.

Title concepts tend to just pop into my head, and *Vulnerable* was saying something about myself which maybe people hadn't realised, about my shyness, and looking at my background in a different light.

The cover pictures were taken in my apartment in Venice Beach, with the big window that opened out, and where I had to get the guns in because there was only one way out. I took the front picture with my own camera, on timer, with this mad messy green and brown wall painting a woman did for me in the background. The little mohican I've got grew pretty long in the end! You can see how hot it got in there from the back picture with the light streaming in, and me with a towel on my head.

To be honest, being with Hollywood Records was just something to do. I'd got to the point where nothing was ever gonna be like Island again. I didn't have much motivation, and after doing those two records with them, I floated around. Somehow, being in LA, I stumbled into the movie world, doing music for this huge producer called Jerry Bruckheimer, who'd done stuff like *Beverly Hills Cop*, *Armageddon* and *Pirates of the Caribbean*.

My connection came through a very powerful Hollywood woman. I was in her office and she goes, 'Do you want to do any film scoring?' She starts punching into the phone, then it was, 'Jerry? I'm sending Tricky over,' and suddenly there was a car there for me. I said to her, 'Listen, you've got to watch this actor in a little Australian movie called *Chopper* – he is amazing!' She wrote down the guy's name, Eric Bana, and the next thing you know this guy had the lead role in *Hulk*!

I went over to meet Jerry, and he turned out to be not what I expected. He was actually a proper music fan, and I did soundtrack work for a couple of his movies and a couple of his TV shows, including *CSI: Crime Scene Investigation*. I said to him, 'I'll find it difficult watching some film and then writing a score to it.' He said, 'Don't worry, I'll set you up with the studio and you just do loads of sixty-second bits of music.'

He put me in this little garage with all the gear I needed, then I'd write loads of pieces of song that were about a minute long, and go into his office and he'd say, 'I'll take this one, this one, I don't want that one.' What's funny is, I'd give him maybe ten dark things and ten lighter things, thinking he'd choose the lighter stuff, but every time he chose the darkest stuff. From how he dealt with me, he was a very good guy. Instead of saying, 'Tricky, we need you to do this and this and this,' he just let me do what I wanted.

In one of his movies, *Bad Company*, I went in front of the camera, singing a song called 'Breakaway' onstage then doing some dialogue afterwards. I was also on two or three episodes of this black TV show called *Girlfriends*, which was like *Friends*, but black. To be honest, I never watched it, but it was a huge show in America.

My first experience in movies came a long time before, in 1997, in Luc Besson's *The Fifth Element*, which I didn't enjoy. I was playing Gary Oldman's sidekick, called Right Arm, which sounds fun but it really was the most boring thing. It was great meeting Gary Oldman, though, and that's how I got him leaving messages on my ansaphone in Jamaican patois.

On one of them, he went, 'Yo! Trick-ay! Where the bloodclaat … where you at? Pick up the fuckin' phone!' Gary Oldman, all in Jamaican patois! Now I realise I should have kept that apparatus – imagine having Gary Oldman talking Rasta on the beginning of a record.

Acting in movies is tedious, because you are just sat around waiting for hours, and you might not even do your scene that day, but you have to be there just in case. You could be there for eight hours in a room, not doing anything. After that experience, I was like, if I ever do a movie again, it would have to be something where I don't have to do a screen test. If you want to put me in a movie, and I like the script, I'll do it, but I can't learn lines. I'm not going to rehearse for it, and I have to be able to talk off the top of my head, where I know what it's about and then I can just shoot.

I just found it all to be bullshit. I didn't get it, and you have to go through the same thing over and over. It wasn't inspiring for me. Learning lines and trying to get a part in a movie? Forget it. After *The Fifth Element*, my thing was, 'You either wanna put me in the movie, or you don't!'

But I do like directing. Most of the promo videos I've ever done, I have either done myself or at least it was my ideas. I'm not trying to be a video director per se. I just like having ideas, and letting someone else execute it, so all I have to do is turn up. I don't mind someone else getting the credit. As long as the video was good, I never cared too much about the credit.

Through reconnecting with Chris Blackwell, I ended up starting my own label, called Brown Punk, and kind of directing a movie, also called *Brown Punk*, starring the real people who were signed to the label. The concept was for a street version of *The Office*, which was definitely what it was inspired by – like a documentary almost, but in this case, we blurred the lines a bit more.

The plot was loosely me scratching around, trying to hustle money to get the label moving and to make music. It wasn't scripted. There was just a general story outline, so each scene would be improvised, kind of making it up as we went along. For instance, with Elliott Gould, who was the only famous actor in it, I would give him the general idea – like, 'Alright, you've lent this guy money, and you want your money, then you make it up from there.' I would put people in the situation – no writing, just, 'Okay, this scene is, you are trying to get your money back off me, and I've had this idea: say, "What do you mean, you'll get it to me in two days? You've got forty-eight hours!" Then make it up from there.' Elliott was great – he knew what he was doing.

We had a screening of an unfinished cut in a cinema in London, and a girl said to me, 'Is that your life?' I was like, 'If that was my life, I would either be dead or in prison now!' Some people honestly thought it was real.

One of the guys in it from the label was Kyrill, from the white punk/blues band The Dirty, who has actually passed away. He died of alcohol poisoning in a little hotel in Thailand. He was born in England, but his parents were Russian, and he was a very troubled boy – you could see that on screen, and you could tell when you met him that he wasn't going to make all of the bonus.

Unfortunately, neither did *Brown Punk*. Chris Blackwell put quite a bit of money into it, and when he watched it, he said to me, 'This is so good, it changes movies! We need bigger distribution. I don't think my company Palm Pictures is big enough.' He was describing stuff with serious directors, like I'd seriously changed the face of movies. But the trouble was, I didn't know the movie industry well enough to get it off the ground, so I couldn't get it released, and nothing happened with it. I put a few clips up online, but apparently Chris still wants to release it properly.

Also working on this movie was a guy called Lee Jaffe, who is a weirdo and a bit of a legend, because he actually lived with Bob Marley.

LEE JAFFE: I met Chris Blackwell in 1972 when a girlfriend took me to one of the first screenings of the Jamaican rude-boy movie *The Harder They Come* in London. I went to see one of Chris's acts, Traffic, at Madison Square Garden the following year, and when I went back to their hotel suite afterwards Bob Marley was there. I was a multi-media artist, doing conceptual art, photography and film-making, and Bob and I really hit it off.

I went to Kingston with Bob and Chris in '74, and Chris had bought this house uptown, a few hundred yards from the Prime Minister's residence at 56 Hope Road – an old colonial house with a backyard, and in the backyard was a shack which had formerly been the slave quarters, but The Wailers had transformed it into a rehearsal hall. When I arrived there, Peter Tosh and the Barrett brothers were rehearsing this song, '400 Years'. Just, wow! I didn't want to leave.

I didn't know what I was gonna do with my life at that point, but I felt there was nothing more interesting going on in the world. There was an extra bedroom in the house, and I just stayed. At that time Island didn't really have a presence in the US, and Chris asked me to help organise a tour for The Wailers. I organised the first two North American tours, and eventually played harmonica on *Natty Dread*, and worked with Tosh producing *Legalize It*. Soon after I'd moved out of Hope Road in '77, people came and shot Bob, so who knows, I might've been dead if I'd still been there.

After *Legalize It*, I moved to New York, and started making political art again. I did a load of photos with Jean-Michel Basquiat, and we made a trip around the world together.

By the 2000s, I was living in LA, and when Chris Blackwell came to town, I would drive him around, because being alone with him in a car, you get to have quality time. One time I picked him up, and he said, 'I have to go and meet Tricky.' I was already a fan, and I'd seen Tricky play at the El Rey Theatre, maybe in '97. I was a little late, and the stage was completely black. There were no lights on any of the musicians, or Tricky. I thought that was brilliant. It was so anti-pop. He is very anti-celebrity, and my work is very much about that, too, so the work I went on to do with Tricky definitely pursued those ideas.

He was starting this label with Chris, and I was going to be the cameraman, shooting videos with some of the acts that were gonna be on the label. I suggested Tricky make a story out of it and use some of those people as actors. I considered him a bit like Bob and Peter, or Jean-Michel, on that level of importance and brilliance. He's an amazing video artist.

Doing the movie in the UK, there was a lot of bad weather. It seemed like it was cold and raining for months. That was actually good for the pictures, and the video. The title *Brown Punk* started to make a whole lot of sense to me. We went to Bristol and met some of his family. He has family who are social workers and have PhDs, and then others who are gangsters – or rather, former gangsters! But they all love each other.

It was Easter and they were all getting together. His auntie told me this story about Tricky's great-great-grandfather who was a slave in Jamaica, but then when they freed the slaves, he got a job on a boat bringing bananas to the UK. He gets off the boat and he sees this white woman in Cornwall, they fall in love, and that was the beginning of the end of the idea of race in the UK. It was like, wow!

The idea of race started with colonialism; it was a construct that was built to justify the subjugation of people in other parts of the world. A lot of Tricky's work, I think, is deconstructing that idea, it runs through all of what he does on some level.

The scenes we shot with Bob's daughter Cedella were just beautiful, I thought. We also shot with Elliott Gould, who's a friend of mine. He said, 'Just tell me where and when, and I'll be there!' He didn't even know who Tricky was, but they got along great, and we shot in my apartment in Santa Monica.

So many things happened during filming. Flat tyres in the middle of nowhere. One time we were shooting a scene with a lot of money, and the rapper guy we were shooting with brought his own money – £30,000 in cash – and his own blood. The scene needed blood. We didn't have any fake stuff; he actually kept vials of his own blood in case he got shot or stabbed or something.

We shot with these kids in Manchester who were working for organised crime. They had new clothes and new bicycles; they were too young to be driving. It was pretty intense, and visually it was powerful. There were a lot of real guns – and people think there are no guns in England! That was not true. It was more prevalent at that time than people realised. Two of the kids got shot right after we were filming with them.

We made some great music videos, too. Tricky edited one really cleverly with this boxing match between two girls – one of them was a welterweight Muay Thai champion that Tricky knew, or some gangster was managing. It was like *Raging Bull*.

Tricky thinks the movie is finished, I don't. You can see it in pieces online. We actually shot quite a bit more. I think he's a great director, but he quickly moves on to other things. It needs so little to finish it off. Maybe it'll happen someday!

TRICKY: What's crazy about LA is, with all the partying, five years went by, just like that. It wasn't even planned. I just went to LA, loved it, made a couple of records, then half a decade disappeared in a flash. I was hardly making music myself, just trying to get artists on my label recorded, and partying and having a good time. I didn't have to work, because I had money, and I could do the odd little bit to keep it coming in.

Mad things were still happening to me. One morning I woke up and looked out of my apartment, and I had paparazzi outside. So I went out

SHOOTING *BROWN PUNK* WITH ELLIOT GOULD, 2012 (PHOTO © LEE JAFFE)

David Bowie

London
Aug - 95

Dear Tricky,

Iman and I loved the show the other night. I've loved the album for some time.

'Q' asked me to do a small piece on anything I wanted so I chose to do a fictional on you! Hope you enjoy it, or find it interesting/annoying/something.

Not sure when it's coming out, next month I think.

Anyway, Oh great-gun, hope we get to meet again.

[signature] 95

DAVID BOWIE'S LETTER TO ME

WITH TERRY HALL

LA LIFESTYLE

JIN, PARIS (PHOTO © CHARLES DE LINIERES)

AT 104, PARIS (PHOTO © CHARLES DE LINIERES)

LIVE IN PARIS, 2017 (PHOTO © VERA RODRIGUES/VERACITY MUSIC)

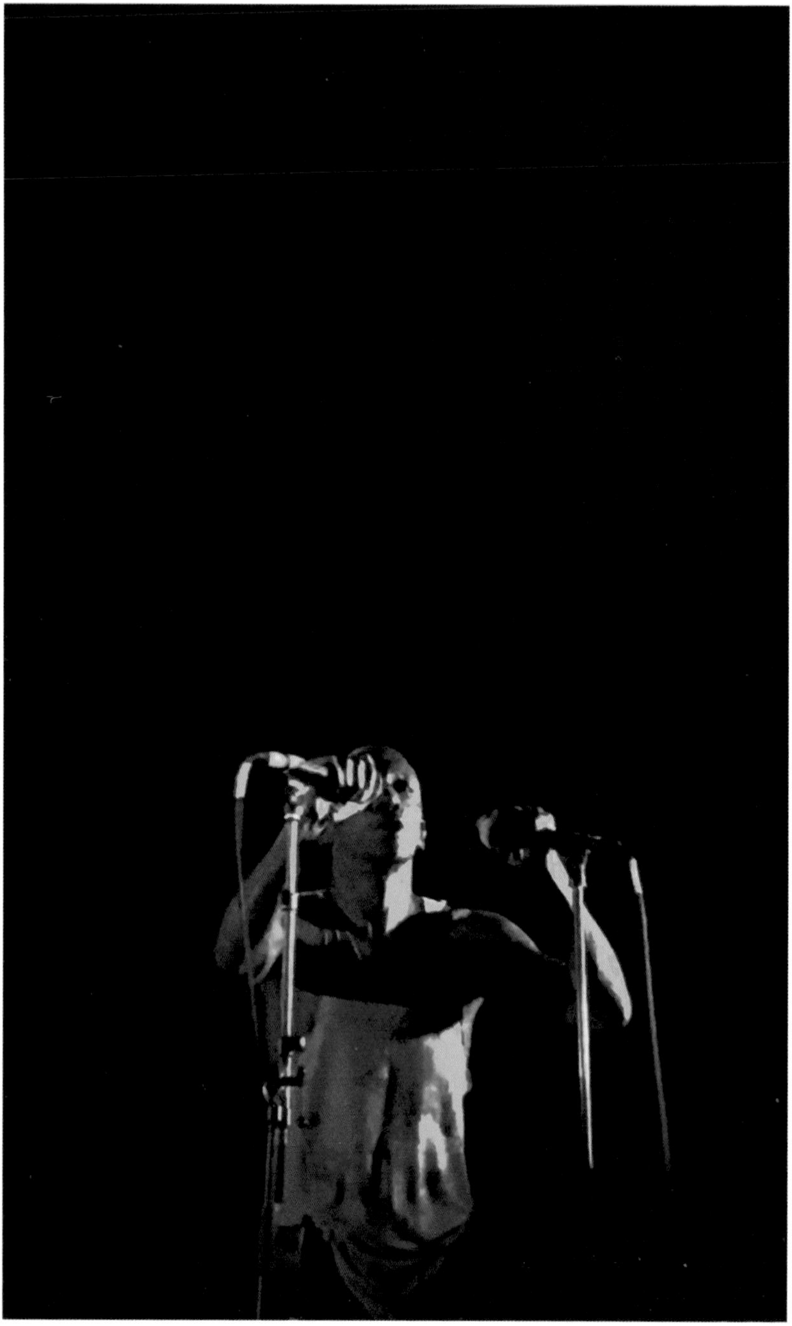

SHOOTING *BROWN PUNK*, 2012 (PHOTO © LEE JAFFE)

CHRISTMAS IN BRISTOL WITH SOME OF THE FAMILY

– 'What the fuck is this all about?' Because I was in LA, I wasn't hearing about what was in the papers at home. One of the photographers goes, 'Did you play pool with David Cameron's missus?' It turned out that his wife Samantha went to college in Bristol years ago. She used to go to this particular pub, and she reckons she played pool with me there. Bizarre. I can't remember that, obviously. Anyway, I never hang out in Clifton pubs, know what I mean?

Being in LA I was very cut off from home, but I'd also lost my motivation. As long as I had enough money rolling in for my daughter's school fees – that was all I cared about. Martina wanted Mazy to go to good schools. Martina is a Somerset girl herself, and she made the decision Mazy should go to school in the UK – the same sort of boarding school that she went to herself. I would have just let her go to a school around the corner, but Martina is a good mum, because she was like, 'No, it's got to be the best school,' so she went to Roedean, just outside Brighton on the Sussex coast.

Martina and I weren't in a relationship anymore but we were always happy to collaborate as parents – we never had any problem with that. She planned it all out school-wise, and I paid for it. Roedean is old English – old money! Put it this way – I didn't see many other black parents. And there were definitely no guys from Knowle West sending their kids there.

The facilities are unbelievable. They have a proper theatre and a proper recording studio! Mazy loved it there, and it made a very English girl of her. For me, it became all about paying the fees. That's when things start getting real, isn't it? Every quarter of the year, I had to have her school money. Before that, I could just spend whatever I had. In a way, though, it made life easy, because as a dad you don't care about yourself anymore. You care about the kid. I didn't give a fuck about anything else, so long as I had the money to send Mazy to school. I could be broke and living in a bedsit. It put everything else in perspective. What's mad is, I knew she wasn't going to use any of this education. I knew that she was going to be a musician.

That chapter was closing, and my stay in Los Angeles was coming to an end. The problem there was, it's Party City, and I ain't got no discipline. The hardest part about being a musician is that you ain't got nine-to-five, so you ain't got any reason *not* to party all night. It was time for a change.

MASTER CHEN

The reason why a lot of musicians have drug or alcohol problems, I think, is because we ain't got no consistency, no routine. Most people have a nine-to-five, which for better or worse gives their life a regular pattern. Whereas a musician might tour on and off for six or seven months of the year, then all of a sudden you might have three months off. You ain't doing anything, and you've got money, so what are you going to do with that time?

If you don't fill the gap with some form of physical exercise, then maybe you're gonna do it with drugs or alcohol. When I come off tour, what I try to do is have a week where I train hard two or three times, and then I'm knackered, and I wanna do things like cook food and chill. If I don't do that, I'll want to go out and do stuff, and I'll end up partying all weekend.

I've found that if I don't train in winter, I get depressed. At that time of year, I can't sit outside and have a coffee and watch the world go by, so I have to do some form of exercise otherwise I start to feel down. I'll get up and it's a shit day, and I'll be like, 'Fuck, I don't want to leave the house,' so I'll go training, then I'm ready to tackle the winter. I'm a guy who never stops thinking, so exercise helps occupy my mind.

I don't consider myself to be a fighter, but I've always gravitated towards boxing or some form of martial arts, because I can't exercise without learning something. If I'm not learning, I'll quickly end up not wanting to do it. I'm not going to do circuit training, or run on a treadmill just because it makes me fit. In hotels, I rarely use the gym. It always has to have an element of education to it. If I'm learning moves, and I know I'm getting somewhere, then I love it. But going to the gym to get your body looking good, or just feeling good – that's not for me.

Lots of people play football: that can be fun for about ten minutes, then I'm bored as fuck. Running about chasing a round thing seems ridiculous to me, even though I was actually a good footballer. I was in my school team all through school, and if I'd have focused, I probably could have got somewhere with it. I was always a left-winger: I had speed and I was left-footed, so I could play left wing, which can be a hard position to fill, but ultimately I found it pointless. You know, chase the ball, run around, pass it, score a goal – after ten minutes, my mind would lose focus.

If I'm learning how to do something, however, like a kick or a punch, that keeps me focused and entertained. I can get into something when I know that I'm learning something people have been doing for hundreds of years. That helps me get through, when I can't be bothered to go.

I think doing any discipline is good. When I was fifteen, my auntie Marlow sent me to the boxing gym. I wish I'd stayed with it, because that's good discipline. When I moved to London, now and again I did a bit of Muay Thai, or Thai boxing, in a club above a shop in Harlesden. I went to a boxing club in Notting Hill a few times when I was living in Kensington, and then when I moved to New York, I started doing a bit of Muay Thai again. I've since gone on to do Brazilian Ju-Jitsu, and some Russian martial arts. Wherever I travel, I have always found a place to do a bit of something.

The longest I've stuck at anything was Tai Chi, which I did in New York for seven years, with a guy called William C.C. Chen. He was taught by Cheng Man-ch'ing, so he is second generation from one of the all-time originators of Tai Chi, and that was my first time doing it, which was an amazing experience.

Tai Chi is the closest I've come to meditation, but it's different, because it's all about learning 'a form', or a routine, and having patience in that process. It takes seven minutes to do the form: you think seven minutes is not a long time, but that seven-minute form could take from eight months to a year to learn. I learnt it in about seven months – but that was still a long time to do something for seven minutes! That blew my mind – patience!

When you get the form, your hands heat up and then you go somewhere else – you stop thinking about the outside world, and then you start thinking, 'Ah, negative, I know that word, but what does it mean?' and you can't figure out what negative means. You think, 'Depressed – I know that word but what does it mean?' Then you think of happiness: 'Oh yeah, I understand that,' and, 'Oh yeah, I did this in the womb!'

It just makes you realise that all of these things are just words, and if you didn't know the words, would they really exist? So when you've got the form down, and you know it well enough, it can take you somewhere else where you can't think of the word. You'll be like, 'I know I know that word, negative, depressed …' but you just can't think of it.

So, it's not typical meditation, but it is kind of close to that.

After a while, I was teaching in Master Chen's class as well, for the old people. He gave me the old people because he was teaching me more about patience – to teach someone who is eighty years of age requires that virtue in abundance.

From being my teacher, Master Chen became more like my dad in New York, this little Chinese guy. I used to hang out with him and go to his house. We would have dinner together.

When I played shows in New York during that period, he would be my support band. He would do a form onstage, and the crowd would go totally silent. They would go from talking, then they would see him, and then you could hear a pin drop, because they were feeling his vibe. Then me and my band would go on afterwards. One time, I did TV news with him: some big American news organisation wanted to do a feature on me, and I said, 'I don't really want to talk about music, but you can come to Tai Chi with me!' so they interviewed the two of us together instead.

Tai Chi is the sort of thing you would want to keep up, but I was unlucky in a way, because the best guy in the world taught me at the start. I've been to teachers since, and they think they are just doing a meditation, but Tai Chi is a fighting art without the contact. Its origins are in disguising fighting movements. Master Chen used to be a competitive fighter – I think he won a silver medal for China in the Olympics or something crazy like that. Tai Chi is still very healthy for you, it produces blood flow in your body, but everything you're doing is actually a strike.

After Master Chen, I've gone to clubs, and I'll do the form better than the guy teaching me. I've gone to classes and they don't even know why they're doing it. They think it's all for health and relaxation. 'No, that move you're just showing me – that turns into a strike!' I've been to a class in London, and I said to the teacher, 'That's a good strike!' And he went, 'What do you mean, "strike"?' I said, 'What you are doing is a strike. Like, this one is a strike to the throat, you do it slow, but if you speed it up, it's a strike to the throat. This one is a fist. That is a push …'

I tried to keep up with it, but when my form is better than the guy teaching me, it's hard to stay motivated. I was incredibly lucky meeting Master Chen, but also very unlucky. It was almost a curse, because after you've trained with someone like him as your first teacher, where do you go?

After I moved to LA, I never did Tai Chi properly again. Instead, I did a little bit of Muay Thai – never competitive, just training, and then I did some Brazilian Ju-Jitsu for about three years. I happened to bump into this Brazilian guy, who showed me some moves. If you've ever seen UFC, aka Ultimate Fighting Championship, it's a bit like that – wrestling, with submissions. If a fight ain't over in the first thirty seconds from a punch, it goes to the floor and then it's basically fighting on the floor – grappling, chokes, arm bars, ankle locks, wrist stuff, all leading to submissions.

I've also done a Russian martial art called Sambo, which is punching, kicking and wrestling – like Ju-Jitsu but Russian style – and then a Filipino martial art called Panantukan – affectionately known as Filipino Dirty

Boxing – which I found by accident near my home recently. It's boxing, punching, kicking, but in the Philippines they start with knife-sticks, and when you are really good, you move up to hands. This is because it's easier with sticks – like in real life, if you have a problem, pick up a stick (or a bottle or a knife). That is their culture: they learn to fight with weapons first. Once you master the weapons, then you go to hands. But in Europe they teach it differently, it starts with hands, then after two years I started learning the sticks.

Again, it's contact – elbows, punching, knees, kicks, and stick fighting. You're not padded up – if you're getting a leg kick, you're getting a leg kick! It has its own form, but not like Tai Chi or even karate. You learn forms like moving forwards and backwards, using both elbows – punch, elbow, elbow, elbow. Or – left, right, front kick, right left, back kick. You learn both sides as well, so you do a technique one side and then the other side. Palm, elbow, hook, strike, do that forwards, then you do it backwards on your back foot, then you do it to the side.

As I mentioned earlier, the only sport I actually watch is boxing, to see what they're doing technically. When you're watching someone like a Floyd Mayweather, he can do stuff that other people can't. The guy's skill level is amazing, and the attitude as well. I really respect the work ethic. With someone like Mayweather, it's art – a top level of talent and intelligence. People think boxers are dumb, but you have to have Ring IQ.

Everyone watched Muhammad Ali in the '70s, even all the little white kids in Knowle West. I can remember staying up really late to watch his fights on TV. He was a very intelligent man, and what a life he had. I was too young to know what he did outside the ring, but I would stay up with my uncles and great-grandad to watch him fight, because he was just such a huge figure.

With the various disciplines I've attempted myself, it's never been any kind of spiritual quest. I don't know about that shit, or care. I'm probably looking for discipline – imposing a structure that I never had when I was growing up, what with being allowed to bunk off school and stay out all night. It's also about learning: I didn't learn anything in school, because I wasn't interested, so now I can learn in my own time, and learn something I *am* interested in. Apart from that, it's about keeping me entertained while I'm getting fit. It keeps my mind occupied.

When I'm training my way, by contrast, I'm not thinking about anything at all. I'm focused on learning something in the moment, and when I come out of there, I'm so tired that I can't even manage to think what I'm going to eat that day. And that's a good thing.

CHAPTER THIRTEEN
GHETTO YOUTH

In June 2008, I had a couple of TV appearances lined up in Paris, so Cesar and I decided to escape from LA's unrelenting heat and book a week or two's holiday in the French capital, just to hang out in a different environment. Our usual lifestyle came with us, though, and one lovely spring afternoon, we dropped loads of Es and sauntered around the city enjoying its famously romantic atmosphere. We were meandering down this tree-lined walkway in the middle of a particular boulevard – I'm afraid I don't remember which one, for obvious reasons – and suddenly all these pigeons flew from the branches up into the sky. We watched this private display the birds had put on for us with a mixture of joy and wonder.

'Woah, this is so beautiful,' I said to my buddy. 'I'm gonna live here!'

Within two or three months, I had moved to Paris. I'd been feeling it was high time that I changed things up in my life. I'd realised that I needed to get out of LA because, much as I loved knocking about with Cesar and had been having the most fantastic time, I was simply not doing anything productive out there. All I was doing was partying.

One day, I was doing an interview, and the journalist said in passing, 'As you haven't done an album in five years …' I was like, 'Fucking hell – really?!' I knew I hadn't made a record in a while, but hearing it said like that – 'no album in five years' – was a real shock.

I loved America and, after thirteen years of living over there, I actually thought like an American. The shops, I could relate to. Going to supermarkets in America, everything, I could relate to. While I was living Stateside, I didn't go to many places outside America. When I was living in LA, I hardly travelled at all. I would fly over to Bristol to see my family quickly and fly back again. Or go to London, do a few work things, then rush back. With no albums to promote, my touring schedule had all but dried up, so my only excursions would be with Cesar to other places within the US. I'd been in America so long it was like I was Americanised.

When the two of us went to Paris, it was like discovering Europe again. Even though I'd been to Paris many times before, I thought it was incredible. It was like seeing the place with fresh eyes, and that experience made me want to discover Europe again, to live in a different culture, with more variety. In America, you could go to one city and then go to another city, and they will both be quite similar. Go from New York to Philadelphia – yeah, there are differences, but still …

Paris was something else – just 'wow', after all those years away from Europe, so I thought, 'Okay, I want to live here for a while, and I want to start recording again.'

I ended up living in Paris for six years and, like in New York and LA, I had loads of different apartments, in very contrasting areas. Sometimes I'd live really ghetto, sometimes really posh – from as expensive as fuck, to very poor. I didn't feel outside of things because of the language. The language barrier didn't bother me at all. I don't feel any different in London or Paris. It's just another very different culture. It's also quite a small city in the centre, so I walked everywhere and got to know the streets well.

LA hadn't really been like a home, it was more like a party city, all about going out three or four times a week and getting fucked up. I was going out sometimes just because I was bored, because I wasn't doing anything substantial. I still went out in Paris, but more because I was actually invited somewhere. I became much more settled there. Sometimes I would just sit around at my place, chill out, record some music, then go out and eat. I had a favourite butcher's shop where I would buy fresh meat, and I knew where the health food stores were to get my special bread that I need to eat. I had a couple of favourite restaurants I'd go to regularly, so it was all about living like that, simple and regular, rather than partying, and that's how Paris became my home.

· ▪ ▪ ■ ▪ ▪ ·

Right at the start of my time in Paris, I got involved in the opening of a new arts complex at 104 rue d'Aubervilliers in the 19th arondissement. Called Centquatre, or just 104, the building used to be a morgue, and the idea was that they'd invite artists in residence to use its 29,000 square metre space for installations and contemporary art events.

Through a Parisian girl called Mai, who I'd first met in New York in '95, I was initially asked by the Mayor of Paris to play a free gig in their vast hall to mark its inaugural evening in October 2008. The whole point was, Centquatre is right in the middle of one of the inner city's poorest neighbourhoods – the 19th is ghetto as fuck – so for them to throw open these big wrought-iron gates at the front and let the locals in might've been seen as risky.

On the night, there were 3,000 people crammed in there, and apparently there were just as many outside trying to get in, but we never had no trouble. The mayor and the organisers were so happy with how it went that they asked me back there in December to do some kind of installation – whatever I wanted, for three months.

They were really cool, and weren't trying to force me to do one thing or another – it was all up to me. I said, 'Listen, if I can work with the ghetto kids there, I'll do it.' On the first day, I had them just open the gates, so that anybody could come in and mill about in the main space. In one of the side studios, there was all the stuff for painting and drawing, while in another one, I got in some musical instruments and recording equipment.

One day I would do football in there, then I'd have a martial arts teacher, or I would be sparring with the guys. Then sometimes there'd be a graffiti studio, and usually a studio where they could record music. And then other times we would just hang out.

It soon fell into two shifts, with young kids dropping in at 4–5pm on their way home from school. By about 8pm they would all go home, then at about 10pm, thirty ghetto guys would waltz in and they'd do graffiti or make music into the small hours.

In all the three months I was in there, we didn't have one single fight situation, even though everybody was telling me beforehand what a rough neighbourhood it was. Initially, they didn't want the ghetto kids coming into their expensively renovated cultural centre. In fact, crime went down locally while I was there – all kinds of crime just stopped, because these kids that had been causing it actually had somewhere to go.

We had really good fun in there, although I did have one guy who brought a gun in. He took me into the bathroom and said, 'Hey, Tricky, check this out!' He was very polite about it. I don't know why he was showing me the gun – maybe it was his way of telling me, 'It's real here.' But you could see it was real – you didn't need to see a gun to know that.

I said, 'I can feel your energy, I know you're for real, but you don't need that. Can you not bring it in here?' The guy was cool after that. He never brought the gun back again, and we never had any problems with that kind of thing. Paris is kind of hectic like that. There are loads of ghettos there, and 19th is only one of them. While I was in 104, I lived around the corner in Rue de la Chapelle, so I got to see it for myself every day.

I got a lot of love for letting these kids hang out, which was very touching. After a while, I had people's families bringing me food and presents. Mums were coming down, dads were coming down, hanging out with their kids.

When I used to walk out to go to the shop, all these kids would follow me. Sometimes I was buying pizza for them, or cans of Coke, but a couple of guys would always come along, making sure I was okay. Even though I was good there, they were looking out for me. It was like I joined the family.

MAI LUCAS: I'm a photographer from Paris and my ethnicity is half Vietnamese, half French. I've known Tricky for more than twenty years, and I consider him family – he is the godfather of my first daughter, Taika.

We met in 1995 at a very bright moment in both of our careers, when we were defining our lives and who we were. I was doing street photography in New York, and one day in downtown Manhattan I saw this guy with an amazing face – Tricky. I asked him, 'Can I take your picture?' He was smiling at me, and he was like, 'Yeah, no problem! I'm an artist, maybe I'll use your photos. Come to my hotel tomorrow.'

We took photos out on the street and had a lot of fun. When we were done, I told him that another musician I knew, Ben Harper, was staying at the same hotel, and wanted to meet him. We made our way up to Ben's and I rang at the door but there was nobody there. I was behind Tricky with my camera, and he was like, 'I'm sure I can hear someone in there,' and he got onto his knees, trying to look under the door. I took a picture of him with his feet sticking out behind him looking under the door.

I went back to Paris but we stayed in touch. He called me: 'Yo, Mai, I want to see all the photos you did,' so he made me come to London, and he loved the picture of him on all fours looking under the door. He said, 'Wow, that is so deep – it's going to be the cover of my next album.' We talked to the record company and they said, 'We need more pictures for the CD booklet,' so we did a proper shoot on that idea, and that became the artwork for *Nearly God*.

We spent time together in New York, but then I lost touch with him while I got married and had kids in Paris. For five years I didn't see him at all, then one day he called me soon after he'd moved to Paris.

At that time, I'd had a chance to work at this new museum, 104. Their people called me, saying, 'We loved your exhibitions about New York ghetto street life, and we would like you to do the same thing in this neighbourhood.' I'd never worked in that way in Paris before, only in fashion. I was working with 104 for two years taking those pictures, while the building was being renovated.

After Tricky got in touch, I introduced him to the two bosses of 104, theatre directors Robert Cantarella and Frédéric Fisbach. They'd loved Tricky since the beginning, and so the opening concert was arranged. The 19th arrondissement is a very bad neighbourhood, with a lot of people crammed into high-rises, and a lot of guns in those buildings. There's a lot of violence, a lot of drugs, and a lot of poverty. Relations with the cops are always tense – Tricky was actually arrested in this neighbourhood, and the cops put a gun in his face as they took him in. That never happens in Paris anywhere else.

Tricky's plan was to record an album with the people we met in the neighbourhood. Sometimes it would be an Arab guy from the café next door, other times some kids we met on the street – the rappers of the neighbourhood. For three months Tricky created his own world there, which I soon realised was all about working in total chaos. He thrives on chaos, whereas I struggled to cope!

Tricky made this beautiful album, and we made some videos of the music, but then none of it ever came out because he took it to various record companies and they just didn't get it. That's the problem with both of us: we have vision, and a way of seeing interesting things, but sometimes the commercial world doesn't understand.

Sometimes he was more attracted by a nobody that he met on the street than by working with some well-educated creatives who respect him for who he is – but if he doesn't feel it in that moment, he won't do it.

We also have thirty-six hours of documentary footage that I never found the money to release, but what was magical was the time itself. Tricky made a connection straight away to people on the street, from the ghetto, and we took them into 104. Everybody was scared, but there was no reason to be scared. Tricky was the person who broke the stupid rules.

After that, he made the space like a playground for the kids of the neighbourhood. They would come in, play football in the studio, screaming, smoking, and Tricky didn't care. He was recording stuff, and at the same time buying them food, drinks. Total chaos, and he loved it! Tricky was never mad at them. Amazing tolerance!

In the French media, there was a lot of attention, because this well-known English star was mixing with kids who were drug dealers. After we finished, we learnt that some of the guys we knew were arrested because they'd kidnapped people and burnt them in their house. But when they came to our place, we just had fun, talking about their parents. It was a place of release, and acceptance.

The sad thing from that time was the story of Jin. Tricky had moved to the 4th arrondissement, and he'd befriended this Korean girl, a video-maker who was so beautiful and special. She was like Nina Hagen but Korean – an amazing artist, and the things she made were very close to Tricky's imagination. She had a special style of her own, very quiet, very smart – the kind of girl who doesn't say much but is really in tune with everyone's feelings.

When we did the 104 installation, she came with us and participated in a video we wanted to do, and she kind of peaced everybody out. She was part of our friend circle when we went out to clubs and parties, but one day we heard she'd been found dead in the river. I went to her funeral. It seems she was on her way home after a party on a boat, and she slipped and fell – a stupid sad accident.

Jin was like an angel who came into our lives, and she disappeared just as quickly as she arrived. After she died, Tricky made a tattoo of Jin on his hand. So that was the big sadness and pain in the story of 104.

One of the many positives was that it was also when we met Charles. He arrived on the first day with his story of being in the French Foreign Legion and listening to Tricky's music on his many postings around the world. He was a photographer, too, and he began to join us there every day.

TRICKY: Charles is a white Parisian who was a Legionnaire for fourteen years, and who comes from a Foreign Legion family. I've since learnt a lot about it: that it's not what everyone thinks, where once you join, you can't get out. It's the opposite: they look after you all your life – not like the British Army. People don't run away from the Foreign Legion – people run *into* the Foreign Legion. What used to happen was, if you were on a murder charge in England, you could run away and join the Foreign Legion, and you couldn't be arrested. The Foreign Legion is its own territory.

When Charles came down on my first day at 104, we started talking and soon realised there were some unexpected parallels between our two lives. His mum had epilepsy, like mine did. Before he met me, they were fans of my music and she would play songs off *Maxinquaye* on the piano.

Stranger still, he was in the Foreign Legion with a guy from Manchester who knows my uncle Tony. This guy was Charles's sergeant, and his brother was the famous boxer, John Conteh. Charles said to me, 'I was in with a Liverpool guy,' but he never knew that the guy's brother was once the world light-heavyweight boxing champion! It sounded like, for Charles's sergeant, it was either boxing, or the Foreign Legion, or get into trouble.

Another thing Charles said that interested me was how they don't see race in there. Once you join up, you are no longer Japanese, black, white, nothing – you are Foreign Legion. One day someone will make African food, the next Japanese, and there's no race or colour division whatsoever. Charles said that when he first came out, it was difficult for him to adjust back to normality in Paris, because in 'real life', people were rude and prejudiced. Even going to buy something from the corner store, someone would be horrible, whereas in the Legion everybody respects each other.

Charles was a part of how I became settled in Paris, because the two of us went to boxing training three times a week, which brought a regularity and regimen to my life after all my late-night antics in LA. Once I'd got back into it, I went into an amateur boxing competition there – club against club.

By nature, Charles is very much a no-trouble guy. If you met him, you'd never believe that he beat up two policemen! There was a protest in Paris, and this one policeman was beating a girl. He said to the policeman, 'Stop!' but the policeman didn't stop, so Charles beat him up, and another one who was heavy-handed, trying to intervene. He had to go to court afterwards, but the charges were dropped.

Charles has become almost like my brother. He's been back to Bristol for Christmas with me a couple of times, and he talks to my cousin Michelle sometimes more than me. He could go to Bristol tomorrow and stay at her house or my auntie's, and I wouldn't even have to know about it.

He cooks good, but he eats very simple. Sometimes, he will eat literally only mashed potato, and that's it.

'How can you eat that on its own?' I'll ask.

'It's fine for me!'

We'll go out to a restaurant, and he'll order a plate of mashed potato! That's not very French, is it?

CHARLES DE LINIERES: I met Tricky at 104, not long after I left the French Foreign Legion after fourteen years. I guess we bonded because we have some similar things in our background: both our mothers are dead, and they were both epileptic. My mother's epilepsy started when she was two years old. Tricky's mother died when he was four, so he never saw his mother suffering with it. I say to him, it was much better not to see that.

For both of us, it was our grandmothers who took us in and brought us up, because my father died when I was fourteen years old – from a bee sting, within thirty minutes of being stung, because he was allergic to the venom.

We have a lot of soldiers in my family, but I'm the only one in my generation who was in the French Foreign Legion. I did it because I wanted to be stronger in my life, and I thought the army would help me to achieve that. I'm not particularly a fan of the army, only the concept of the French Foreign Legion. There are 150 different nationalities accepted into it, so there's no racism, no history of religion, no history of politics or family. They don't care about your past. You enter into it as a new family, and it's amazing!

I stayed with it for fourteen years because it was super-interesting, and cool, although the discipline was difficult. Initially I was stationed in the south of France, in a cavalry regiment at Orange. After that, I travelled all the time, serving six months minimum in a different country every year. The first two years were the most difficult, as I got posted to Yugoslavia in 1992, to work alongside the United Nations. Everything I did after that was easier, because I started with the most difficult thing.

I would sleep in a room with a Russian, a Swede, a Brazilian and an African, and there was never any problem. We shared everything: cigarettes, socks, T-shirts ... Every day something funny would happen, because everyone brought his own culture with him into the group.

When you come back to normal society afterwards, you're alone. You've forgotten all the things from normal life, like waiting for your pay and paying rent and bills, but mostly I missed the mentality that we would help each other. Normal society is hard – no one wants to help you if you have a problem in the street. It took at least a year for me to turn it around and start another chapter in my life.

It was the death of my mother that helped me to leave, because after fourteen years I wanted to have a normal life. When I left the Legion, I became a photographer for the press army back in Paris, and it was then that I met Tricky. I knew his music from the beginning, with Massive Attack, and I followed his progress right the way through.

I saw the 104 concert and took some photos. Afterwards I had them blown up really big. I went to see him at his installation and gave him all the photos. We arranged to see each other the day after, and for the next three months I went every day after work, just to see him and have fun with all the people there. It was a massive place, with ceilings twenty metres high, and somehow Tricky made a different vibe every day – like a party, with all these children.

Normally at places like this, you might open the door once a month just to show people the work you're doing. But Tricky opened the door every day. Loads of boys and girls, after they finished school, all wanted to go straight to see Tricky – not their parents! He would buy sweets, cakes and Cokes for them, and all the children loved him. Not for his music, or because he was famous, just because he was super-cool with them. Many of the parents invited him to dinner to say thank you.

Before 104, my morale was not good, but with Tricky my smile came back, and all my sadness went away. In some ways he directly changed my life, and after that, because we had a good vibe together, we decided to keep seeing each other.

That was hard for me to imagine, because I'm not a musician or in the music business; I'm just a photographer and a soldier. How many singers or successful people do that? I was shocked by his character, his openness. During nearly six years we were together all the time.

He knows Paris like the back of his hand, because he walked everywhere while he was here. Not many Parisians do that. He probably knows more about Paris than many Parisians, because he moved around so much. We liked to take coffee together – to stay in a café and watch people, and have fun.

Early on, he asked me to find an English boxing club, and I found a really cool one, so we did the beginners course together. I was shit at it. I had no technique, but he helped me with every lesson. We went sometimes three times a week, just him and me and a teacher.

He's a very good boxer, and he can teach it too. Like his uncle Tony, he can knock someone out with one punch. He did a competition with the club, and he knocked a guy out in two minutes flat. He's very quick and has great technique. He follows a lot of boxers, follows the culture, and can speak about the big names. Personally, I don't have that culture, so he was my introduction, and since then, I have never stopped boxing. I love it.

For me, Tricky is an anti-superstar. He's really open with people, but if you treat him like a celebrity, he will close up or throw you out. He uses his instinct all the time, and he's super-honest. Many people think he's dark, but he is totally the opposite – super-funny, and very positive. If you give him a bad thing, he will do something good with it. It's a rare quality.

I couldn't possibly have had a relationship like that with another singer. I don't think many people can open the door like Tricky opened the door to me. I'm a simple person, but we have a cool vibe. And he never forgets me. He is loyal.

TRICKY: During the move between LA and Paris, I'd got myself a new label deal with Domino in London. I liked their vibe: they were an independent company with a lot of young people working there, and they'd just had some serious success with Franz Ferdinand and Arctic Monkeys. They were nice and enthusiastic, but honestly, after a while, I didn't get what they were trying to do with me.

The first record I did for them was *Knowle West Boy*, which was made in London in '08. The owner of the label, Laurence Bell, wanted me to work with Bernard Butler, who had been the guitarist in Suede. It was Laurence's label, so I kind of had to agree to it. I went into the studio with this Bernard and, in the end, I took the tapes, but I didn't really want to use anything we'd done.

Laurence talked to him and said, 'Sorry, you're not really on the album now,' but the thing was, I'd done a deal with him, so I had to give him a production credit, even though he didn't do all that much on the finished record. Now, no offence to Laurence, who is a really good guy, but I wouldn't have made that mistake because I would never have worked with Bernard Butler in the beginning, because I knew I didn't need to.

Calling the album *Knowle West Boy* was important to me. I've always been proud of coming from Knowle West. I always thought it made me who I am. Knowle Westers are individuals, and the place has many fond memories for me – things like Guy Fawkes' Night. I can still smell the bonfires. We always used to be out on our bikes till late at night, all the kids. Everybody knew each other in the area, so whoever I hung out with, my nan usually knew their family. You didn't hear about a paedophile running around the streets. It was a tight community. It was the days when you could borrow sugar off your next-door neighbour, and the back doors were always left open. I could go from my nan's house to my great-grandmother's house, and just walk straight in. Good days, fond memories.

The further I went away to live – from London, to New York and LA, then back to Paris – Knowle West has had more and more pull for me. When my uncle Tony was on the road with me, sometimes we would drive back to Bristol, just to go past 13 Padstow Road, because that's where his best memories are as well. One time, we saw a proper Rastafarian on the street – not just a Knowle West mixed-race kid with locks, an actual Rasta! We were like, 'What the fuck!' Things have changed a little, but not much.

On the album's back cover, and in the picture section of this book, there's an old picture of my great-uncles Martin and Arthur, my great-auntie Olive, and my great-grandad, taken in the house in Padstow Road, when they were all dressed up to go out. Back then, they all used to dress like the Rat Pack. They look like gangsters as well, don't they? It makes you wonder, what were they going to do that night? What happened after that picture? If you look, you can see that I've got the same eyes as my great-grandad.

It's funny: after that album came out, you suddenly had people who talked about Knowle West. That never happened before. Me and Whitley know a couple of DJs from there, and they would have never mentioned it before. Now when they do interviews, they are like, 'Yeah, I'm from Knowle West!' It was as if this album made it cool to be from Knowle West.

Over in Paris, I did a video for the song 'Council Estate', in a real ghetto neighbourhood there. It was actually a lot worse than Knowle West, that place – next level! A dangerous fucking area! We had to have permission to film there, because it was totally controlled – I think the director knew someone. We were there for a couple of days and we didn't see any police the whole time. The people controlled the area.

Another song on the album, called 'School Gates', had a huge and unforeseen impact on my life. It was how I ended up finding out for sure that I had another daughter, Marie, who was born when I was seventeen. I never knew about her, and she never knew about me, until her mum heard the song, and was like, 'Okay, it's time to tell her.' She went to Marie and said, 'I think this is your dad.'

I don't know if I could say that the song was me trying to find her. The lyrics are about me hanging around outside her mum's school waiting to see her when we were kids. But the song is what found her. My whole life revolves around the music.

Both my kids look like me, and nothing like their mothers, but Marie, who was eight or ten years older than Mazy, is the image of *my* mother, Maxine, who would've been her grandmother.

Her mum went to Merrywood Girls' School, while I went to Merrywood Boys', but she lived in more of a black area than I did, and her family is all Jamaican, so Marie has very Jamaican roots, and she knows them well. Her grandparents are Jamaicans, and she grew up with Jamaican food. She listens to the same music me and Whitley listened to when we were kids, and she even used to go to the same places where me and her mum went, so she is very much involved in Jamaican culture.

I'd gone through life from the age of nineteen or twenty knowing she was my kid, but *not* knowing she was my kid, if you know what I mean – it was one of those. One time I was with her cousin in Totterdown, and her mum went past with her – she must've been about three or four years of age, and this guy Leon said, 'That is definitely your kid – she looks just like you!' After things like that, you kind of know, but you can't be a hundred per cent.

In the 2000s, on my intro tape, which I used to go onstage to, was a song called 'Lost and Looking' by Sam Cooke. I used to cry whenever I heard it, and I couldn't really understand why. Like, alright, you just love the song! The lyrics go, 'I'm lost and I'm looking for my baby, Lord knows my baby ain't around', and I'd read that Sam Cooke wrote that about his kid that died in a swimming pool. He had a very tragic life.

One night, I'm just about to go onstage, and my phone rings, and it's my sister, who I've rarely spoken to over most of my life. She goes, 'Hey, you know Marie's your kid, right?' She'd seen the mum, and the mum admitted it to her. Then I went onstage to 'Lost and Looking', and I realised that's what I'd been crying about – I'd been looking for Marie.

The funny thing is, I always knew deep down that it wasn't about my mum. It was a totally different vibe to how I feel about my mum. I know when something is about my mum, because I've lived with it all my life. This was just different. Lost and looking … I didn't understand what this was about, but that night it all became clear to me.

Still, her mum needed another few months to sort it out in her head: imagine having to tell a girl of twenty-two or twenty-three, 'Look, the man you thought was your biological dad is not your dad – this is your dad.' Eventually she told her, then, to make sure, we did the DNA tests and they came back 99.9 per cent certain that she's my kid. That's a match right there, isn't it? Now she's got three dads: me, the guy she previously thought was her biological father, and her stepdad who brought her up from the age of seven, with her mum.

Being well known is weird for me, let alone for her by belated family association. Right from the start she said she doesn't want to live off me, and I've always taught both of my kids that. Having famous parents doesn't help you. Marie is thirty-three now, and she's been through university to get qualified as a social worker – which is kind of weird, because I could have done with some social work myself!

MARIE: I'd just come back from Notting Hill Carnival in summer 2009. I was about to go to my third and final year at university in Cardiff, and my mum was like, 'I need to tell you something.' I thought she was gonna say she was dying or something. She said, 'Your dad ain't your biological dad.' I knew of Tricky, because I went to a school where everyone hyped up Massive Attack. I knew my mum was friends with them back in the day, but I never really thought anything more of it.

After I found out, to be honest I think I was a bit shocked. I'd grown up with a different dad until I was twenty-two or twenty-three, and I was spun out about it. I had to go back to my final year at uni, and to start with we just spoke on the phone for a good few months. Then, in August, we met in London. He was staying in a hotel there, so I went to meet him with my friend.

It was weird first of all, but he was very relaxed about it. He phoned me up after the DNA test, and went, 'Oh, I *am* your dad!' I was just going to work, as I remember.

It was easy for him to get involved in my life, but it was very strange for me. Gradually, I started making contact with my biological family. I got his cousin Michelle's number off him and found out that her daughter Tasha lived literally five minutes around the corner from me – we'd even worked in the same office. I got her address and went to meet her, and with her it was really easy. We've been like sisters ever since, and we're really similar considering we weren't raised together.

I started going over to Paris to see Adrian a year or two later, and then I went and tracked down grandad – Adrian's dad, Roy. I just started looking people up, because Bristol's black community isn't that big, so you can phone someone who knows someone, and say, 'Where does this person live?' Grandad was really cool, immediately just like a proper grandad, and

I started going there every Sunday for dinner. He is so chilled out – he just goes to church and does gardening.

When people find out about it, they are always like, 'Oh my God,' so yes, it was pretty odd, but after that it's just like extra family, isn't it? Suddenly, Father's Day is a bit more expensive, but I don't listen to Adrian's music. You don't listen to your dad sing or rap or whatever – that would be weird.

Having a dad who's well known can be a bit annoying, especially because I live in Bristol. To begin with, I would be quite open about it, but now I tend not to tell people because people can get really intrusive. They ask stuff they wouldn't ask someone else, so I turn it on them and ask them to tell me shit about their dad, and they go, 'Oh, yeah, it is a bit fucking weird, innit?' I think when someone is famous, people don't look at them like they're human. It's like they're property, and people just want to know everything.

Some people start behaving differently, but to be fair, most of my close mates who I've known since I was five years old, they couldn't give a shit who he is. They just talk to him like he was anyone, and that's why they are my close friends.

What I don't like is the assumption that I've come from money, or that I've got everything. I've just lived a normal life. Dad says I met him at the wrong time – when he was broke! When he was a millionaire, I never had a clue, so I got fuck all, ha-ha.

I think if I'd I found out when I was a teenager, it would have fucked me up definitely, it would have been too much of a head-fuck. When you're a teenager, you're figuring out your identity anyway, and you are just a dick in the way that you manage things. I probably would've gone off the rails or something.

One of the weirdest things is: I grew up in an all-black family. There were no white people in my family, then all of a sudden I've got a white auntie, mixed-race cousins and a mixed-race dad – so that will fuck with my head!

When I was doing my training to become a social worker, you had to do your own family tree, to analyse your family – so how do you put three dads on your family tree? That was complicated, and it was a lot of explanation in the middle of a lecture. I think I was pretty non-judgemental anyway, but this experience has probably reinforced that. You don't know anyone's background – you don't know what they've been through, and what their family set-up is.

I now know that I'm not totally black, but it hasn't really changed my outlook, because I've grown up in Bristol which is quite multicultural anyway. I went to Cotham School, which was predominantly white middle-class, so I'm used to being in a mix anyway. I suppose it was just a shock, because you grow up thinking you are one ethnicity and then you find out you've got other bits in you. I don't think it's changed me otherwise. It's hard to know what life would have been like if I hadn't found out. How would you quantify it? I'm not sure.

TRICKY: Marie reckons I would have been a crackhead, if I hadn't found music.

MARIE: Yeah, because you've had a horrible life, and I think you've got awful coping mechanisms.

TRICKY: I don't think I've had a hard life.

MARIE: You've had a horrendous life!

TRICKY: But I had fun! I could go out at fourteen or fifteen and go to a blues …

MARIE: That's not normal.

TRICKY: I could not go to school if I wanted. I could go rabbiting, I've been around guns, when I was a kid. I've seen fights and stuff, and my uncles were well known. It was exciting – but you think I was neglected.

MARIE: It was neglect. Auntie Marlow looked after you well, but apart from that, if I'd been your social worker, you would've been on a child protection plan.

TRICKY: Are you serious?

MARIE: *Neglect!*

TRICKY: Being in Paris, I was able to see a lot more of my family than I had while I was living on the other side of the Atlantic. Various family members would come to visit me, and I was often back in Bristol myself. Now I had a record deal, however, there was a whole lot more incentive to hit the road, and tour to support my latest album.

To be honest, I was bored of playing in England. I have many great fans in the UK, but fashions change so quickly there that you never know what you're flying into. I was more excited about playing all the other different countries in Europe, where they welcome you with more warmth, and less preconception, and it's just about appreciating good music.

I was also branching out more into the 'emerging markets', as far as Western popular music is concerned, making regular visits to places like China, South Korea and Russia. I'm pretty sure I was one of the first Western artists to play in China beyond Beijing and Shanghai: I went to places like Chinese Outer Mongolia and Inner Mongolia, which were weird, but much more rewarding – just weird places where I thought, 'Why the fuck am I going here?' which was reason enough in itself.

I toured numerous times in South America, visiting every territory there, including Venezuela. I have a really strong following in Mexico: there's a Mexican gangster guy I've been in contact with who used to do crimes to my music. He posted a picture of my album on Instagram, saying, 'It reminds me of my gangbanging days.' He'd listen to my music in his car, and probably shoot people, for all I know. I have a big Mexican following in LA, too.

I never thought I would be doing tours all over the world. I never envisaged myself going to China. If you'd told me that years ago, I would have said, 'China?!' I thought I would just be doing little shows around England. The only places I haven't been, that I can think of, are Africa and Vietnam. The travelling part of my job, I love. If you can be in different cultures and be okay, it's good for you. You can't be ignorant if you go to other people's countries. When you're travelling all over, you've got to fit in, and I think it takes the ignorance out of you.

It's brilliant seeing other people's cultures. People tend to go to the obvious places, working or on holiday, but I love going to places where no one else goes. Like, I've spent a lot of time in Russia, and I've just been to Chelyabinsk – find me a person who has been there! There's no reason to go there unless it was on business, which would be very rare. When I go to Russia, I go to places that Russians go, not tourist places. I've played shows in places like Perm, Krasnodar, Nizhny Novgorod and Yekaterinburg, and the crowds are good all over – very passionate.

If I'd known beforehand how dangerous Russia is, I probably would never have gone. The first time I went, I had a guy with guns looking after me. I had a guy sat next to me at the bar with a newspaper with a fucking machine-gun underneath. As soon as you get off the train or plane, security take you to the hotel, and when you come down from the room, they're sat there, waiting. I had a guy follow me to clubs, everywhere.

I kept hearing that Russia is racist, but I've never experienced any racism there. I've been all over Russia, and I've never seen a black person there – cities where there are no black people, guaranteed, and I've never had a problem. There's nowhere I haven't gone – no club, no restaurant, nothing I haven't done, and I've never experienced any racism, apart from the occasional customs guy. I get more actual racism when I fly into London than I do flying into Russia. Travelling and experiencing places for yourself makes you realise that a lot of this stuff is propaganda.

I loved it there from the off, and I've always had a strong listenership there. They have always been with me, the Russians. It's not just that I keep going there, it's the music. Hard times make hard people, right? They love the struggle in my music. They can feel what I've been through. That's why they connect with me. My music is struggling music – it's blues, and they recognise it. The most Tricky fan tattoos anywhere is in Russia.

In the early 2000s, when I first went there, I was doing a show, and backstage this promoter showed me a letter from a kid called Alex, saying, 'I learnt English from your music, you are like a father to me.' A really nice letter. Before the show, I was getting bored, so I went down into the audience, and I was hanging around. The promoter said anxiously, 'Hey, come on, we'll go back upstairs because people will start recognising you.' I was like, 'It's okay, relax!' Then I saw a kid with my T-shirt on and I thought, 'How the fuck did he get that?' because I wasn't selling it on the tour. I asked him, and it turned out that he was the boy who had sent me the letter. He was only eighteen at that point, and he'd driven sixteen hours on his own to be there. Totally, it was fate meeting him.

We exchanged numbers and started calling each other, and when I came back to Russia, we met again. It all happened so naturally, and we have never left each other since. He has been to Paris, and one time he came to Istanbul to surprise me. Once, he took me to the mountains out there.

He is from this place Chelyabinsk, which is in west central Russia, close to the Ural Mountains. It's the most polluted city in Russia. It's seriously fucked up, not a pretty city, but he's lived there all his life. I find it depressing there, but I doubt he would consider it hard at all. He is almost like a son to me. I don't know if he thinks that, but I feel like he is. Now he's older, and has a wife and kids, he might be more like a little brother. But we are close.

· ▪ ▪ ▪ ▪ ▪ ·

Unfortunately, I didn't really have a good time on Domino. I did another record with them called *Mixed Race*, which again was themed around making sense of my upbringing, and my family, and how that had made me the person I'd grown into as an adult. Domino were nice people, and I think they cared about the music, but there were certain ways they wanted me to work that didn't suit my style.

Their plan was that I'd record demos for them, then they could pick the songs they thought I should record. Once I'd recorded them to their satisfaction, I would go to a meeting, to then be told I was allowed to go ahead and mix them. I'm afraid I just didn't understand that way of doing things.

It was like you or me telling a professional boxer how to train, or what to do in the ring. Like saying, 'Hey, listen, you're ready to fight now!'

The team there knew about their label, and their business, maybe how to get on the radio, but how do they know when I'm ready to mix? I just found it weird.

I do an album in about four or five weeks, recording, mixing, everything. When you think there's only ten tracks on an album, then I mix at home nowadays, I don't have to go into a studio anywhere – four or five weeks does it. If I'm finishing an album, I don't wanna take four weeks off, thinking about mixing. And if I do, then it'll be my choice.

It just didn't work out. I know Laurence thinks I slag him off, and maybe I've said a couple of negative things about him. I understand now that I was bad on him, but I'd become comfortable with my own methods of creating. Chris Blackwell, of all the label owners, has had the best artist roster ever, and he never came into the studio and told me what to do. Me and Chris never even had conversations about my music. If I wanted to go and record in Jamaica and he didn't hear from me for two months, then I came back and said, 'Here's the record!' He'd say, 'Ooh, great!' So maybe I was spoilt.

Are these labels only into radio today, or are they thinking of tomorrow? Someone saying to me, 'I need to give you permission before you can mix,' or 'You should work with this guy,' I think they're not forward thinking, because what you might initially think is a mistake might become a classic album ten years later. It was like this conversation I had with Marc Marot at Island, when I was frustrated at the beginning.

'Marc', I said, 'sometimes I feel like my music just don't fit in.'

'Tricky, don't worry,' he replied with an encouraging smile. 'One day people will catch up with you!'

GLASTONBURY

You might be getting the impression that I'm never to be persuaded to capitalise on a no-brainer career opportunity. Well, that isn't true at all. The most obvious example is when I agreed to join Beyoncé onstage during her headline set at Glastonbury 2011, for the song 'Baby Boy'. It was apparently her choreographer who suggested me to her because they were a fan of mine, and it was my manager at the time who persuaded me to do it.

'Look,' they pleaded, 'you have to do this, it's Beyoncé!'

'Nah!' Not because I didn't want to work with Beyoncé, but because that ain't my scene.

'Tricky, come on, you have to! There is no one on earth who would say no to going onstage with the biggest pop artist in the world!'

'Oh, fuck it – alright!'

Big mistake.

We met up a day or two before the actual show. She was staying in this country house near Glastonbury, which belonged to some executive, who must've been a very wealthy guy – that place was serious! Obviously, her being Beyoncé, it wasn't going to be easy getting in and out of the festival. She had to have a police escort.

Meeting her that day, she didn't at all have a superstar vibe about her. It was like meeting a normal girl, just very simple and down to earth, which I was really surprised by – not the person you would see in a video. She was rehearsing the dance routines with her dancers, but we didn't do much of a rehearsal for the music. It was just to say hi.

In the daytime, before the actual show on the Sunday evening, I was visiting my nanny Violet, who was about to pass away. When visiting time was over, I drove straight down from Bristol to the festival site.

Walking onstage as a guest is the worst thing anyway: you have all the build-up, all the waiting around – and it's Glastonbury, where everybody else is partying hard – and then you get your three or four minutes.

This was something else. This was nerve-wracking. Ten minutes before my slot, I realise: oh shit!

I go on, and it's like I just walked inside a giant TV set. This isn't a show in front of a live crowd. The whole stage is a TV screen. Smoke everywhere, dancers, bright lights. Bright as fuck! TOO MUCH!

I instantly feel very out of place. Rabbit in the headlights. Overwhelmed, I freeze. I grab the mic, but my mouth isn't working. The backing track plays on, with a huge gaping silence where my voice should be.

I dare not look up, where 200,000 pairs of eyes are gawping at me, waiting for my contribution. Nothing will come out of my mouth. Beyoncé knows what's going on, that I'm fucking up, and she tries to cover for me. She comes over and dances close to me, professional, vibing with me, trying to make it better. But that's making it worse.

I look at her. It's fucking Beyoncé, dancing beside me. I look down into the pit, and there's Jay-Z gazing up at us. My verse has passed. Too late. The song is over.

Confused cheers, as I go.

Oh God.

As soon as the show was over, people were asking me in interviews backstage, 'Like, what happened?' I said my microphone wasn't working because I wasn't gonna admit at that stage that I just froze. It was a lie. I was speechless. It was that no words would come out of my mouth. Nothing! I just got on, saw all the lights, grabbed the mic, and it was almost like everything was happening like it was supposed to, but then my mouth wouldn't let me say anything.

I only had one verse to do – I could easily have freestyled that. I could have made up something off the top of my head. I could do that onstage, fucking no problem. But I froze.

Anything that happens to me, people think, 'Oh, he was stoned or he was fucked up!' People are ignorant. I was totally sober, and it was too much for me. It was nothing to do with Beyoncé; just, that kind of show really wasn't me. I'm a fish-and-chip guy, very simple. I'm a 'stroll onstage' kind of person. Beyoncé is professional, one of the best performers around, when you're talking about a big showbiz production like that. It was too professional for me.

Afterwards, she was as cool as fuck, and Jay-Z as well. No one said much. It was funny being backstage with them. You think, 'Beyoncé, biggest artist in the world,' and she's got a dressing room like everybody else's dressing room – one shitty portacabin with that horrible hospital strip-lighting, nothing going on at all, just a bit of music, boring as fuck. You remember how I was telling you about Elvis? Well, she'd just been in front of 200,000 people, and then she's backstage, no vibe, back to reality. It's like that even for the biggest stars of all.

I was quite shocked by how down to earth she was. I thought, 'How can you be so grounded when you're that famous?' Onstage, she's so immaculate, but backstage so normal. I couldn't work it out. She could be here now, and you would forget she's Beyoncé. You see artists where the fame gets to them and you can tell that they're not mentally stable, but she just manages to be herself. She hasn't lost herself. She is not needy. That's very unusual.

I was just looking at her, and I actually said to her, 'You know you're the biggest artist in the world, right?' And she kind of looked at me and shrugged.

I don't know her, but from what I saw, she seemed like a normal grounded person. People would be running around after her if that was what she wanted. I was there when she was around her dancers, and it wasn't all about her. I've seen her in her dressing room – the same. She doesn't have to dominate the room; she doesn't need the attention. And she worked really hard. I saw her rehearsing and she worked – work, work, work, work. I was really impressed. Maybe some people are built for it.

Jay-Z was a good guy, too. I'd met him once before, and he was very polite. I would say that if you've got that much money, you must be a powerful guy. He was nice to me, though, very humble.

At Glastonbury, a girl came over to me, and goes, 'Do you want to meet Jay?' I said, 'No, I'm good, let him do his thing.' I just stood where I was, and she came over again, and she goes, 'Come and meet Jay!' I'm like, 'No, I'm alright, I don't need to meet him.' That's never going to happen, I don't care who you are! If you wanna meet me, I'm cool – *you* come and say hello – but I don't care how big a star you are, it's never happening that you could send someone to *me* to come and say hello to you. I don't know if it was that, or he might have been shy. I'm thinking he's probably got enough people who want to meet him backstage in Glastonbury. But then, finally, he came over to me, and he was just really nice.

And do you know who's really nice as well? That guy from Coldplay – Chris Martin! It's funny – the ones you wouldn't expect … You know, there's artists out there who think they are really cool and credible, and they are not, their music is shit pop music. But they think they're credible – they ain't worth talking to. Save your breath. The days of credible pop ended with Marc Bolan.

Then you've got huge pop artists like Chris Martin, who is actually a good, good guy. I met him at Glastonbury. It took me aback, because first of all I didn't want to talk to him. I just thought, 'Coldplay singer, hello, goodbye.' I had totally judged him before meeting him. He is someone I really respect in that industry now. It's hard being nice, when all eyes are on you. I wished I'd said certain things to him. Like, 'You're a good fucking guy, mate!' But I was so overwhelmed at how nice he was, I came over a bit speechless again. He caught me off guard. It totally threw me. He was with his wife at the time, Gwyneth Paltrow, and then they hurried off before I could say anything.

So, these were great people, who I felt fortunate to meet. Glastonbury itself I was not impressed with. The food backstage was ham, egg and chips! The food they do for you backstage at a French festival, say, is fucking ridiculous – proper food. At Glastonbury, it was shit, with all the money they're making off television rights. Crazy, right?

There's another thing:

'Why is the fee so low?'

'Oh, because it's Glastonbury!'

'So?'

'Well, it's because bands *want* to play here.'

What is that about? I'll never do Glastonbury again unless they pay me properly. I won't do it 'just because it's Glastonbury'. Fuck Glastonbury! It's not even Glastonbury anymore, like it was when me and Whitley used to go there. Imagine trying to get side of stage for Beyoncé like Anthony did, with his face painted and a spliff on the go? It wouldn't happen nowadays.

CHAPTER FOURTEEN
THE TAXMAN

Money-wise, I've lived a ridiculous life. All through my years of making music, there was so much cash around, I never thought of saving, or minor details like tax. I could spend 200 grand on a car service, or hiring a private jet that I never ended up using, and make it back in a few days. I had cheques coming in from all the different labels I'd been signed to. Little did I know, I would spend money even when I hadn't got it. I had no concept of not having money. Why worry?

What I earned went on my daughter's school, and a couple of houses – I bought Mazy's mum a house in London, so they had security, and the place in New Jersey, and I don't even know what happened to that one. I remember living there for a few years, then all of a sudden, I was in LA. Really, whatever happened to that house?

Maybe I should've kept a closer eye on stuff like that, because all of a sudden in the early 2010s, I found out that I was flat broke. I owed 500 grand in unpaid taxes on both sides of the Atlantic, with interest rapidly accumulating, and I was getting sued by my manager because I hadn't paid him either. With all my moving around, and changing managers and accountants and advisers, nobody had ever looked at the big picture of my finances, and the whole thing had got deeply fucked up.

My attitude at that stage was, 'Fuck it, I'll move back to Bristol and live with one of my family! I'll quit music, I don't give a fuck!' That's where I was at, when my new manager approached Horst Weidenmüller, the boss of a German label called !K7, to do a new record. As soon as I did the deal, the advance went to that manager, with all those taxes still outstanding.

I was in a very, very bad place, but over the next four or five years, Horst put my career back together. He became my manager, and set me up with publishing and my own label at !K7, called False Idols, so I could eventually have a fresh income. This wasn't like a major record-company deal. This was a long-term commitment, where he was sorting out my problems, and setting me up for the future. He didn't make any money for himself for three years or so: it was all investment from his side.

For the first couple of years, he funded me to live, not just to make music. He rented me an apartment, gave me money every month to live on, put in money monthly to pay off my debts, and eventually got me to the point where I no longer had any debts to pay, where I had repaid him and could start rebuilding my financial affairs.

He looked into everything in my business dealing. Was there anything I owed? Was there anything people owed me? He'd say, 'You produced this, this, this and this – let's see if there's any money out there for you.' He'd try to see what contracts I'd signed at different stages. It wasn't just difficult, it was a puzzle, because no single person knew the past of what I signed, and what I had done. Once you stop working with someone – an accountant, say, and you aren't paying them anymore – they aren't rushing back to give you info. Or an old lawyer – they don't give a toss.

Horst went through it all from top to bottom, and without him I don't know what I would have done. It was more than just a leap of faith on his part, he helped me survive. He is a different type of guy – not your typical industry person. It's been hard for me to have trust after I've been fucked over so many times, but this man, I trust.

HORST WEIDENMÜLLER: I started !K7 in 1985 as a media production company. I did a lot of documentaries, and live videos with people like

Nick Cave. I created the DJ-Kicks compilation series; through that came Kruder & Dorfmeister, and from there I developed a label group.

In 2010/11 we started a management company, and it was about a year after that that we got approached by Tricky's management, asking if we would be interested in releasing his upcoming album. We suggested it would make more sense to do a label service deal, whereby we'd facilitate the release, and Tricky would remain the full rights holder. As we were setting that up, Tricky decided to leave that management company. That's how we started to manage him, too.

At the start, I just tried to understand what had happened. Tricky had made so many records, I imagined there must be a really healthy flow of money coming in from many sources, including the live side. When he was living in America, he had the convenience of having the income of all his past music, which is why his productivity had stopped by the time he lived in LA.

I soon realised there was no longer any income from the history of Tricky: when the tax bills had first landed, he was advised to sell all his claims and shares in his own publishing to another company, so he could pay them off.

It took me a while to understand, because Tricky would say, 'Yes, there was a deal, I sold something,' but there was never any paperwork, and he didn't remember the details. I was finally able to find that agreement, and also to look into his former accounting: Tricky used to make a healthy six-digit figure, before tax – nothing through the roof, not popstar living, but appropriate for an artist with his heritage. When you then deduct cuts for all the people you need, like managers and tax advisers and lawyers, that figure would be reduced by half.

Then, to pay his tax bill, he was advised to sell his publishing share, for a multiple of 2.3. That means, for less than two and a half years' worth of that income. Of course it's attractive to make such a deal, because it's a large lump sum on the table, and it was recommended that he take that money to pay off the taxman – two and a half years' worth – but then never to receive any back-catalogue publishing again, and that lump sum was subject to management commission, and fees for lawyers and tax consultants.

After that Tricky's manager, a guy called Matt Willis, started to sue him and he ended their agreement mid-contract. A court case then developed, and it went on a long time, so there were various teams working on it. For some reason, it got to a stage where there was a hearing at which Tricky was not represented, and in this court hearing, there was a ruling against him, that he had to pay that money, plus interest.

He had a lawyer, a new manager and an accountant, and all of them were involved in the case, but for some reason there was another court hearing where nobody disputed the ruling, and it was an irrevocable ruling against Tricky, and the money owing to Willis's company was a substantial six-figure sum.

That is when I got involved. I looked into the accounting, and there really was no more income from the past; the only place where it could come from was for Tricky to play live, and to release his first album with us, *False Idols*, in 2013.

What then happened was, every time he toured, the legal team who had the court ruling against him seized the money. That meant that if he was playing at a festival, suddenly he would get a call from the agent, Ben Winchester, saying, 'I'm sorry, they just seized the deposit.' Even after that, you still have to go and play at the festival – you are under contract, and you go there not even sure if you will get the back end of your fee, or if that has also been seized directly from the promoter. So, you actually get deeper in the hole, owing your band and crew their wages.

It got very tense for a couple of years. Tricky said to me, 'I don't know what's going on here, but I'm going on tour and I'm coming back with even more debt than I had before I left, and I can't pay my band.' There were so many uncertainties – the opposite of what an artist needs when he goes on tour.

His debts were substantial, and if we hadn't settled the management suit quickly, it would've gone on forever, and even if I'd wanted to build a new business for Tricky, I would never have been able to, because it would've been constantly attacked in an ongoing war of hide-and-seek and revenge. The end result would've been Tricky living under a bridge. He was like, 'I don't care, I can live under a bridge!' But we had to end it, so I put my own money in, and settled with the management people for something around £200,000. It was actually on my fiftieth birthday, in 2014, and the following day I wired over the money. Then at least we could say, 'No more war!'

I had just cleared that payment, when we found out about Tricky's storages. 'What the fuck are these?' When Tricky left New York, he put all the furniture and contents from his house in New Jersey into a storage facility, and every month the storage had to be paid for. The same happened for LA: Tricky probably said, 'I look only into the future, not into the past – put it in storage!' We had no money, so we decided to let LA go – without looking in there, we just told them to delete it, destroy it, sell it, whatever.

We decided to focus on the New York storage, and we had all these DATs and discs. By now, there was no catalogue business for Tricky, but with this wealth of unreleased material we were able to create a digital archive, and give it to Tricky, like, 'One day, in case you ever get bored and want to look back, here's a load of stuff you did with Neneh Cherry and Björk, amongst others – uncleared, but unreleased!' There's also a demo recording of just Bob Marley singing with an acoustic guitar, which Chris Blackwell gave him at some point – the only copy! Probably he has never looked into the archive so far, but the good thing is that it's there.

At this stage, in 2014, Tricky wasn't enthusiastic. He said to me, 'Hey, you're my manager – where's my money? Can you make me a deal? I need money!' With good reason, he felt threatened.

I realised that what he really needed was an independence from that syndrome where the next cheque is needed to pay his latest bills – because if you are dependent on them, they get smaller; they only get bigger if you don't depend on them. I said to him, 'We have to build a catalogue for you again, because you don't have a catalogue that you own and get income from anymore – the only thing you own is what you produce now. I suggest that you create your own label and publishing, and therefore have a monthly income from those. That monthly income will hopefully, in the future, if everything goes right, give you a financial freedom again because you own the rights, and you will make the lion's share.'

I told him I was happy to bridge that for him, and I did, but it was a difficult time, of maybe two or three years, from 2014 to 2017, where we were building up that catalogue. Sometimes Tricky was saying, 'What the fuck are you doing, Horst? I trusted you, but I have no money in my account!' At times, I was also questioning myself, and I had my financial people saying, 'Horst, what the fuck are you doing?' I was just passionate about it, like, 'This is such a fucked-up situation, and I'm going to fix it.'

I said, 'Look, we'll turn it around. It just doesn't make sense right now for you to spend all the money that's coming in, because it's needed elsewhere. Just for these couple of years, you'll get an auto-payment every month to live on, and I will manage all the rest.' In one year under that new system we'd paid off half of the debt. That was the first ray of sunshine coming – the turning point where Tricky started to trust me. I don't think he necessarily understood what I was doing for him in detail, but he realised that something was changing.

It was getting better all the time, because the albums he was creating with us were making money. We also had to scale down his live band, so that touring turned a profit. He loved me for that one! It was risky because we were selling it as a Tricky show, but there were just three people – Tricky, a guitarist, and a drummer, with no female singer – and the drummer was the tour manager! There were no projections, not even a lighting person – just Tricky and his voice. If the show hadn't turned out well, it could've been damaging, but luckily he pulled it off. He really bit the bullet and gave an amazing performance, and every day it was easing the financial situation.

As management and label and live coordinators, we were able to look at things holistically. After Island, Tricky hadn't toured Latin America, for instance: we were able to put marketing into place, working with Latin American bands on vocals of versions, and building a Latin American profile with tours there, which then really opened up that market.

Now we are there. I think if I'd known from the beginning what I was getting into, I probably would have said no. But I'm happy that I forced myself to do it. Tricky can leave me tomorrow, and he can take all his catalogue with him, and !K7 have no rights to it. It's his. There are no strings attached. I think that's important. He could roll everything together and sell it tomorrow.

In the seven years we've worked together, he was never interested in doing something that was related to the past. If you go to most concerts by artists of Tricky's generation, the average age there is forty-three. Go to a Tricky concert, and you'll see that 60 to 70 per cent of the people are around thirty. That's because he doesn't look back, he always looks forward, and he's been committed to creating a new, younger fanbase.

People come to him and want to work with him because of now, and not because of 1990-something. He's not a heritage artist, who gets engaged for heritage reasons. He is current, he is performing out there, and I think that's something that we should be proud of. Nobody foresaw that.

This approach makes Tricky one of the last few remaining hundred per cent pure artists. Where do you find that purity in music these days? It hasn't been easy, but at the end of the day we preserved Tricky as an artist, and we released some albums we are really proud of, and all of them were completely what Tricky wanted to do. There was no A&R-ing involved, just Tricky.

The financial pressure was definitely forcing his creativity. There was pain, hunger, frustration, anger. There was, 'I wanna get out there and scream about how fucked up it is.' It put a lot of useful energy into the mix.

TRICKY: Every move I made for two and a half years, whether it was touring or making a record, was done under the shadow of the taxman, to meet those monthly payments. Inevitably, that purpose was always in the back of my mind. I found that I was trying to get things done fast, because I felt this constant pressure to cough up the money. It was almost like, 'Alright, that track's done – next track!' It felt like I didn't have time even to sleep on things overnight, or think them over. I just had to get them out there as fast as possible, to reduce the burden.

The records weren't done in a hurry exactly, but I realised that it was stressing me. My lifestyle didn't change, I was still travelling all over the world, but when you have a responsibility every month, it's bound to affect you.

In 2012, *False Idols* was made at my home in Paris, and even for me it was done pretty quick, as the money problems were starting to unfold. There are a few good things on there, but people seem to be getting to it now, and loving it more and more, like happened with *Pre-Millennium Tension* and *Angels with Dirty Faces*.

Two years later, I did another album in Paris titled after my real name – *Adrian Thaws*. Now I was back living in Europe, it was about looking back at that journey I'd been on, and finding my way back home to see who I really was. It was another solid record which went under the radar. Everyone missed it – it's only now that it's getting some love. *False Idols* is turning into a bit of a classic, and *Adrian Thaws* will eventually do it as well. Like Marc Marot said, people are catching up with me!

After I toured that one was the time when I began to get disillusioned with Horst's strategy. I couldn't see an end to it. I would go to the ATM, and there was nothing coming out. I didn't understand why. That's when

Horst came up with the idea of cutting down the size of my band – losing a few members, because it's harder to make money touring when you have to pay a full band's wages. Before hitting the road, I made an album of more stripped-down music to play with this new line-up, called *Skilled Mechanics*. To be honest, it was produced pretty quickly, and it's definitely my least favourite album that I've ever made, but it helped pave the way to paying off the rest of my debt.

I toured for most of 2016 with just a guitarist and a drummer, and for the first time ever, I was doing all the vocals myself, without a female singer onstage. One of the first shows was at the BBC 6 Music Festival in Bristol. The plan was like, 'C'mon, we're gonna go out and do it!' But when I first went out onstage, I realised, 'Oh fuck, I've got no singer!' If there's only three onstage, there's nowhere to hide. Just the thought of doing a whole show by myself was scary, but I learnt a lot from it. My performance changed because I had to focus. It made me better because I had to work harder, and be present for the whole show.

That year I was doing some of the worst festivals I ever did in my life, but we couldn't say no to anything. Even for low fees or in places I didn't wanna go, I did them to pay the rent. That was how bad it was, and it's so disheartening being in that position. I would play in a bar if the price was right. And it's a vicious circle, because you need money to tour: to pay for flights, hotel rooms. And if you're only there to pay your rent, how are you gonna do a good show?

We had a lot of good press and good vibes, but some people were like, 'Why are you using backing tracks when you are a rich artist?' It's funny how people ain't got a clue! They think you are wealthy, but I was nearly at the end of my debt: it was, 'Alright, let's just get this done!' We toured a lot, and it was hard work, but afterwards a lot of the pressure was finally off.

In 2017, I made *Ununiform*, and it felt different. I noticed that I would complete a track, and then it would be, 'Okay, let's put that aside, sleep on it and listen to it tomorrow' – a luxury I didn't feel I'd had for a good few years. And instead of just sticking everything I made on there in a rush, I'd sometimes say, 'No, that's not good enough, I don't want it on the record,' because there was no pressure to bring the album out.

I actually recorded some of it in Russia. I spent Christmas 2016 over there, because Christmas isn't such a big deal in Russia. Since I'd been back in Europe, I'd spent the odd Christmas in England, and it gets too much. I liked going back to see my cousin Michelle, my dad, and having a drink with mates, but that is exhausting as well. So I thought, 'You know what, I'm gonna escape there instead.'

My 'son' Alex came for some of the time, but most of it I spent by myself. It didn't even feel like it was Christmas out there – you wouldn't really know. You don't see all the Christmas things on TV, and it's not all consumerism gone crazy like in England. Russia has become my second home almost. I went in the studio, I just got away from all the Christmas bullshit. I worked with some Russian producers and two rappers, Scriptonite and Smoky Mo – I like having people on my records who maybe aren't known all over the world, It's too easy having a name person.

With that record, I finally felt like Horst had put me in a position where I could focus on my music and my shows. I can't be focusing on my business *and* being an artist. After becoming so involved in getting myself set up financially, I now feel engaged with my False Idols label and making the right decisions.

I now travel Economy, for instance! Before, if my label put me in the cheap seats, I'd be thinking, 'Why the fuck am I travelling Economy?' Now it's like, 'This is my business.' The five grand that I would spend on a First Class ticket to America – I could make a video with that.

I've started thinking like a businessman, which is really good for me. Instead of all my money going on stupid shit, it's going into the music, and I get something out of it. I didn't think like that as a 25-year-old, but as a mature person, I suppose I'm thinking more realistically and logistically – okay, maybe not totally like a businessman, but thinking *of my business*, and through that my business is growing, and some really good things are starting to happen. Because who gives a fuck about a First Class ticket? It's mental, when you think about it: you get on there, you get off, and that's it, and you've wasted five grand. All I need on a plane is some books.

When I did labels before like Durban Poison and Brown Punk, the trouble was that I was signed to a label, but trying to do my own label as well. With this, I'm on my own label, and so are the artists I sign. You can't do it when you're on a major, because the major only really cares about you.

People are catching on to False Idols, posting things online about my releases – they're like, 'Wow, this song!' The more I'm touring, the catalogue is becoming special again. When we tour, people go crazy in the crowd for certain songs. It's about building, and I can choose what shows to play. It makes a big difference to your performance if you're there because you wanna be there.

In some ways it's an injustice that I don't get any income from my old music. But fuck it, I'm about my new music now. If I can record and have somewhere to live, I'm good to go.

. ▪ ▪ ▪ ▪ ▪ .

You have to sell like Drake or Kanye West to make money out of the recording business these days. There ain't no in between or half measures: you only make any cash in that game if you're a mega-popstar, so you have to make it work as a live performer.

In 2012, my manager at the time persuaded me to do some UK shows playing *Maxinquaye* in full. I only agreed because of the money, to pay off my tax bill. Why would I do a *Maxinquaye* tour otherwise? It's in the past, get over it! This old guy said a brilliant thing to me in a pub once: There's a reason your rear-view mirror is small – because it's the past! Don't keep looking back!

Once I'd signed up, I was scared, and it felt horrible actually doing the shows. Every night after a couple of songs, I kept bringing on some people from Bristol and London, basically to kill the boredom. I'd say, 'Jump in!' and they'd freestyle unrehearsed over the tracks. It was about having my little brothers and other friends with me, so it was a party, less boring.

BEN WINCHESTER: That tour didn't work, and in retrospect it was obvious that it wouldn't. That was a different time. Matt Willis was managing Tricky. He thought it was a way of getting back into the UK market, but Tricky's show had moved on so far, and trying to wind the clock back wasn't a good fit. The original *Maxinquaye* shows had a session-musician band twenty years older than him wearing black tie. It was a showbiz feel, but the contemporary show was dark, powerful and intense, and the tracks Tricky plays from any given album are nothing like the recorded versions. He'll jam and riff on them, and that's why his shows are so special because most people can't and won't do that. So rewinding to those days where he was playing a faithful reproduction of the record with a big band, but today with his current band – that wasn't a good idea.

TERRY HALL: Me and my kid went to see the *Maxinquaye* show at Indigo in London a few years back. It was in the period where Patti Smith did *Horses* again, and Pixies did *Doolittle*. He was doing his big album, but after two songs he got bored, so he called some of his cousins on and it went somewhere else! I was cool with that, because I didn't expect him to do it religiously anyway – but I didn't expect him not to do it at all!

But I admire that. That's what I would consider a great artist: you're never quite sure what's gonna happen next. It could be terrible, but it doesn't matter. It could be fantastic! Just keeping yourself fresh in your own head is the most important thing. You do what you wanna do, and people either go along with you or they don't. Tricky always does his own thing, and I think that is his greatest attribute.

TRICKY: I haven't performed 'Hell Is Round the Corner' onstage for fifteen years or more. I stopped doing it, because as soon that starts, everybody goes, 'Aaaaaaah!' and it's like, 'We haven't even fucking done anything yet!' Fuck that. It's the same with 'Black Steel'. Recently I've been doing 'Black Steel' with my guitarist guy singing it, which changes the vibe. Touring gets so boring if you don't keep yourself excited.

When people get me nowadays, they don't really know what they're getting. It ain't like you're gonna get any *Maxinquaye*. I'm always doing the last couple of albums. You just keep moving on. Sometimes I do still feel uncomfortable onstage, but I think that's part of the journey as well.

After that *Skilled Mechanics* tour, I got a new singer in. It was going well, but sometimes I can be pretty particular with my crew on tour. I was giving what I would call constructive criticism to her, and maybe I came down on her too strong, because she quit the next day.

That was the opening night of a tour: after that we had four more to do in Poland, before going on to the UK, so I said to myself, 'Okay, we've lost seven songs in the set now!' When we arrived for the next show in Krakow, I said to the Polish promoter, 'Can you find me a singer to do a couple of songs, and then maybe I could do a song in Polish, to please the crowd?' Almost immediately this girl called Marta Zlakowska turned up.

'Do you know a song in Polish?' I asked.

'Not really,' she replied, 'but I have learnt one of your songs!'

She tried it in soundcheck, and I said, 'Can you learn another one before the show?' So she did two songs that night, four the next, and five or six the night after, and she has been with me ever since. She has toured America, she has been through Europe and I'm signing her to my label. She'll be on my next album, too.

Marta is a sweet girl, but tough as well. At the time, she was working in a bar in Krakow and wasn't sure if she wanted to take doing music seriously. Her choice was like, 'Am I just going to work in a bar all my life?'

The first proper show she ever did was with me in Krakow. At the start, she was often totally uncomfortable, but she didn't try to hide it or strike a pose. She got it, without me having to say anything. It was like, 'Ah, this is the perfect girl!' You could say it was luck, or you could say it was meant to be. It wasn't like we auditioned fifty singers, she was the first girl who came in. It was through no choice. And from no choice, she was exactly what the show needed.

She is in her own world. She ain't got no fake about her. Sometimes me and my drummer Luke will smile at each other onstage because she is so honest, so fucking real. She has done shows in front of 3,000 people in New York, and not only is it the first time she's doing that show in front of 3,000 people, it's the first time she's been to New York! She is a hard worker, and she's got a good spirit, and this amazing soulful texture to her voice.

· ▪ ▪ ▪ ▪ ▪ ·

There's a lot of freedom when you perform. When you're up there and everything's working, you don't need anything: you're not hot, you're not cold, you're not thirsty, you're not hungry. You forget about someone calling you, you forget what you've got to do tomorrow, you forget everything. In that respect, it's a form of meditation, like you're going somewhere else – getting away from the world for a couple of hours.

After you've been in the game for a while, you realise that touring is all about those two hours every day: they are the reason why you put up with the other shit stuff, because they are the only thing in your day that really matters. Beforehand, you could be in paradise, you still don't know what to do with yourself. Then after the show, it's finished, game over – even if you go out and have the best fun at an after-party, whatever, the only thing that means anything is the show itself.

Beforehand, I'll usually go to the venue with the band around 2pm for soundcheck. They'll usually leave around 6pm after the soundcheck, and go to the hotel and get some food, but I'll stay at the venue from 2pm until the show is over at midnight or whatever, because there's nothing else for me to do.

As I said before, dressing rooms are always shitty, and venues in general are horrible, but I'll sit in the dressing room and I literally don't leave there, because in my mind going back to the hotel just breaks the cycle. Once I'm in there, I'm in 'do the show' mode and I can't go back into the real world. If I go back to the hotel and shower and crash out on the bed and turn on the TV, I won't want to go back to the venue again. I could have the nicest room ever, but I'm not there to enjoy the nice room.

Most of the time I'm by myself in the dressing room, because none of the band are gonna sit there for eight hours. To while away the time, I listen to music, watch YouTube and have a whisky. It's my own space, so I'll bring some speakers in there, and I listen to all my favourite music really loud, like having my own little private DJ set. I'll play the first Specials album – the whole thing – because at home I never seem to find the time. I've got eight hours to kill, so I get to do the stuff I used to, when I was a kid. I'll get all my old hip-hop out, and old reggae. Old dancehall compilations, David Sylvian, or old hip-hop classics by Rakim. It's like catching up with your past almost.

Otherwise I might watch a movie. I don't smoke weed much anymore, so I'll have a couple of whisky and Cokes, and chill out.

When I'm doing that, I really don't want people coming in there. I don't want to be hanging out with people in their cities, pretending we are friends. I'll see Charles in Paris, Alex in Russia, and my family when I'm back in England, but anywhere else in the world, no one is coming in.

Coming offstage is the hard part. Even if I've had a few drinks and you're the friendliest person on earth, you still ain't hanging out in the dressing room. Sometimes I let some of the audience back to get something signed, but not often because people always want to talk about me. I say to people, 'Tell me about your city, tell me what good music there is here, otherwise you're gonna have to leave!'

After the show, that's where alcohol comes into it. You're buzzing, you come into that shit dressing room, and it's a real big comedown. What now? I rarely go to an after-party, because I want to keep myself to myself – socialising with fans can be difficult, especially right after you've been onstage. You need something to keep the buzz going, to make the transition, and I think that's why lots of musicians get a drink problem. Like any other job, you use it to kill the pain of the shit part of your profession. You know it's coming, and that's how you deal with it. Sometimes we'll go out for some food, or I'll cook backstage, then we'll go back to the hotel, and it's on to the next one.

I've found the best way to avoid getting a drink problem is to be fit, and to train regularly in the daytime. When you are fit, after a show you'll want to eat, and then you'll sleep properly. It takes about an hour and a half for the band to pack down, so I'll cook something, we'll eat, go back to the hotel, sleep, get up, and I'll train. When I'm training, I can sleep well and I beat my insomnia. When I don't train, I don't sleep, and I'm always trying to knock myself out with alcohol. I have to be exhausted to want to sleep in the dressing room, and I don't like it. I'll wake up feeling grouchy.

The travelling, though, I love. It don't matter how tired you are. Recently, we drove through Colorado, through the mountains and the redwoods – fucking amazing! We were pulling over and walking in the country, then you're by the sea, walking on the beach for twenty minutes. How many people get to drive all the way through America, from Philadelphia across to California?

Also: when you are on holiday, you are a tourist. When you are touring, you aren't a tourist, and people will show you the best places. On holiday sometimes, you feel a bit outside, and it's not real. When you're on tour you don't feel like that. If I say to a promoter, 'Where is the best Chinese food?' they'll set up a place for you to go, without you having to go on the internet, where it's pot luck. You don't get that holiday strangeness. Straight away you're welcomed into the city, and people will take you anywhere you want to go.

When I did a show in Sardinia, the doorman – I'm talking the bouncer, a street guy – cooked traditional Sardinian food for me afterwards. You ain't gonna get that if you go to Sardinia on your holiday. I wouldn't go to Sardinia without doing a show, because I wouldn't know what to do with myself there. That's why I don't go on holidays, and why I haven't celebrated a birthday for years. How can I beat that life I already have with a birthday party? Every day is a birthday for me. On my actual birthday, I do nothing. I don't know how I could do anything better than what I do ordinarily. I suppose I'm celebrating my birthday all the time, every time I tour. My life is a constant birthday, a constant day off!

Still, touring is *hard*. People don't understand how hard it is. There's nothing glamorous about it at all. For me, it's pressure, because it's all under my name. The band are just hired guns, whereas it's my name on the ticket. There's a lot of eyes on you. It's all about *you*. It's not the pressure of doing a good show; it's just that everything revolves around you, which is kind of a pain. With Massive Attack, say, they've got this huge lightshow, they've got each other to lean on, under this collective group name. When I go onstage, it's Tricky. That ain't easy.

That's why the last tour I did in America in October–November 2018 was so brilliant, because it wasn't my tour. We were supporting A Perfect Circle, which is Maynard from Tool's other band. They play hardcore rock, not heavy metal exactly, and they were on a big arena tour, which was fucking tough, but really fun.

Maynard is a huge fan of mine, and the feeling is mutual. I didn't realise that until we were talking to his manager. That's how we got the gig, he plays my music. Like me, he's very non-celebrity. He doesn't play that superstar game, which is very refreshing. He's been doing Ju-Jitsu for twenty-odd years. He knows my uncle Tony, through touring with me. When I first saw him on this tour, he went, 'How is your uncle Tony? He is one *hard* motherfucker!'

MAYNARD JAMES KEENAN: I was introduced to Tricky's work by a friend called Martina Salerno, who, along with her incredible friends, used to follow my band, Tool, and Rage Against the Machine throughout the UK and parts of Europe. This was long before Martina went on to debut her talents with the track 'Songbird'.

So, I can't say when I actually heard *Maxinquaye*, whether I heard it before it crossed the Atlantic to America because I was receiving it from clued-up young Brits, but I immediately became a lifelong fan from that moment onwards.

I finally met Tricky on Lollapalooza '97, which was a good year for camaraderie, with people like Porno for Pyros aboard. Our paths crossed many times thereafter, such as when we had Tricky as Tool's tour support in 2001–2, and when he secured a work-release programme to star in our video for 'Parabol/Parabola'. Was there money? Not a lot, but apparently enough. I have few memories, I'm afraid, as I had a penis hat on, and couldn't see much. On tour, he would actually play keyboards and sing with us on 'Reflection' and 'Opiate'.

It would be erroneous to suggest we spent any time together outside those glorious but random moments – I lived in Arizona when he was in LA – but we have always been excited to run into each other. There are usually conversations involving 'boxing versus Ju-Jitsu', some day-to-day banter, then a snack.

Tricky has gone on to get regular airplay with me. That he was available to open for my other band, A Perfect Circle, in 2018 was a blessing. It was good to see first-hand that he has evolved as a musician and producer, in my opinion, in a positive direction.

TRICKY: Most of A Perfect Circle's crowd didn't know us, and their fan base is so fanatical, they don't really want to see anything else apart from A Perfect Circle. I thought there was gonna be hardly anybody in there for our set, but it was packed out in these arenas when we were going onstage, and we had to work to win them over. I like that fight, trying to break into someone else's crowd. The best compliment we had was in Vegas, where a guy in the crowd shouted out, 'Yeah! Play some more of that weird shit!' What a beautiful compliment – you think it's weird, but you still want to hear it.

For me, it was no pressure, like a fucking holiday. When it's all about you, it's a bit obvious. I've been doing that for twenty-five years. I've been a headline act almost since the beginning. The only artist I ever supported for a whole tour was PJ Harvey, right at the start.

So, after this tour with A Perfect Circle, I'd like to do more shows opening for people. I would support Madonna. I would support Britney Spears. I'd support anyone, honestly – Britney Spears, U2, fucking any of them!

. ∎ ▪ ◾ ▪ ∎ .

As a city, Paris is small in the centre and crazy-busy. I'd started to dread the summers, when there are tourists crawling around everywhere. That had started to get on my nerves, and I was feeling like it was time for another move. In autumn '14, I bailed. Initially, I moved back to London, of all places. I got a place in Hampstead, because it's beautiful up there, and quiet. My neighbours were famous footballers and, a couple of doors down, Liam Gallagher (our paths never crossed, though!).

I never quite acclimatised to life there. Because I don't drive, I had to get car services and taxis just to go to the supermarket, or the health food store. It felt weird after Paris, where I had everything right on my doorstep. Also, in Paris I used to walk everywhere, but I soon remembered that in London you walk for an hour and you haven't really got anywhere, so you never have that feeling of knowing the place.

I'd forgotten about the whole class–race thing, too. One day, I came out of my house and started walking up the hill into Hampstead village, and there was a woman parked in some average car – she definitely didn't live in that super-affluent area. It was broad daylight, and as I turned around the corner and walked past, she locked the door on me. Crazy, right? With the car she had, she's locking the door so I don't rob her!

I never felt that I re-engaged with London life. I wasn't going out much. One day in early summer '15, I was talking to Horst on the phone, and I was like, 'I don't know if I like it here.' And he said, 'Well, you don't use it for networking, so there ain't no point in you being there.' I used to go to clubs now and again, but it wasn't clubs where you're going to bump into the 'right people'. I wasn't using London for what it's good for, as an artist, like doing red carpets and movie openings, and getting noticed, and hanging out with other artists. People travel to London from all over the world just to do that stuff, but I can't be arsed with all that.

A week or two later, I was over in Berlin with !K7 to do some press. It was summer, it was so chilled out, and I thought, 'Do you know what? I'm going to live here!' and a month later I moved my studio there.

I suppose it's down to getting older, but I like slower places now, rather than being so busy and cramped all the time. Berlin was just easier for me. You don't need a car, because you can walk everywhere, like you can in Paris.

When I first moved, I lived in a little council flat in a small block, with piss in the fucking lift – a stinky elevator! I don't have a problem with living rough for a while, and money was tight at that time, as we sorted out my finances. Horst came round to visit and he said, 'This is really nice!' and I was like, 'Are you kidding?' Shortly after, I found a proper place in Neukölln – coincidentally, the same neighbourhood where David Bowie and Iggy Pop went to 'disappear' in the mid-70s.

I immediately felt good in Berlin. Berliners know how to live. It's so cheap there, and they are not monetary people. The really wealthy people there – you wouldn't know they are wealthy. They ain't driving around in Rolls-Royces, they are more into quality of life than quantity, so they're a lot less stressed out. Coming to London, you can see that people are stressed there, because you have to get so much money in just to survive. It ain't like you've got a choice. In Berlin, wealth is a choice.

In the three years or so that I've lived there, my life has become much calmer. I'm a lot more relaxed. I tour a lot, and tours are mad enough as it is. You don't want that life when you get home, so it's better for me to live where I don't know anybody. I've got no discipline, right? If I lived in London, I've got loads of friends and family so I'd be going out all the time. If one of my cousins calls and says, 'Let's go for a drink!' I'm gonna go, and it'll be a long night. In Berlin, nobody's gonna call and say, 'Let's party at the weekend!' because I don't know anyone.

I rarely see anyone. In three or four years in Berlin, I've been to a club maybe once a year. I never go to the cinema, or to museums, and I very rarely go to a live concert. I train three times a week, and I see my management now and again at the office. The majority of my time is spent by myself, and I'm really happy with that. I cook, I train, and I sit outside cafés, watching people. Seriously, that's all I do.

Hanging out with me would be totally fucking boring. I also love walking – that's my favourite thing. I come outside my house, I choose a direction and I just walk, anywhere. To a lot of people, that would be as boring as fuck. I don't even go out to eat that much, just when I can't think of what to cook. I always cook the same things anyway: vegetables, meat, shepherd's pie, very English stuff. If I do go out, I go out by myself.

I like being under the radar. I like chatting to people on the street, or at my local shop. I go in and say hello, and everybody says hello back. I suppose that's how I socialise. I don't know, I'm not very good at making firm friends. Well, it's not that I'm not very good. It's just that, to be honest, I'd rather be by myself. I can't imagine living with anybody. It wouldn't matter how big the house was, I'd prefer to be by myself.

I think I'm going to be by myself till I die. I'm fifty-one now. I'm distracted. I think about music 24/7, and it's hard for me to be interested and enthusiastic about anything or anyone else, and that's because I'm obsessed.

I – am – obsessed. I could sit in a room and listen to music, and you are no longer there. If you're with me in a room and you think you're listening to music with me, you're not. You are by yourself, because I am *gone*.

All I do is think about music, lyrics, my next show. I've got no space in my brain for someone special in life. Girlfriends have said to me, 'Where are you right now?' We'll be sat on the couch watching a film or whatever, and she knows that I'm not present.

I'm dysfunctional. I don't have a normal life. My whole life since I was a kid has been based around music, but I know other musicians and their lives are not like mine. Their life is like, 'We do an album, we tour, and then after that we go back into normal life.' I don't have a life. When I'm not touring and not making music, I do nothing,

I've always put my music first, and left myself without any other life, which I'm prepared to do, because whether you're gonna be a boxer or a footballer, you've got to give your life to it to be the best. I've lost loads of relationships and friendships to music. I've always been a bit of a loner anyway. Whitley will tell you that, even though me and Whitley are best friends.

Sometimes I think I find it difficult interacting with other people. I can see it sometimes when I'm at festivals, with other artists who have met me before – I can see it in their eyes that they don't like me.

I put my foot in it sometimes, for sure. One time I met one of the Chemical Brothers and said something dumb like, 'Fuck me, you look old, mate!' I could just see his face drop, he looked so hurt. I didn't mean it maliciously, and I don't see it as like, 'Oh, you're an artist, and I'm an artist.' It was just how I would talk to a mate in the pub.

I've had friends say that they think women are drawn to me. What I think is, there are some women who have a natural maternal instinct, and they can feel that I'm a motherless child. Maybe some feel sorry for me, or others see my vulnerability. It's not even just girlfriends or partners, it's in general life too.

We were in an airport in Russia one time, and I'm sat there, and there was this older lady next to me, with her son and her grandchildren. My hair was just one dreadlock at the time, and without saying anything she reached over and felt my dread. She started talking to me, communicating that she was from the mountains, and she told me about her music, and then she just held my hand for twenty minutes. After that, she went off and got her plane.

Another time, me and Cesar were in Mexico. A lady was sat with her granddaughter, and the granddaughter said, 'Hey, how are you? Where are you guys from?' We talked for ten minutes, then when they were leaving, the old lady came over and said something in Spanish and kissed me on the forehead. I said, 'What did she say?' Cesar said, 'She just fucking blessed you!' The motherless child thing – I can't explain it any other way.

I feel like it's too late for me to settle down. I imagine dying by myself: just pass away somewhere on my own and my body ain't found for days. I don't want the fuss. If I was ill and dying, I wouldn't want to put anybody else through that. I don't want the drama. I would just like to die in a room, and then my body is found two days later, and it's over. I don't want to go through all that real-life shit.

I was saying all this to my brother a while back, while we were at a funeral.

'Wow, what a send-off!' he goes, as we were filing out of the place.

I don't get it when people say that.

'You know what?' he adds. 'If I have half as many people at my funeral, I'll be happy!'

I was like, 'But you won't be happy – you'll be dead!'

I often say to my family, 'Just let me rot where I am. Funeral stuff – don't worry about it! Leave me where I lie. If I die in Berlin, or Japan, let them deal with it. Don't get involved and just get on with your life!'

I don't believe in the afterlife, or any of that spiritual shit. I just know you live and then you die, and that's it. Everything in between is good, bad or whatever. Just do what you wanna do, not working for anybody, not being told what to do. On those terms, I am a success, whether I've got money or not. I've maybe had one or two jobs in my life, short jobs, so I've got through life without playing the game they want me to play, like going to work in a factory or on a construction site – without being involved in the system. I've gone where I want, I've been around the world, I've done what I want when I want. I haven't got trapped in the rat race.

My life has been too amazing, too good. I get up, and I choose what I want to do. I don't have to go to work, I don't have to do anything. You think: how many people really love their jobs? People work because they have to, right? There's so many people who do that. I'm lucky, because I've managed to survive without it. Doing interviews can be a pain in the arse, but it's easy really, you're just sat around. I'd say working in a factory or on a construction site is a lot harder in the freezing English winter.

But settle down? It's not gonna happen. I could go to Holland tomorrow and decide I'm going to live there, and I could leave everything behind. Living like that, how can I have a relationship? I could have a wife and kids in Berlin, but then I could go to Holland and think, 'I love this city!' and never come back again.

I could move to Vietnam tomorrow and I would be alright – find a place to eat, somewhere I can train, a café to drink coffee, and that's it. I moved around a lot as a kid, from my grandmother to my auntie and what have you, so I guess it's my natural life.

I've always wanted to live in Asia. Somewhere like Vietnam, just to see. It's probably not the time to do that yet, but I wouldn't mind going for a year, because I love Japan, Hong Kong, Beijing. I'd love to live and record there for a year, in an Asian country. Japan would be good for my diet, because they don't really do dairy, and they don't do bread. Perfect!

You wouldn't believe my place in Berlin. It's a beautiful apartment, but there's nothing in there. I live out of a suitcase, even now. I ain't got no furniture. There's nowhere to sit, so I can't invite people round: I've got one studio chair and a table, and that's it. All my clothes are on the table or hanging on the door. My bags are packed, ready to move.

CHAPTER FIFTEEN
SEARCHING FOR MAXINE

I've got away with murder in my career, all because my mum committed suicide. People have got behind me and supported me because of that story in my early years – not just for the music itself. I think people can tell that I've been searching for my mum in my life and through the music, and maybe that's the thing they identify with most, for whatever reason. I'm only really noticing that now, years later, because when you're living it, you don't see it, do you?

When I found out that my mum wrote poetry – which was after I'd made *Maxinquaye* and become famous – it made me really think about my place in everything. Back in her day, there was no outlet for a mixed-race woman living in Knowle West to write poetry. I started to feel like my mum gave up her life so I could have my life, because really, without her death, there ain't no me.

Some people look at it like, 'Oh, your mum committed suicide, that's like the ending for you,' but that was my beginning. If she'd not killed herself, I couldn't have written any of that early music. I certainly couldn't have written any of the lyrics. I felt that she was writing through me. I've realised that many of my lyrics are written from a female perspective. 'Overcome', all those songs – it's like a woman wrote them.

'Broken Homes', the one I did with PJ Harvey – I wrote those lyrics, but it's not a bloke writing them. How did a young guy from Knowle West write those lyrics? It's not a man's way of thinking: 'Those men will break your bones, don't know how to build stable homes' – why am I writing from inside a woman's head? Eventually, when I sat down and thought about it, I realised: it's my mum writing them.

Everything I did was based around my mother. Without her committing suicide, there is no Tricky, no albums, no nothing. I might've had a good life with her being alive, but there would've been no music, which I find kind of weird, because you would think of suicide as being negative, wouldn't you? Like, fucking hell, my mum killed herself, but I can't even think negatively of it, because without that there is no me.

At least my mum killing herself means I never had to go through that thing of grieving for her passing in my adult life. To me, it's worse when you're older. As a kid you just get on with it, but how the fuck do you deal with the loss later on? That's one of the worst things imaginable. People feel sorry for me, like, 'Aw, your mum committed suicide!' Listen, losing your mum or dad when you're already grown up and you know about life, and you know about love – my mum committing suicide maybe looks sadder on paper, but *that* to me is the most awful, cruel thing I can think of.

I realise that I've spent much of my life so far thinking about losing my mum, trying to understand it, trying to remember things about her (even though I can't), and trying to process the feelings I must've had back then as a four-year-old boy.

There was a song on my last album, *Ununiform*, called 'When We Die', which was about the younger me having a conversation with me now. The younger me is saying, 'My mum's dead, what do I do now? Where do I go? What happens to me? I don't die young, like Michael?' Michael was my uncle, the one who got murdered in the blues in Bristol, but it was weird because around the time I wrote the song, George Michael passed away, so a lot of people connected that lyric with him. Anyway, the older me says to the kid, 'Everything's going to be alright, you're gonna end up going on tour, going on trips abroad – it'll all be fine in the end!'

Between those two versions of me, I suppose there have been many years of searching for the truth about Maxine. As you've already heard, there are many secrets in my family through the generations. Not everything is crystal clear. Things get buried and not talked about for years, if ever again. Only very gradually have I found things out about her from family members who were around at the time.

MICHELLE PORTER: Being seven years older than Adrian, I have a lot more memories of Maxine than he does. She was amazing, and me and my brother Mark absolutely adored her. She was very tall, slim and attractive, and also very bubbly and outgoing. You definitely knew when she came into a room – she would be chatty and friendly and really vibrant.

She and Roy were so different. There was Roy – very tall, too, but very quiet – and he was happy to just sit in the background, because it would all be about Maxine. She always had something interesting to say, and there was always some drama going on. She was very drama queen-y. Everything in her life was a crisis. She definitely should have been in the theatre. She dressed really outrageously and was a bit adventurous for her era. She always had that spark in her eyes, a bit cheeky.

Considering her upbringing, she was very cultured. She was really into poetry, and theatre, and she was always going on about these French actresses she idolised – I swear she thought she was French!

Put it this way: she wasn't a dull auntie. She used to tell us fantastic bedtime stories. Mark and I would go to bed, and she didn't read a story from a book – she would make a story up, seemingly off the top of her head, about someone in the jungle, or whatever. The only one we can ever remember was about Sabre the lion having this great adventure. After a while, she would finish the story off, and we would have to wait till the following night before she told us any more, so she would leave us hanging there in suspense. It wasn't your usual Disney stuff, and we absolutely adored her for these wonderful stories.

My mum, Marlow, was like a mother figure to Maxine. They were incredibly close. They often used to go out together, and then they would go out with Roy and my father Ken, the four of them, to clubs and shebeens, so their social life was very much bound together. Maxine would always look amazing in what she wore, with her hair all done up. She was always one step ahead with the fashion of that time.

Maxine was always at our house, with Adrian and Leanna. If my mum didn't see her for a day, she would think something was wrong. She wasn't an aunt that you saw every now and then, she was someone who more or less lived in our house. My mum used to laugh and say, 'Haven't you got a home to go to? Roy will be back from work soon.' She would say, 'Oh yeah, yeah, in a moment ...' Adrian would be like, 'It's late now, Mum, we may as well stay.' They were always with us – they never went away! We had such a lovely relationship with Maxine, and my dad absolutely adored them both. He had a real soft spot for Adrian, and I think it was because he was cheeky like Maxine.

When she passed away, we were all obviously devastated. We came home from school, and Roy was there with my mum and dad, all of them sobbing. I don't think my brother Mark has ever spoken about her again, since that day.

It must have been hard for Adrian – at that age, having your mother around, and then she's gone. I remember my mum saying he'd done something naughty, and she'd said to him, 'You've got to be a good boy, because your mum is looking down on you from up in the sky,' and later on he was in the garden, saying, 'Look at me, Mummy, I'm being a good boy!' It was heart-breaking at times.

Adrian used to stay with us a lot anyway, but all of a sudden having to do it without Maxine – that must've been really tough for him. What must've been going on for him emotionally, I hate to think.

MARLOW PORTER: When all the Godfreys went to Manchester, Maxine went for a while but ended up staying in Bristol and living with me in Hartcliffe. Though she was actually my younger half-sister, I was like a mother to her.

When she was fifteen, she found out she had epilepsy. She had the idea, which was probably true back then in the 1960s, that people would think she was mental. The day it first started, she was in our kitchen making a cup of tea and she lost control of her hand, so she missed the cup. People made a joke of it because they thought it was an accident. She said, 'It's not funny.' Little things like that were happening, until she started getting the full fits.

She went to the hospital and had all the tests done, where they put the electrodes on the brain. She got prescribed phenobarbital, which is what they gave you in those days. It was a heavy barbiturate with very bad side effects – depression and things like that.

Still, Maxine was a free spirit, and as a young adult she loved the excitement of life. I think she was born before her time. She would fit in now, you know, but back then? I would say to her, when she was off to a club with Roy, 'You're *not* going out like that, are you?' She was very close with Sandy – a lovely girl – who was married to her brother Michael, and Sandy used to make a lot of clothes for her. Say she'd made her a shirt, Maxine would have it tied above her tummy! You didn't do that in those days. She didn't see the wrong in it. She liked it, so that was what she was going to do.

The four of us – my husband Ken and I, and Maxine and Roy – often used to go out on double dates together. There was one funny time, when we were going to the Mayfair Suite, which was a big club in the centre of town, with an ice rink, and Roy was having a Christmas do there or something. This is where she was wicked: Roy had given her some money to get a dress made, but she didn't have enough for what she wanted, so what she bought was a night dress, and she had Sandy put in a lining for her. It looked beautiful – long, flowing and grand, a bit of a strappy number, better than any dress you would buy in a shop these days – but it was still a night dress, for going to bed in. It wasn't for wearing out!

'You can't wear that, Maxine!'

'Of course I can,' she shrugged, twirling in the mirror, 'look how beautiful it is!'

'But it's a fucking night dress!'

She liked the attention, and creating a scene. One time we were laughing and joking, and Maxine said, 'When I die, I want to go out like Edith Piaf! I want all the people there …' She thought Edith Piaf was wonderful: she had seen pictures from her funeral with all the people of Paris lining the streets and that was what she wanted too.

With her having fits all the time, it was good that she almost always lived with me. By then we had a bigger house in Bishopsworth, and she pretty much had her own room there, once she'd had the kids. Often Roy worked nights at the bakery, long hours, so it made sense for her to stay with us. It didn't break them up because he was at work anyway, and otherwise she would've been on her own. I suppose he felt better with that too, that she was with someone.

Once the kids got a little older, though, they got a flat not far from us, and my husband Ken went down and sorted everything for her – a nice bedroom suite, all nice things.

She could get my husband to do anything. They used to go off to bingo together, and I would be looking after the children. I loved her that much, I liked it. It was never, 'Oh, they've left me here on my own,' or 'What are they up to?' I never once had that feeling.

Once, she was in the house and she was trying to aggravate me: she was putting music on loud, and I still wouldn't say anything. Afterwards, she wrote me a note saying, 'I'm so sorry, you are my crutch,' all this. There was never a confrontation between us, ever. There were never arguments. Mark and Michelle have never argued, Adrian has never argued. There were no rules, except we always sat at the table for tea, everyone, and they were good as gold.

The trouble was that she didn't like the new flat. It was too much for her to do all the household chores on her own, and look after the children, do this, do that, and she was frightened about having a fit. She'd had to have nurse visits because of her epilepsy. It was too much, but she stayed there, and that's where she passed away.

On the actual day, she'd come out of hospital on the Sunday, and on the Monday she was down at our house, wasn't she, putting my clothes on, and 'I'll borrow this and that,' doing her eye make-up. I remember saying, 'Maxine, are you going? I've got work to do.' We were in the kitchen, and I had my back to her and Ken, and there was cake on the table. She said, 'Look, Mar, he won't let me cut my cake – he's only doing it so he can hold my hand!'

She'd got all dressed up in my clothes. It was what you wore in those days, black trousers tight at the waist and wide at the bottom, with a long-sleeved camel-coloured dress over the top, and a belt at the waist. She had my coat on as well: it sounds horrible, but it was lime green with big collars, which was very trendy at the time. We both liked to be in with the fashions – different from the norm.

That was the last time I saw her alive. She went down to Sandy and Michael's, and Ken dropped her home. She said she would be over at one o'clock the next day, but no, that was it.

When we heard the news, Ken went up to her flat. I couldn't. I froze, and that's not me at all. Just, 'No, I can't do it.' It would've killed me. Ken went up, and he said that she was still warm, and that she had a tear in her eye. I thought, 'Well, if she was still warm, did she and Roy have an argument?' They didn't have an argument at all apparently, but it leaves you thinking all sorts of things – like, did she really mean it? Did she take the phenobarbital tablets near enough to when she knew he was coming home, but it went wrong?

She was only in her early twenties. I still think she might have meant it as a cry for help. I told you, she was a drama queen. The things I used to have to do ... I would get phone calls, like, 'Could you come up and talk to Maxine? She says she's taken some tablets.' Because I was like her mother, I'd go up, and I'd say, 'Maxine, I haven't got all day! I've got a family to go back to! Have you taken tablets?' No, she hadn't. That was that, so I don't think she had actually tried it before.

The night she died she left a note on the table. I didn't read it, but my husband did. I don't know what happened to it. They wouldn't have let me have it. It was awful when she died, because all the Godfreys turned against me. Even then, nobody talked about Violet being my mother. Maxine always wanted me to come out with it. I'd say, 'But I can't, Max, I'm too afraid of them. They would come and harm me or my kids.' I couldn't come out and say that Maxine was actually my sister.

I went up to Violet's house in Barnstaple Road where they took her body, and all the Godfreys were there talking. Arthur was bossing everybody about – not Martin, because he was in prison, and anyway, with us Martin wasn't as confrontational as Arthur. Martin did things openly with his mouth, whereas Arthur was very sly. Anyway, Arthur said, 'In the first car, there will be Violet, Tony, Michael and Winston.' I don't know where I got the courage, but I said, 'No way on earth! I'm the eldest, I'm going in that car. Winston can go in the other car!'

I also took charge of writing the notice to put in the paper. At the bottom – oh God, I can't believe I did this – I put, 'From your devoted sister, Margaret'. They went mad with me. When I next went over there, Maggie said, 'You let me down – now everyone knows!' I said, 'But everybody knew anyway!'

I went up to see Maxine in the bedroom and she had her hair all over the place. I thought, 'No, people can't see her like that.' I got some elastic bands and clips, and I did her hair up in a bun. She used to shave her eyebrows, and as I was doing her hair, I looked at her and I thought, 'Your eyebrows need shaving, girl!'

When I went to the funeral down at Arnos Vale, nobody was speaking to me, and I sat in that car and I stayed looking at the coffin, and I said, 'Maxine, you've got your wish. They're all out watching you.' Loads and loads and loads of people had come out to see her go. I was smiling at her: 'It's your birthday, innit, Max, and you've got your wedding dress on!' – they'd put a white shroud on her – 'You've got your wedding dress on ... you're loving this, aren't you, girl?'

When she died, I wrote a letter. I ain't no good at poetry, but I wrote the most amazing thing. I can even remember parts of it: 'wherever I am, I look up through the window, you're reading a book ...' In later years, I thought, 'How did I manage to write that?' I think it was her doing it.

When Adrian left us and went to live with his nan Violet, we were heartbroken, but now I can see that maybe his passion wouldn't have come out if he'd stayed with us. We were just a happy family. His rawness has made him who he is, in the music. His songs are very deep and meaningful, aren't they? They go right down. I don't like listening to them, because sometimes it's like, 'Oof! I'm seeing what's in his head!'

For many years, he was angry – very, very angry. When he first made it big, and he was in America, and he had the most beautiful house in New Jersey, and the grounds it was in – it was amazing, but he didn't know who he was. I went over, and it wasn't the Adrian I knew. One thing I have always done: when he called himself Tricky, I wanted him to know that he is still Adrian to me. I have never once called him Tricky. He is not Tricky to me. He is Adrian – that is the real person. Tricky is the persona. With him, I think it was like a lot of people: too much, too quick.

Since then, coming back to Europe, and settling in Berlin, he's not that person anymore – he's Adrian again. He has changed immensely, so much for the better.

TRICKY: For the last five or six years, I've been getting on with my dad again. When I was in my late teens and early twenties in Bristol, I'd see him out and about in clubs. I'd go into places like The Tropics, and he would be stood there, with all his gold on, and his green safari suit, with the green waistcoat, green trousers, with the safari-style pockets. I'd go in there and say, 'Alright, Dad?' He'd be out with his mates, stood against the wall like a bad man, and he'd nod back.

Back then he wasn't the angelic grandad he is today. He was a Jamaican with a bad temper. He might pull a switchblade on you, and he sold the best weed in Bristol, but over the years he has mellowed.

A few years ago, I was in London, maybe doing some shows, and I was staying in this apartment in King's Cross. Out of the blue, my dad called me.

'Where are you?' he asked.

'I'm in London.'

'I'm going to come up!'

'What for? I'm only here for a couple of days.'

'I need to talk to you!'

I was sitting in this apartment waiting for him to arrive, and I was getting uptight because I didn't really have a relationship with him at that point. I didn't know what he was coming all the way up to London for. I thought maybe he was just coming to hang out, to see me, but why so urgent?

His wife dropped him off and left, and it was a really weird vibe.

'Alright, Dad, how are you?'

'I need you to know something,' he said. 'The reason I didn't come to see you when you were a kid was because, if I had, I wouldn't be here now.'

'What do you mean?'

'I would've been dead!'

It was cool that he finally said that to me himself. I'd found it out through whispers years before, about the letter Martin sent from prison basically threatening my dad, but it wasn't coming from him. You don't know what's true. I know that my nan didn't like my dad. I can understand that, because my nan lost her daughter, but that was nothing to do with my dad. She was terrified that she'd be on her own at home with me when I was a kid of three or four, and she'd have a fit, and no one might find out until the next day. I think she killed herself because of that.

My auntie Marlow tells me that my mum was a force. She used to bully my dad, almost. It wasn't like the stereotypical situation of a Jamaican guy cheating on my mum, hurting her. My mum used to take money off him and spend it. She was a force – she was a Godfrey! It sounds like it wasn't easy for my dad to be with my mum.

Once I got into music and I left Bristol and travelled, I would forget to call my dad for maybe a couple of years at a time. I didn't grow up with him, so it was natural – his life was one way and my life was another way. Maybe back then I thought he wasn't interested, so why should I give a fuck? When you're young, you don't so much, do you? My life went to London, then America, so he wasn't someone I kept in contact with.

Even now, it's my half-brother Kevin who will sometimes say, 'Hey, have you talked to Dad?' My brother has to remind me to call my own dad! Kevin is really close to him. It ain't a problem; it's not like I forget about him – it just hasn't been my habit to speak to him often because I didn't grow up with him. He's got twelve or thirteen kids – I'm not sure exactly how many. There are some I don't know about, apparently.

It's kind of amazing, but he can't read and write. He's gone through all his life, living in Bristol, driving everywhere, living in different places, and he has survived without being able to read and write. He still can't now. You take it for granted, don't you?

Me and him were always cool, but in the last year or two, we've developed a really great relationship. He's telling me stuff I never knew. He's got a good memory, but when he was younger, he wasn't so outgoing with his information. He wouldn't say a lot. Now, as he gets older, he's telling me stuff about my mum, and my grandad – Tarzan the High Priest.

He has mellowed out a lot. He's a lovely man. He's quite quiet, and not like Martin, all about money. He has found God at the moment as well, but I don't know if he really believes it. He feels bad about things. You know, he found my mum's body. That must be pretty devastating. He's a really good man, but I didn't see it when I was younger. What I realise is, we just had a separation, and now our relationship has evolved naturally, and it keeps getting better and better. It's crazy – he's one of my best mates!

I might not talk to him for two months, so this is the first time it's been like this. I'll call him now and say, 'Hello, Dad?' And then we both just start laughing. And when he goes, 'Adrian?' we start laughing at that too. It's like we both know we fucked up. We both know we ain't very good at this thing called life. He ain't been a great dad, I ain't been a great son, or a great boyfriend, or a great family member. We are mistakes. We laugh, and it's like, 'Yep, I know you're crazy, Dad,' and, 'Son, I know you're even crazier! What a mess we've created, but we're still here!'

He puts up with me. I'll say to him, 'Oh, I'm coming down in May,' and he'll laugh because he knows I probably won't. I had to call his wife the other day.

'Tell Dad I love him a lot,' I said when we'd finished.

'Why don't you tell him yourself?'

'You know I can't do that,' I replied, and I put the phone down on her.

▪ ▪ ▪ ▪ ▪ ▪

I used to avoid Bristol at all costs. I'd go and visit when I had to, and my cousin Michelle would say to me, 'You should just go home now, you're hating it here!'

In all the 25-odd years since I moved away, getting back to Bristol from Berlin these days is the easiest it's been – the shortest journey time so far, including from London. It's literally only two hours on the plane, so I nip back for a weekend quite often.

What's mad is, I quite like Bristol now! I appreciate how peaceful it is. I couldn't see it when I was a kid, but what a beautiful city! I wasn't really interested in beauty and things like that back then. I go to see Michelle, and she is just amazed. I come out of her house, and I'm like, 'I can't hear any cars! Wow, there's no traffic noise!' When you're young, things are moving so fast that you don't notice things like that. As you get older, you slow down and the penny drops.

Back then, my life was nuts. I wanted excitement, and Bristol wasn't the place for that. It ain't a place you go to party, because it's not got great nightlife. It used to bore the fuck out of me, because there's nothing to do and nowhere to go.

Nowadays, by contrast, going to a pub is good enough for me. I want less from life now. If you wanna have a beer with your mates, Bristol is a great city to do it. There's nothing that appeals to me more than drinking in a totally crappy pub – not a happening pub with a DJ, just a shitty little bar – and wheeling out stories from our neighbourhood from years ago, and who is doing what, and, 'Did you hear about so-and-so? Did you hear about that shop that got robbed?' I've found that I can go back there and relate to people again.

Not much has changed in Knowle West. They still need more stuff to do. There's no pubs, nothing there, but what's crazy is, former council flats are selling for 200 grand up there apparently!

I was there for Christmas 2017, and on the day before New Year's Eve, my friend Darryl Pursey's mum threw a party at her house, which is literally round the corner from where my nan used to be in Barnstaple Road. I was at his mum Lynn's house, drunk, dancing, with people I grew up with, in a house right near where I grew up. I was also in pubs seeing guys I haven't seen since I was seventeen years of age.

I went out with my cousins Mark and Michelle, and Trevor Beckford, and my nephew Jeran, and later on me and Jeran went and saw Danny Shepherd, the guy I was at school with from the age of five. Danny was in the pub with his son, and he is actually married to a girl we used to hang out with when we were kids. It was like I never left.

It's funny, because people always associate me with Bristol, and 'the Bristol Sound', whatever that is, but I never made an album there. I don't know if there ever was a Bristol scene. I said that in a magazine interview a couple of years ago, and people down there went fucking crazy. Bristolians were like, 'Waaaaah, Tricky said there's no scene!' I had to laugh, because some guy called in to a local radio show, and he goes, 'What does he know? He's a millionaire who lives in LA!' Which wasn't true on at least two counts. People have no handle on reality.

The irony is, I definitely could see me doing an album there in future. I've even talked to Michelle about moving back. She reckons that I should get a place there, but also live in Berlin. If that comes together, I would love to do an album in Bristol, just to see what the vibe would be like.

I'm back with some of my oldest friends, so even though I've cut myself off in Berlin, it's actually got me back to my essence. I've also been hanging out with Whitley, who I lost contact with for a while. When I did my 'Aftermath' white label and moved to London, he stayed behind and was kind of done with music. He didn't like how people change around it. He thought it was all bullshit, so he went and got a job, and now he works for a company delivering mobility equipment to people's homes. He just didn't want to be involved in it anymore.

WHITLEY ALLEN: A couple of years ago, I got a message from a mate out of the blue, saying, 'Tricky wants your number.' I was like, 'Yeah, sound!' We didn't see each other for years. I can't tell you the details of where he was career-wise, because I wasn't around him then. I only remember him as the guy I mucked about with, and the couple of times when I have seen him, he was that same guy.

I saw him in London one night when he was over from LA. Someone was going up to see him, and I said, 'Yeah, I'll come,' because I hadn't seen him for twelve or thirteen years, since the mid-90s when he left Bristol. We went to his hotel in the middle of the night and I could hear loud music in the foyer – I thought, 'That'll be him, won't it?' Next minute it was thump-thump on the door, and then, 'Aaaaaaah!'

At that point, I think he was getting caught up with serious people out there in LA. He had a girl in the bed, and I can't remember which one of his brothers was around, but he was talking all this stuff about guns with someone. We were going down in the lift to get some food, and I was like, 'You ain't a gangster and I ain't coming to your funeral!' Thinking back about it, people might have thought, 'Who are you to say that?' That's just me. Like, 'You are still that person I know and you're messing with the wrong crowd.'

He grew up in that gangster background, and I didn't – but we did get up to a lot of mischief together. Even though we were kind of amongst it, we both got out of there. We dabbled. He said a funny thing to me: 'We were a car ride away from being proper gangsters.' He was really talking about Shaun Fray, the guy who got killed in East Ham. Sometimes we would jump the Tube, but just imagine – if we'd had a car, we would've been going out there all the time, and we could've got seriously embroiled in his world. That was a realisation for me, even all these years later, because we were hustlers, and once you start getting that type of money, you'll get used to it and it's a slippery slope.

We lost a lot of people we knew in Knowle West who fell off the edge. I go up there now and there's a lot of people missing. Girls as well as boys, who just didn't make it out. A few people OD'd. You see the people who are still there now, and it's just like, 'Wow …' Going back is a bit painful sometimes, but it was good times when we were up there. It was clean – it was just a bit hard. We drank a lot of cider, and it was good fun. When we vacated the place, that's when the drugs came in and started wiping everybody out.

Me and Adrian got back in touch properly in February 2016, when he played at the BBC 6 Music Festival in Bristol. We'd been speaking on the phone, and my missus was like, 'He's chatting to his girlfriend again …'

She didn't know that I knew him. Even my daughter was like, 'Why is he always chatting to this Tricky guy?' Then she looked him up and was, 'Oh my God, my dad knows *him*!'

He's been around the world doing this, that and the other. I was always happy for him, but he was on a different level to how I was living. He was like, 'But you could have called?' I was like, 'I know Adrian Thaws – that is my mate. You're the guy from Knowle West and I'm that guy too, and that is our relationship.'

My wife and I went down to the 6 Music show with Michelle and Marie, and I was absolutely blown away, like, 'That's my mate, I've been with him all day, and he's onstage!' I don't know all of his music. It's not like, 'Oh, he's my mate, I've got to buy every album.' I've only really got into it recently through my missus. She plays it more than me. I don't play it – that would be weird.

As I said before, he's a nightmare and he knows it. He ain't changed. The other day he told me that he's moving.

'What? You've only just moved!'

'No, I'm going to another place …'

'But you only just moved!'

My saying for him is, wherever he lays his hat is his home. He keeps it moving constantly, but he's still that person I knocked about with all those years ago. I piss myself, because I see it – you're still the same person, and you're not gonna change. I don't want him to change – that's why I like him.

Our getting back together, I class it the same as knowing someone who has been in prison. They get put away at eighteen years of age, say, and they do ten years, and when they come out, they're still eighteen because their life goes on hold while they're in there. It was like that, straight back to those eighteen-year-olds, as if we'd never been apart.

TRICKY: Someone else I've been talking to again in the last few years is 3D. It's only him and G left in Massive Attack now, which is kind of crazy when you think there were six or seven of us to begin with. They should be called Missing Attack! Seriously, though, it's amazing how big they are, playing arenas and stuff – it blows my mind.

Me and 3D are getting on really well. We call each other and talk to each other. We meet up sometimes and get pissed up together. He's known me since I was a kid. I've known him so long, it's almost like he's always been there. He's about three years older than me, but he doesn't seem it. He ain't like an old man. He's youthful-thinking.

A year or two ago, I was talking to him on the phone, and he goes, 'You've been listed as one of England's Top Five Rappers!' And then he goes, 'They didn't put me in there!' He's really funny, D, he's got a great sense of humour, I must admit. He can make fun of himself.

He knows me so well that I could say anything to him, and he wouldn't take it personally. I've said stuff about him in the press which, if someone said that about *me* in the press, I wouldn't be talking to them! Maybe that's pissed him off, but he's still my mate, because he knows deep down I'm not like that, and I don't really mean it. It's either what I consider funny at the time, or I'm just not very cultured. I'm a Knowle West guy – the one who's pissed up and might say something stupid. The guy who when he's drunk you can't take him places. But D knows I'm a good guy. I've got a good heart. I just put my foot in it sometimes. I can be a dick, and he can totally put up with that.

My nickname for him is Vlad, or Vlad the Impaler – like Dracula, because he's like a vampire. When I text him, I say, 'What's going on, Vlad?' I could post something on Instagram, and he'll see it on there, and he'll like the vibe, and do the same thing. He calls me Ivan the Terrible.

In 2016, I did a track with him for a Massive EP, called 'Take It There', and I felt like some of the old competition between us was creeping in again. When he sent me back the mix, he'd got effects all over his voice, and mine was dry – no effects at all. I'm like, 'Vlad, why is my vocal dry as a bone? Why don't you just put a little bit of reverb on there, seeing as your vocal has triple reverb, delay, echo – every fucking effect in the book!'

I came onstage with them when they headlined at Hyde Park that summer. It's like a machine when they play live: it costs so much money that if they don't have a certain amount of success, they can't tour. I couldn't work like that, as the pressure to be a mega-success every time would do my head in. I'd feel trapped. But as I say, it blows my mind how they've turned out.

I also really rate Nellee Hooper. He is a legend, and he could be playing off it big-time, but he doesn't seem to give a fuck. He was one of the founding members of Wild Bunch, and he produced Soul II Soul, Björk and Massive Attack. He could be giving it, 'I'm the ambassador of this, that, whatever,' but he doesn't live off his name. He's just walked away and is living his life. He doesn't do the celebrity thing. I really rate him for that.

I'd say Massive Attack's music is 'better' than mine, but I think the reason why people relate to my music is precisely because there are mistakes all over the shop. People could never listen to Massive Attack and think, 'I could do that,' whereas I've put out tracks I should never have released. I don't know how I got away with it! But that's how I make music, from the hip, and once it's done, I can't take it back. I think that's why I get a lot of love, because I risk putting it out there. I read a comment about me on YouTube that said, 'Tricky has always been the dark spirit of Massive Attack,' and I thought, 'Now, I get it – I was the mysterious guy!'

Nowadays if I record something and I don't like it, I'll usually just erase it. Back in the '90s when studio time was so precious, you kept everything and there's a lot of stuff from that era that I never released – music no one has heard that I made with Cyndi Lauper, Björk, Grace Jones, Neneh Cherry and probably a load of hip-hop people. A lot of it may be in amongst the stuff we got digitised from my lock-up in New York. Horst has been trying to get me to listen through that archive. I'm crap at that, though – sitting and listening to hours of old music just doesn't seem exciting to me. I feel like if I listen to it I'll get caught up in the past. I'm into doing new music, and I certainly wouldn't want to bring any of that old stuff onto a new album, as I don't feel like I need to rely on it.

The way I record today is almost exactly the same way as it always was. When I start off, it's a completely blank page. I don't make music, music makes me. If I sit with the keyboards, hit 'record' and play around for a bit, I'll play it back and what I've got tells me where I'm going from there. The keyboard part will tell me what the drums need to sound like, then the drums will tell me what the bassline should be, then that piece of music tells me the lyrics – I start hearing words in the music. It really is that easy. There's no thinking process in it at all, no danger of writer's block, nor any need to have confidence. It's always gonna work; you don't have to do anything – just be present and the music will do all the work for you.

I still can't read music, and I don't know notes, but I can hear. I'll set a beat going, and just play keyboards on top, muck around. I still play keys with two forefingers sometimes. The technology doesn't interest me at all. I still have an engineer, and that's because I don't want to press buttons, I don't want to know about what Pro Tools can do, or be reading a manual. I don't want to be thinking about watching a screen, and plugging things in, and shuffling things to get them all in time, like a maths project. I don't wanna do any of that shit. I wanna make music!

. ▪ ▪ ▪ ▪ ▪ ·

I can't sing like Bob Marley, I can't play guitar or write songs like him, but Island saw me as the right man to keep Marley's tradition alive. In my way, I was a musical rebel, and outspoken too. That has always been my place in music. I've always been the outsider who got in there somehow. I got my foot in the door, but I definitely shouldn't be in here – especially after all these years!

I always got advice from Chris Blackwell, even after he left Island, but I sometimes still wonder: if he hadn't sold up, would things have been different? I think I would've done all my best work by now, but seeing as he did, and I went through all those years of disappointment vainly trying to find 'another Island', I really believe that some of my best work is yet to be made. It still lies ahead of me. All the problems in the last twenty years or so – that's all good, because now the best stuff's coming again. I'm constantly recording, and I know things are getting better.

By nature, I'm an experimental artist, and to be able to experiment you need time. You can't rush it. You have to have a bit of space to realise which experiments have worked and which ones haven't. Instead of polishing up everything you write for release, you need time to step back for a bit, then have a listen and say, 'Actually, half of this is shit,' and throw those tracks away. Before, those tracks would've got released. Now I've got the luxury of recording for a couple of weeks, going on tour for a bit, coming back, sifting through what I've done and keeping only the top-notch tracks – and my music has gone up another level again. It's got a new energy about it. Now that I'm doing my own label, as the boss of False Idols, I'm almost thinking like an A&R man – dip a toe in the water and see how we work together and what the reception is like.

I'm excited about bringing up other artists, too. When you get to a certain position, you're meant to be bringing others through, introducing them, giving them the opportunity. I feel that's part of being a musician. Plus, I'm not inspired when it's only about me. It's always been that way. I've got some incredible artists on False Idols.

I'm learning a lot from doing the label. The new singer in my live band, Marta, is doing an album, and I know I have to treat her as I would hope to be treated myself as an artist. She might play me a track she's made with another producer, and all I can do is offer advice. I might say, 'I don't think it's good enough for your voice,' but at the end of the day, it's her album, and if she really wants to put it on there, it's her choice. I can't tell her what my record label needs. I have to go with it. She will either listen to me or she won't! That's how I'll deal with an artist.

As for my own music, I'm really excited about where it's going. It's weird timing – with this book, and the label, everything is coming together at the same time. The other day I said to Horst, 'I'm back! I – am – back!' It's like, I'm getting to know myself a bit better now, and talking about my life in here has definitely helped. It's like getting something off your chest, isn't it? It's helped me be logical, to understand myself more, and to realise, 'I am like this, because …' I'm more comfortable with myself and all my mistakes and who I am than I was even a year ago. Now, I feel like I don't need to do music to feel better about myself. It's easier to do music because I'm not doing it to survive. I'm doing it because I love it.

I'm different in the studio now, I'm having more fun. It's more natural, but more thought about. Sometimes in the past my music has been all energy, and not thought about. It's been like puking up. Often there's been confusion, because I don't know how to express myself. Now, it's still from the hip, but I sit back, listen to it, and arrange it. You've still got the darkness, and the tension, but there's some thinking behind it. It's more focused than ever before.

It's still kind of like Tricky, but this is *new* Tricky! And what else is there to do? I couldn't stop doing it, or retire. How do you retire from something you've done all your life? What do you do for the rest of your time? Ever stopping – that don't make no sense to me!

WHAT A FUCKING GAME

Mina Mazy Topley-Bird

This book starts with my mother's suicide. If I had known that it would end with my daughter's suicide, you wouldn't be reading this now.

When I was young, my uncle Martin told me this story. He'd just got out of prison after seven years, and he was in the centre of town. It was raining, he had no money, and he had one cigarette left. He put up the collar of his coat, lit the cigarette and said to himself, 'What a fucking game!'

'Lie awake and let the visions take me, think of life and how it tried to break me'

I was rewriting those lyrics the day before I found out about Mazy. My baby died. My world over. The person I was, he's gone. Everything looks different, sounds different. Like I'm in a world that doesn't exist.

What a fucking game.

ACKNOWLEDGEMENTS

Thank you to all the family and friends who contributed to this book, to Andy Perry for interviewing them, to my management and to the team at Blink, to all of them for making this book happen.

INDEX

(Page numbers in **bold** refer to contributor entries and main entries)